ZULU TIME

when ireland went to war

MARK LITTLE

**NEW
ISLAND**

ZULU TIME
First published 2004
by New Island
2 Brookside
Dundrum Road
Dublin 14
www.newisland.ie

ISBN 1 904301 52 5

British Library Cataloguing in Publication Data. A CIP catalogue record for this book
is available from the British Library.

Typeset by New Island
Cover design by New Island
Printed by CPD, Ebbw Vale, Wales

10 9 8 7 6 5 4 3 2 1

Mark Little was born in Dublin in 1968 and educated at Trinity College and Dublin City University. He joined RTÉ as a television reporter in 1991, and in September 1995, he was appointed RTÉ's first Washington correspondent. He returned to Ireland in January 2001 to become RTÉ's foreign affairs correspondent. In 2001, he was named Television Journalist of the Year for his reporting in Afghanistan. He spent seven weeks in Northern Iraq reporting on the War in Iraq in 2003. He is currently a presenter of RTÉ television's current-affairs programme *Prime Time*. His first book, *Turn Left at Greenland*, reached number one on the Irish non-fiction bestseller list in 2002.

CONTENTS

Acknowledgments

This book is partly the result of an ongoing dialogue with my best friend, Tara Peterman. It was shaped by conversations with many others, including Tom, Anne, Eoin and Jennifer Little, Trina Vargo, Ryan Tubridy, Ann-Marie Power, Darius Anvari, Richard Martin, Mark O'Connell and Paul Cunningham.

If I have managed to bridge the gap between the flash-bang language of daily journalism and a more literate form of expression it is because of the wise counsel and good humour of Jonathan Williams. Once again, it has been a pleasure to work with New Island. Emma Dunne, Joseph Hoban and Fidelma Slattery have the uncommon talent of making a complicated process seem so full of passion and commitment.

I owe my continued sanity to Tom Vantorre, who was with me every step of the way in Northern Iraq, and thank Sean Swan and Mark Davies for their friendship in hard times. Thanks also to David Hammelberg, Philip Boucher-Hayes and Blnd Amedy. Back at RTÉ, Margaret Ward and Cathy Milner showed me great kindness and understanding during the war. I am grateful to Noel Curran and Ed Mulhall for their guidance.

During the writing of this book, I have relied on numerous experts, writers and sources. There were too many to credit directly in the body of the book, but among the essential texts were *The Iraq War Reader*, a book of documents, speeches and opinions edited by Micah L. Sifry and Christopher Cerf; *Islam* by Karen Armstrong; *The War We Could Not Stop*, a collection of essays by reporters from *The Guardian*; and *The Reckoning: Iraq and the Legacy of Saddam Hussein* by Sandra Mackay. For information on land-mines, I relied on the Mines Advisory Group, Human Rights Watch and the Mines Action Information. The *Columbia Journalism Review* was an invaluable source on embedded reporters and White House spin.

Where my memory was an unreliable guide, I drew on a wealth of reporting from Northern Iraq. Among the best observers of the 'Northern Front' were C. J. Chivers of the *New York Times*, Jim Muir of the BBC, Julius Strauss of *The Daily Telegraph* and Luke Harding of *The Guardian*.

Some of the very best journalists did not come back from Northern Iraq. In particular, Gaby Rado is never far from my thoughts.

Introduction

A Thousand Shades of Grey

'Every day, new signs of impending war appear. Sunday brought the disclosure that today all forces poised to attack Iraq will switch to Zulu Time, an adjustment often imposed before military operations to keep everyone in sync.'

Washington Post, March 11, 2003

The soldier's name was Nye. If he had been any more anonymous, he would have disappeared. His camouflage jacket was stripped of any significant detail; there was no first name, no indication of rank and no battalion insignia. Soldier Nye was an officer with US Special Forces. We knew that much because he told us so. He could hardly pretend to be anything else. He had emerged from behind the smoked glass of the Land Cruiser surrounded by his counterparts in the Kurdish militia. Their baggy trousers and headscarves were reflected in his wrap-around shades.

Soldier Nye smiled at us. We smiled back. We shared the implied joke. For months, US Special Forces had gone

1

to extreme lengths to elude journalists in Northern Iraq and now they were hosting a press conference. There was not only a trace of suspicion on the wind, but also a heightened sense of irony. Soldier Nye was clearly enjoying the company of people with the same sarcastic affectations as him.

'How about we buy you a phone so we can keep in contact?' suggested one of the reporters.

'There's a good idea,' said soldier Nye flatly, fixing his new best friend with a stare of comic intensity.

The wariness returned briefly when a reporter at the back of the huddle asked soldier Nye why he and his Special Forces comrades were late. We had been waiting at that Kurdish militia base for more than an hour.

'We're on Zulu Time,' soldier Nye replied.

There was something about the way soldier Nye spoke those words. In strictly literal terms, Zulu Time is military jargon for GMT (Greenwich Mean Time) or its new incarnation UTC (Universal Time Coordinated). At some point in recent history, Zulu Time became the temporal glue that held the US armed forces together as they extended their reach across the time zones of the world. On this particular day, as US forces closed in on Baghdad, Zulu Time had become the prime meridian for the entire planet. The invasion of Iraq had removed the last trace of doubt: no matter where you lived or what language you spoke, in the age of the lone superpower you were on Zulu Time.

There is one dominant force in the world today, and the rest of us live in its shadow. It is not America so much as 'Bush's America': a potent mix of raw power and emotion. If Zulu Time had a beginning, it was September 11. From that moment on, the American people demanded a foreign policy that took account of their legitimate fear of attack.

For better or for worse, they got the 'war on terror', complete with its doctrine of pre-emptive military action. You could use the word 'empire' to describe what Bush's America has become, but that would miss the point. It may dominate, but it does not control. It fears the world as much as the world fears it.

As it set off in pursuit of its enemies, the United States collided with Europe, which was distressed by the new warrior tendency in American foreign policy. There was a time when accommodation seemed possible, but hope faded fast once the die was cast in Iraq and Zulu Time became world time. For Europeans and Americans alike, however, there have been comforting certainties to fall back on. The Americans have their self-serving clichés about European weakness, cowardice and ingratitude. We have our smug assumptions about American arrogance, ignorance and paranoia. The parodies are compelling because they act as an antidote to the uncertainties around us, making us believe they are someone else's fault.

Beyond Europe and the United States, Zulu Time is characterised by a volatile combination of heartfelt grievance and prehistoric hatred. The forces of moderation in the Islamic world have been handicapped by decades of home-grown repression and political failure. For millions of young Muslims, Zulu Time has moulded a landscape littered with burning resentment and broken dreams. Radical forces have been able to exploit this profound alienation, thanks in no small measure to the blunt instrument that is American policy towards the Middle East.

The primary conflict in Zulu Time has been the war on terror, but the uneven progress of globalisation still shapes the contours of our age, and in its slipstream are unresolved struggles over world trade, global inequality, climate change, human rights and AIDS. The cumulative effect of all this discord is to inflict a mighty shock to our collective equilibrium. As we struggle to regain our balance, we tend to reach out for the simple answers to the complex questions. In the mind of the dominant power, the answer is to wipe out terrorism. Across a large stretch of the globe, the answer is to stop the Americans. But the important question remains unanswered: if George Bush and al-Qaeda disappeared tomorrow morning, would our problems disappear with them?

On one level, Zulu Time is defined by how Bush's America has chosen to act now that it is the dominant force; on another level, it is shaped by our reaction to the big kid on the block. The danger is that our fixation with Bush's America will make us blind to our share of responsibility for the problems of the world and our obligation to help make things right. It is quite possible that hating Dubya really won't save the planet.

There is one last characteristic of Zulu Time that is worth considering. People who live Dublin, Des Moines or Dubai have radically different ways of looking at the world, based on their values and ideals, and their fears and prejudices. We may approach an issue with an open mind, but all too often we are handed the facts that conform to our expectations and not the objective truth. The opinion formers in our society know which buttons to press, presenting evidence that strengthens our preconceptions and painting the world around us in primary colours, not the thousand shades of grey that define it. When the media give us what we want, we end up seeing the world as we expect to see it, not as it actually is. In truth, the realities of Zulu Time are the same the world over. They just look different, depending on what part of the globe you are standing on.

INTRODUCTION

Just in case you are girding yourself for a serious lecture about foreign policy, let me assure you there is no need. This is not a lengthy sermon about the evils of an American empire, and it is not an argument for greater understanding of George W. Bush. It is not a book about whether the Americans were right or wrong to invade Iraq. I have stories to tell about my experience of war, but I am not a war correspondent, and this is not a battlefield memoir.

This is the story of travels in Zulu Time, the record of a personal journey and also a portrait of Ireland in an age of war. It is a book written for anyone who ever wondered how Ireland relates to this moment of madness in history. It is about the alternative reality that lies behind the black-and-white headlines in your newspaper and the shocking images on your television. It is about culture as well as politics. It is about our relationship with Botox and Britney as much as our attitude to Bush and Blair. This book was written for anyone who ever doubted the conventional wisdom about Ireland and the world, anyone who ever paused over an opinion in the paper and thought 'That sounds too simple.'

To me, the Irish represent the fundamental contra-dictions of life in Zulu Time better than any other Western nation. We are held up as poster children for the benefits of globalisation, yet our roller-coaster ride to wealth and affluence has unravelled our identity in ways we are still struggling to come to terms with. While we still shout loudly about the big issues of the day, we seem confused – on a subconscious level – about where our sympathies lie. The massive anti-war demonstration in Dublin in February 2003 put us very firmly in the European mainstream, yet in so many other ways we are drifting farther out into the Atlantic.

Of course, there is no way of understanding what it is to be Irish in Zulu Time without appreciating the mixture of attraction and repulsion that characterises our relationship with the United States. Few Western nations have such close historical links to the world's dominant power as Ireland, and thanks to the revolutionary changes of the Tiger years, those links have morphed into a bizarre, distended entanglement that almost defies description. The tired, old clichés about the USA being 'the next parish' are no longer relevant. In Zulu Time, our relationship with Bush's America cannot be described with words alone, nor even with cold, hard statistics. You have to walk down our streets, see how we look, what we say, what we watch, what we listen to, what we read and how we sound to get a measure of how we feel towards the US. Somewhere in between the unconscious murmur of adoration and the high-pitched squeal of disgust is the sound of Ireland and America.

I have been living with the ambiguities of this relationship for close on a decade now and mentioned some of them in my first book, *Turn Left at Greenland*, a record of my experiences as RTÉ's Washington correspondent. I finished writing the book shortly after September 11, in the warm afterglow of sympathy towards the United States. However, by the time it was published, in May 2002, Ireland had gone stone cold on America and its president. As the war drums became louder, so did our indignant tone. In between highbrow exchanges about American foreign policy was the sound of a cultural shift that was so intense it began to unhinge my own sense of identity.

Like thousands of other returned emigrants, it had taken some time for me to readjust to the uneven rhythm of Irish life. Before long, however, the seductive subtleties that distinguish Ireland were drawing me back in. It was

exhilarating to hear ideas that could have
only in this country and emotions that cam
our shared history. It helped greatly that life i.
gift-wrapped with a luxurious coating of so,
and diversity. H&H Bagels from New York taste   .1
better when bought from a shop in Dublin city c..ire.

However, long after the process of decompression was
over, there was still that unsettling trend in Irish attitudes
towards America. I had become used to the jaded
scepticism of people my own age – the less they felt they
needed America, the less they seemed to *like* America. I
could also understand the general antipathy towards
George Bush – after all, he was planning a war Ireland did
not want. But what troubled me was that feelings towards
Bush's America had become more than the sum of their
parts. Politics and culture had merged to produce a
uniquely Irish vision of the United States that was both
compelling and grotesque. And I could not help feeling
that I had been here before, at a different time, in a
different place.

When I lived in the United States, the prevailing vision
of Ireland drove me demented. There was no room for
reality amid the manufactured clichés that passed for
Ireland in the American consciousness. This is a subject I
will return to in greater detail, but for the moment it is
enough to say that I spent the weeks before St Patrick's
Day wishing I were Polish. I had to give up listening to the
local radio station because their commercial breaks were
stuffed with 'Patty's Day' promotions for local bars and
restaurants, featuring boozy leprechauns with squeaky
accents. However, by far the worst possible encounter with
'makey-uppy' Ireland involved 'the Unicorn moment'.

You have not felt real despair until you have sat in a bar
and witnessed a performance of 'The Unicorn Song'. It

was popularised by a band called the Irish Rovers in the 1960s and stalks the bars of America like an evil drunk. It is not specifically about Ireland, but it is 100 per cent 'Oirish'. As soon you heard the opening words ('A long time ago, when the Earth was green ...'), your teeth would involuntarily clench together and your face contort. Your American friends often mistook this for a knowing smile and began to act out the animal movements that go with the song ('There were green alligators and long-necked geese ...'). You felt like screaming but were afraid any emotion would be taken as approval, so instead you sat in silent agony. I often fantasised about testifying in court against the Irish person who wrote the song, until I found out his name was Shel Silverstein.

Back home in Ireland, I encountered the Unicorn moment in reverse. While the Americans enjoyed their make-believe Irishness, we had our fantasy vision of the Yanks. I could hear 'The Unicorn Song' playing in my head when someone slipped into an American accent to illustrate stupidity or crassness. I could hear it in those word-association games where the word 'American' is followed soon after by 'fat' or 'loud'. As America was discussed through the filter of US television or Hollywood movies, there were plenty of Unicorn moments, and, of course, they were present in every conversation about the death penalty, religion, guns, crime, obesity and Texas.

There had always been some element of fantasy in our assessment of the US, but there was a darker edge to it now, and there also seemed to be a growing tendency to exclude the inconvenient facts. On the morning of the All-Ireland football final in 2003, a radio host remarked to a guest in the US that such a remarkable celebration of community spirit could not happen in America. As I thought about a packed Yankee stadium during the World

Series, and the Friday-night ritual of high-school football in small town Alabama, I had a Unicorn moment.

As George W. Bush pushed forward on the road to war in the Middle East, I started to wonder if any of this mattered. So what if a couple of misplaced insults are thrown America's way? As long as our version of reality raises opposition to Bush and his neo-conservative cronies, does it really matter if we 'get' America?

My journey through Zulu Time leads me to believe that the answer to that last question is yes, that the relentless over-simplification of America has become fundamentally counter-productive for a nation like Ireland at a time like this. It has weakened our capacity to develop an alternative to the actions of the lone superpower and blinded us to the extent of American influence over our daily lives. Even as some of us look forward to a future where the United States does not dominate world affairs, our clichés keep us trapped at the arse-end of an unhealthy relationship with the US. Like all dysfunctional couplings, it is characterised by wishful thinking, mutual misunderstanding and a failure to communicate.

Once again, let me assure you: this is not a lecture about the rights and wrongs of American foreign policy. I have no interest in trying to defend the behaviour of the Bush administration, just as I have no desire to undermine the reasoned arguments of its critics. There is nothing I could say that will soften the images from that prison camp in Guantanamo Bay or explain the absence of proof of Iraqi weapons of mass destruction. By the same token, this is not an exhaustive analysis of American misbehaviour in this age of living dangerously. If I fail to name check everything you think the Americans have done wrong, I apologise in advance. This is not that kind of book.

My priority is not to change your mind about America; I would much rather challenge the way you think about Ireland. It seems to me that despite endless debate about the Americans, Bush and the war, we still find it difficult to work out how Ireland relates to all of this. Certainly, there have been explicitly political assessments of government policy and stark conclusions about the use of Shannon airport by the US military, but there have been precious few attempts to look deeper into Irish lives. What about the change in our gut instincts towards America? What about the subconscious shift in our outlook on the world? And what about our struggle to match our ideals with actions?

At the end of my journey through Zulu Time, it occurred to me that our relationship with the world could do with some of the liberating spirit of post-Tiger Ireland. One of the many pleasures of living in this country is the collapse of narrow-minded orthodoxy under a weight of openness and optimism. The willingness to ask the hard question, to take a risk, to challenge the establishment, has underwritten the social progress of the past two decades, and where we have faltered it is only because we chose to accept the easy answer to the complicated question. Perhaps it is time to use that maturity and courage to work out what we stand for at a crucial moment in world history.

The war in Iraq led to a seismic shift in global politics, but few of the aftershocks seemed to register here in Ireland. Many courageous writers and broadcasters exposed hard truths about the conduct of the war, but there seemed to be something missing from the prevailing analysis of the conflict. As I travelled through Zulu Time,

INTRODUCTION

I found that the objective reality was presented in the starkest shades, even though there was plenty of truth to be found in the grey recesses of our lives; in our subconscious desires as much as our political preferences; in our inherited prejudices as well as our noble ideals; and in the moral ambivalence of wartime as much as the obvious brutality. These are the places where we will find out what makes Zulu Time tick.

PART ONE

BEFORE

1

Family, Religion and Manchester United

'We used to wonder where war lived, what it was
that made it so vile. And now we realise that we
know where it lives, that it is inside ourselves.'

Albert Camus, French philosopher,
September 7, 1939

It was two weeks before Christmas, and the rain had an
arctic bite as it ran down my wrists. My hands were
clasped behind my head, and I was struggling to keep my
balance while pleading for my life with the gunman
behind me. As I talked, I wondered what the pistol would
sound like when it was fired.

The man in the balaclava was a former SAS
commando called Kev, and the gun in his hand was
loaded with blanks. The scene was part of an elaborate
piece of theatre staged for the benefit of sixteen journalists
on the last day of a 'hostile-environment' course. In this
case, the hostile environment was Longmoor army base in
the heart of the English countryside. The executioner was

a fake, but he had created a terrifying virtual reality in that muddy country laneway.

Kev and some of his fellow instructors (also former members of Britain's élite military outfits) were members of a fictional rebel army fighting for control of the Republic of Longmooristan. They had staged a noisy twilight ambush in the woods at the edge of the army base, dragged us – their 'victims' – from two Land Rovers and dumped us face first into the muck at the side of the road. Hoods were placed over our heads. Once blinded by the rough cotton cloth, we were dragged to our feet and led by our outstretched thumbs to a nearby shed where the rebels plunged us into sensory overload. They revved the engines of the Land Rovers to a deafening pitch, fired their weapons in rapid bursts and screamed profanities at the pathetic hooded figures now sitting cross-legged on the concrete floor. When the noise subsided, the rebels walked heavily around the shed shining flashlights at our hooded faces and occasionally shouting abuse at us.

This was the final test of our six days of training. In classroom sessions during the week, the instructors had briefed us on how to make contact with fellow prisoners without provoking our captors. They had told us how important it was to be the 'grey man' who avoids drawing attention to himself in the early stage of abduction. Of primary importance, they said, would be our attempts to befriend our captors and eke out some common humanity to bond us (a process known in the kidnap business as 'reverse Stockholm Syndrome'). The instructors played their roles without a trace of suppressed mirth. Their intensity and aggression made the false premise of the exercise entirely plausible. During one silence, I could feel giggles rising in the back of my throat, but they were soon wiped out by a loud yelling in my ear. As time moved on, the line between real and artificial became increasingly blurred. Could I cope with this scenario if it ever happened for real? The training course had been designed to provide you with an answer to that question, but not necessarily the answer you wanted.

I was not quite clear how the abduction was going to finish: perhaps the lights would go on, and we would remove our hoods to the sound of gracious applause from our kidnappers. Instead, there was more noise and anger orchestrated by the commander of the rebels: a role played by the chief instructor, Mal, a tall and friendly soul who bore a passing resemblance to a young Mr Spock. Amid the chaos of war-torn Longmooristan, Mal had become a vicious nut-job, who was convinced that his captives were trying to make a fool out of him. He conducted a series of brutal interrogations that ended with the victims being led away, one after another.

When it was my turn, the giggles crept up on me again. Running through my brain was the scene from the movie *Life of Brian* where Eric Idle stands waiting in the queue for crucifixion. Michael Palin plays the cheerful Roman centurion who greets each prisoner with a smile and the question: 'Crucifixion?' When Eric Idle arrives at the top of the queue, he replies: 'Ah no. Freedom.' As I was led through the trees towards the site of my certain death, I wondered if my executioner would smile and say, 'Jolly good, off you go then,' when I told him I was actually not marked down for death but rather for a whiskey and a hot bath.

In place of the cheerful face were two eyes peering out of a balaclava. Standing in the muddy clearing on the woodland path was Kev with that gun. He ordered me to kneel in the mud, and as I did, I started to talk in rapid and nonsensical bursts of jumbled words. I calmed myself for a moment and remembered the golden nugget from those classroom briefings – when you are faced with execution, you should engage your captor in conversation about one or more of the following subjects: religion, family or Manchester United. If you can demonstrate religious belief of some kind, there is a chance you will gain the respect of your potential executioner; talking about your family could well provoke pity; and if both subjects fail to provide some common ground, then you should fall back on a discussion about one of the world's most lucrative soccer franchises.

Obviously, this strategy is not designed for use in countries with large, well-armed concentrations of Arsenal supporters. It also does not make sense unless you accept a core premise of globalisation: there is an expanding collection of brands that have bridged global divisions to become universally accepted cultural reference points. This line of reasoning will lead you to another assumption: if two people from incompatible cultures have a shared reference point, such as Manchester United, the risk that one of them will be of a mind to shoot the other in the head at close range will be greatly reduced. Students of globalisation will recognise that this is a variation of the 'Golden Arches Theory of Conflict Prevention', developed by American writer Thomas Friedman, which holds that no two countries with a McDonald's restaurant have ever gone to war with each other. With ice water running down my neck and a gun to my head, I was ready to put the theory into practice.

'Do you have any children?' I asked my executioner.
'Yes, but they were killed in the war.'
'Do you believe in God?'
'Yes. Do you?'
I was momentarily gripped by a religious fervour I had

not felt since I had run beside the Popemobile in the Phoenix Park in 1979. I began babbling about Catholicism and its place in Irish society and finished up with a hopeful little whimper about the role of mercy in all religions. Instead of embracing our common humanity, Kev mocked my new-found godliness.

'So I suppose you will be able to remember your prayers then.'

I was not having a good execution.

'So you know I'm Irish, right? Roy Keane is from Ireland. Well, he's from Cork, a place called Mayfield. Anyway, the point is, you know, he's just back after injury and he'll have his first game for United against Blackburn tomorrow. What do you reckon?'

I am often surprised by how much trivia my brain soaks up without ever officially registering it with my memory. This blast of irrelevant fact temporarily relieved the flow of mania, and with growing confidence I turned my head to look Kev straight in the balaclava. Before I could form a smile, he spat out the final rejection.

'I don't like football. Now turn around.'

The phrase 'That's all folks' popped into my head. I wanted to laugh, but there was also a slight chance I might cry – not out of fear, but out of sadness. This was how some person had spent his or her last moments on earth. Not me, not in this muddy laneway, but someone else, in a far-off place, in another language, for reasons known only to a person with a gun. Our instructors had served up the Manchester United advice in all seriousness, but I wondered if it had been a device to heighten the experience of hopelessness and despair. They had persuaded us to beg for our lives as part of a game with a probable outcome. Then, to show us how pathetic we would be in reality, they changed the rules just when we thought we had won.

Kev did not fire his gun. Without any change in tone, he told me to follow the path for a few yards where I could rejoin my fellow abductees and get a cup of tea. As I rose unsteadily to my feet, he said: 'You did some good work today.' I managed to blubber my thanks and ran away through the undergrowth, almost immediately forgetting the deep melancholy that had gripped me just a few moments before. I climbed in the back of a Land Rover where some of my fellow students sat drinking tea and steaming up the windows. We talked at each other like teenagers, half-drunk on near-miss mortality and the excitement of a week of virtual war.

Most of us had dreaded coming to Longmoor, especially so close to Christmas, but we had had no choice. In most media organisations, hostile-environment courses are now mandatory for reporters who plan to travel abroad, and with war in Iraq looming, there were only a rapidly decreasing number of weeks to unearth the hidden warrior in us all. Most of the journalists on the course were from the BBC, with the rest coming from the American network CBS and smaller European media outlets. It was a surprisingly multinational group, made up of people from eleven different countries including Afghanistan, Kurdistan and South Africa. There were big characters such as George the Greek, a veteran sound recordist with CBS, who showered the rest of us with war stories and old jokes about his identity. 'There are only two types of people in the world,' he told us on more than one occasion: 'those who are Greek and those who want to be Greek.' Our star pupil was Volker, a foreign correspondent from the German network RTL and a former beer-hall bouncer. He was well over six-foot tall and more physically imposing than most of the instructors. While I blabbered away during my mock execution, he jumped his gunman and wrestled him to the ground. He was the only member of our group who had first-hand experience of abduction, having once been kidnapped in the Philippines by the Abu Sayyaf guerrilla group.

Fergal was the other Irish journalist on the course. He worked on documentaries for BBC Northern Ireland, and in the early days of the course, we had both talked about how unnerving it was to be instructed by former members of the SAS. Like everyone else, we worked hard to get the instructors to reveal some of the secrets they were obviously keeping from us. In the beginning, they would not even mention the acronym SAS; instead, they referred to their time at 'Hereford'. As the week wore on, they loosened up a little, sharing some insights about their service in the field, although rarely discussing Northern Ireland in any meaningful detail. One afternoon, while we were being taught the safest way to approach a roadblock, Fergal and I began talking about infamous incidents at army checkpoints in Northern Ireland. There was silence from the three instructors. Not a word, just impassive stares.

The Officers' Mess we were staying in was located at the heart of an active British Army training camp. Every day, we heard evidence of preparations for war, with the sound of gunfire and blast bombs drifting out of the mist. In the early hours of one dark morning, I woke to the sounds of battle erupting in the middle distance. Despite all the activity, there were few security restrictions, and during our lunch break I set off to explore the open areas of the base. An RTÉ colleague, who had completed the course a few weeks before, had told me about 'Paddy-town', the replica village built to train the 'squaddies' for duty in Northern Ireland. I found the village on the other side of a football field, and, sure enough, it was the spit of any number of drab Nationalist housing estates. As I threw one leg over the wire fence at the edge of Paddytown, I heard voices from the doorway of one of the houses to my left. I turned to see a dense wall of cam-ouflage; a group of about twenty or thirty soldiers was gathered in a doorway a few metres away from me. I slowly retrieved my leg and quietly turned around, fully expecting to be stopped in my tracks by the bloodcurdling yells of men with guns. By the time I had scurried back to the other side of the football field, the soldiers were running through Paddytown in a fog of coloured smoke and gunfire.

Of course, times had changed, and this was no longer Paddytown. It might have looked a little like Ballymurphy, but in the minds of the squaddies storming those houses it was a lot more like Basra. Paddy had left the building and been replaced by Ahmed.

The sight of a real army preparing for an almost certain war had made me think hard about what I was learning in the Officers' Mess across the field. Every day at 8 a.m. we would gather in the classroom, and our training would not finish until twelve hours later. During our open-air sessions, we felt more like children in a high-risk playground than professional journalists. The Ballistic Awareness course involved small groups of us running like headless chickens into the woods at the sound of gunfire, or picking good hiding places behind tree trunks or mounds of dirt. The entire group was roused to applause when Volker dodged the blank rounds by leaping headlong over the man-sized bushes at the perimeter of the Officers' Mess. There was a little infantile shiver of excitement in all this, especially when the instructors passed a handgun around the class. Were we preparing for war or just playing at it?

It took a few days, but the profound value of the course began to emerge from our relentless exposure to violence and death. The unspoken understanding in the classroom was that the instructors knew what they were talking about because they had lived through at least an approximation of the horror they were describing. The company that ran the course was called Pilgrims, a title that I believe is taken from the inscription on a memorial at SAS headquarters called 'The Clock': 'We are the Pilgrims, master; we shall always go a little further: it may be beyond that last blue mountain barred with snow, across that angry or that glittering sea.' The company's founder, Dr Mal McGowan, had served with the famous Bravo Two Zero patrol during the first Gulf War. His covert SAS unit had operated behind enemy lines until it was tracked down by the Iraqi military. There were eight men in the patrol. Three were killed; four, including McGowan, were captured and tortured; and just one escaped unharmed.

The first-hand experience of combat came with valuable insider information. Our instructors had once been employed to kill, so who better to reveal the mind-set of the people who might like to kill us? Our friend Kev, and his colleague Karen, introduced us to the world of the land-mine. There was a surreal quality to their briefings. One moment Karen was explaining how you could rig up a booby-trap bomb using a champagne bottle; a few minutes later, Kev was showing us photos of the injuries caused by land-mines: skin peeled away to reveal the white of the bone beneath and, of course, empty space where limbs should be. In the middle of a session on artillery fire,

Kev played video footage taken in the aftermath of a mortar attack during the siege of Sarajevo in 1994. I remember seeing the original pictures of the incident, but this was the footage the television stations never aired. My brain stopped processing the images after I saw a man bent over the railings at a pedestrian crossing. His intestines had seeped through the gaping hole in his stomach.

The collective groan that greeted each grotesque image became quieter as the days progressed, and there was hardly a sigh by week's end. In place of that early feeling of shock, we had become more calculating in our response to the images the instructors were showing us. In the first-aid classes, which made up 50 per cent of the coursework, the primary thought in our minds was how the person in the picture would survive, not how disgusting the wounds were to our untrained eyes. The more revolting the image, the more interesting it became. One instructor flashed up a picture of a young man's face on the overhead projector. He told us that, for some unknown reason, the young man had put a powerful firework in his mouth. When the firework exploded, it had torn his face apart with cartoon precision. His face had literally peeled away from his mouth, in thick strips of equal size. The young man's eyes were opened wide in a fixed look of shock. So were mine.

The value of this course, and all the horror we were shown, lay in a trade-off. We were told that, no matter how hopeless a situation appeared, there was always a chance of survival if we were prepared to sacrifice some of the things that made us human. In war-zone first aid, the trade-off could involve looking at two injured companions and deciding to help the one who had the better chance of surviving. In a minefield, it might force you to leave a companion to bleed to death for fear of risking your own life. Perhaps unintentionally, the warriors and medics teaching this course had shown us the extent to which war can drain our souls of what makes us human.

Here was the antidote to that age-old myth that there is glory in war, for either correspondent or warrior. By forcing us to get used to unthinkable routines, they had helped us to understand that our job was not simply to record the battle. They had shown us that the real story is how ordinary men and women cope with life when all around them there is death. At the end of that week, any glib intellectual pronouncement we could have made about war would have sounded empty and hollow. Longmoor was that kind of place.

Our instructors displayed a dispassionate professionalism that scared me. Broad moral issues were sidestepped and the guiding principle of the course was that war is an unfortunate fact of life. I never heard a hint of relish in the instructors' descriptions of death and injury, but where the appropriate reflex should have been towards outrage, our teachers often veered in the direction of black humour. Be very afraid, they told us, if you arrive at hospital and the ambulance driver introduces you as Mr K. Bundy. This is code for Knackered But Unfortunately Not Dead Yet and means you have no hope of survival. Also, in first aid, we were taught about the importance of dealing with the ABFN when you reach the scene of an accident. It was later explained that ABFN stands for Able-Bodied Fucking Nuisance: a well-meaning bystander who might get between you and the victim. The same instructors were full of off-beat hints for dealing with unthinkable eventualities. For example, one of the most effective pieces of equipment when treating a gunshot wound is a tampon. Perfect fit apparently, as long as you have been shot with a light calibre weapon.

In almost every component of the course, there was an opportunity for light relief. The one exception was the training we received on the threat of nuclear, biological and chemical weapons. Our instructor was called Scotty, which was no great revelation in light of the Scottish accent and the tattoos of the Scottish flag on either forearm. Scotty was a sceptic, and his uncompromising view of the world extended to journalists. He scoffed at the media description of 'weapons of mass destruction', insisting they were 'weapons of mass terror' because it really is difficult to kill large numbers of people with them. Excluding the apocalyptic certainty of nuclear weapons, he said that there are very few effective ways of distributing nerve or chemical agents that do not pose a risk to the people doing the distributing.

This was a rare expression of optimism during a day full of nauseating revelations and acronyms. Scotty explained that inside the bag containing our IPE (Individual Protective Equipment) were our gas masks, which should be held by the PSM (Primary Speech Module) and not the S10 (the respirator). He explained the Chemical Safety Rule (experience, see, smell, notice and hear) and the Chemical Immediate Decontamination drill, and he demonstrated the first basic alarm signal in case of a suspected NBC (Nuclear Biological Chemical) hazard (a loud call of 'Gas, gas, gas'). As Scotty guided us through the basics, he described a specific nerve agent as 'a nasty piece of kit' and constantly referred to 'bits and bobs' when describing the mechanics of germ warfare. Occasionally, he dropped in an American military slang word such as SWAG (Some Wild-Assed Guess).

The jargon gave way to brutally simple language as soon as the practical component of the course began. The symptoms of nerve agent poisoning were described in our handbook as 'Nausea and vomiting. Involuntary urination and defecation. Muscle-twitching and jerking. Stoppage of breath.' On paper it was bad enough, but soon Scotty was writhing on the floor in a practical demonstration of slow and agonising death: 'This is the point at which you start to piss and shit uncontrollably.' To which there really was no appropriate response but 'Good Jesus'.

Once again, we were back to that essential trade-off: you can survive as long as you are willing to do things you never thought possible, such as inflict excruciating pain on yourself. Scotty pulled out a device called ComboPen which contains atropine, the antidote to nerve agent. It looks like a pen, but when pressed to the leg of the chemical suit it will fire a needle into your skin at 147 miles an hour. The effects of atropine are similar to nerve agent poisoning, so this is, to borrow Scotty's phrase, 'a nasty piece of kit' that could kill you if it does not cure you first.

As the day came to a close, Scotty told us to get into our chemical suits and climb aboard a Land Rover parked outside. He drove us a short distance to a line of bunkers at the heart of the Longmoor camp. It turned out they were not bunkers but chambers. Gas chambers. Once inside, Scotty closed the heavy door behind us and told us to stand in a semicircle and put on our gas masks. He bent down, took out a small block, which looked a bit like a firelighter, and tried to set fire to it. After a few attempts, the block started to give off a dense white smoke. But it was not smoke: it was CS gas. Scotty then instructed us to begin a series of exercises that involved taking off our masks, cleaning the components, replacing the canister and masking-up again. The drills had to be completed with our eyes closed and without a breath being taken. Once the gas masks were back on our faces, we could breathe again. If we had completed the drill properly, then the gas would have had no effect on us.

When the exercise was over, Scotty called us before him, one by one, and told each person they would have to remove their mask, look him in the eyes and tell him their name, the position they held and the company they worked for. When my turn came, I stepped forward, inhaled all the available air in the mask and then pulled it away from my face. As I looked at Scotty, the gas seeped into my eyes and started rubbing my nerve endings like sandpaper. When I opened my mouth to speak, the gas raced towards my lungs, burning my throat as it went. Before I could say 'RTÉ', I had to throw my head back in a desperate attempt to find some relief from the pain.

Once outside the chamber, the cold air made me aware of the tears and snot that were flowing liberally down my cheeks and chin. As I turned my face skywards in search of more oxygen, mucous and gas residue collected in the hollows around my eyes. I had to wrap my arms around my ribcage to stop myself rubbing this toxic cocktail deeper into my burning skin. For a few moments, it felt as if someone had plunged my head into a bath filled with hot baby oil and jellyfish.

Like the child who puts a hand on the hottest ring of the cooker, the people in that gas chamber were learning through pain. But while the child will never do it again, we might just have to. During that week in December, I learned how the unthinkable was survivable. Yet, while the realities of a battlefield now seemed appallingly intimate, they were no easier to comprehend, at least not by any standard measure of right and wrong. Then again, as the world moved towards war, the measure of right and wrong seemed to shift, depending on what part of the earth's surface you occupied. We would all be trapped by the same objective reality but eventually find freedom in our various prejudices. Where you were from was what you believed.

2

THE LIBERTY LIP LOCK

'I was at a celebration of India's Independence
Day, and a Frenchman came walking up to me
and started talking to me about Iraq, and it was
obvious that we were not going to agree. And I
said, "Wait a minute. Do you speak German?"
And he looked at me kind of funny and said, "No,
I don't speak German." And I said, "You're
welcome," turned around and walked off.'

US Congressman Tom DeLay, House Majority
Leader, February 11, 2003

An Irish upbringing is a big help in writing about war.
Even if the closest you came to conflict was a schoolyard
scrap, your consciousness was still shaped by all the
senseless suffering and contradictions you were served up
in history class. As a consequence, no matter what war
zone you find yourself in, there will always be something
about the conflict around you that is depressingly familiar.

Perhaps that explains why Ireland was the birthplace of
war reporting, or at least of the man who pioneered the
profession. William Howard Russell may not have been

the first journalist on a battlefield, but he is still considered the original of the species, or, as he put it, 'the miserable parent of a luckless tribe'. Born in Tallaght in 1820, Russell picked up a taste for organised violence in his student days at Trinity College, where he was said to be 'prone to the usual range of adolescent enthusiasms for whiskey and modest riot'. He joined his fellow undergraduates in pitched battles with local Catholic gangs. 'They were glorious doings,' he later told a British magazine. 'We frequently parted with broken heads but sometimes we had it all our own way and made the most of it.' Russell's knowledge of street-fighting techniques gave him a valuable advantage when he covered the general-election campaign of 1841 for *The Times* of London. Three years later, he scooped his rivals with news of the verdict in the trial of Daniel O'Connell.

Russell secured his place in history when he covered the Crimean War. His account of the charge of the Light Brigade and the suffering of British soldiers in the winter of 1854 formed the opening chapter of the war-correspondent's story. Russell's dispatches were laden down with romanticised images and none-too-subtle appeals to patriotism, but there was also an underlying honesty that enraged establishment figures back home. Prince Albert said 'the pen and ink of one miserable little scribbler is despoiling the country', while a former secretary of war wrote, 'I trust the Army will lynch *The Times*' correspondent.' Among Russell's few competitors in the Crimea was another Irishman, Edwin Lawrence Godkin, who was sent to war by the *London Daily News* at the tender age of twenty-two.

Godkin and Russell failed to have the same impact during the next big conflict, the American Civil War, where they had to compete with a legion of recently commissioned war reporters. Much was expected of this new class of wartime professional, perhaps too much. A Union general told Godkin that he wanted reporters to wear white uniforms on the battlefield 'to indicate the purity of their character'. Unfortunately, there was little purity of character on display during the American Civil War, as the profitable search for thrills and half-truths transformed reporters into 'professional observers at the peepshow of misery', as one journalist put it.

There were some novel aspects of the coverage of the American Civil War, including the growing disdain shown by British correspondents towards their American counterparts, a superiority complex that remains in place today. 'Their communications are what you might expect from men of this stamp,' Edwin Godkin wrote of the American reporters, 'a series of wild ravings about the roaring of the guns and the whizzing of the shells and the superhuman valour of the men, interspersed with fulsome puffs of some captain or colonel with whom they happened to spend the night.' There is some evidence to support that view, according to Philip Knightley, who wrote the definitive history of war reporting, *The First Casualty*. He said American journalists did not have the experience to prepare them for the rigours of combat journalism, and he believed the fierce competition between newspapers forced correspondents to sacrifice accuracy and balance in favour of speed and quantity. Knightley cited an order from a *Chicago Times* editor to one of his men in the field: 'Telegraph fully all news you can get and when there is no news send rumours.'

You would be forgiven for assuming the British correspondents were providing a better class of dispatch from the battlefield, but you would be wrong. Most viewed the Civil War through the filter of their employers' bias, and their dispatches tended to pander to the dominant prejudice back home. 'There was not a single British war correspondent who saw the great forces at work in the American Civil War and who tried to convey them to his readers,' said Philip Knightley. 'The British public received a biased, inaccurate impression of the war, and the anger that this created in the American government caused long-lasting mistrust between the two nations.'

History repeats itself, even for the people who write its first draft. The era of Russell and Godkin produced an enduring rivalry that, as the 'luckless tribe' prepared itself for service in Iraq, was incorporated into a contemporary transatlantic battle between two distinct views of the world. Just after my stint in Longmoor, I picked up *The Guardian* and read that BBC World Affairs editor John Simpson had told a literary festival in Cheltenham that George Bush was a man of below-average intelligence and a 'glovepuppet of his vice-president, Dick Cheney, and Defence Secretary Donald Rumsfeld'. Simpson complained that the American public had been horribly misinformed in the wake of September 11, at least in part by the Fox News network, which he said was 'dysfunctional, grotesquely patriotic and embarrassing'. In the midst of his attack on US television stations, Simpson broadened his focus to include the misinformed American public: 'Thank God I don't have to broadcast to them.'

Them. The Americans. Led by an idiot and gripped by ill-informed hysteria. In a time of confusion, within sight of war, this was as close as you could come to a universally accepted premise among Europeans. Like all commonly held assumptions about the United States, there is a shiny nugget of truth buried somewhere beneath the insult. It may not provide the whole truth, but at least there is enough there to sustain the credibility of the premise. Unfortunately for the American media, the premise was taking hold in Europe just as American reporters began to write about their preparations for war, in particular their involvement in hostile-environment courses run by the Pentagon.

The training was offered to reporters who would end up 'embedded' in US military units once the war got underway. By definition, the courses were designed to familiarise these journalists – the 'embeds' – as much with military etiquette as survival techniques. Some participants wrote about being issued with dog tags, riding around in Blackhawk helicopters and Bradley fighting vehicles and eating US military rations or MREs (Meals Ready to Eat). In Florida's *St Petersburg Times* one reporter wrote about the ease with which his fellow classmates slipped into military life: 'It wasn't long before they were making "GI pudding" with the hot chocolate mix in their MREs, hustling to class and using military slang like OPP-4 instead of saying "opposition forces".' A *Boston Globe* reporter had a similar experience: 'By week's end, we know about "sniffle gear" (warm clothing) and are all using the Army's universal affirmative, "hoo-ah," which according to the official definition, means "anything and everything except no".'

This peculiar intimacy was viewed by the optimists as a repeat of the media experience in Vietnam, where correspondents worked closely with ordinary soldiers and still exposed the misconduct of the war. But there were also many pessimists who feared a repeat of the first Gulf War, after which US Secretary of State James Baker delivered a damning indictment of war reporters: 'Who could not be moved by the sight of that poor, demoralised rabble, outwitted, outflanked, outmanoeuvred by the US military?' All that talk of 'hoo-ah' and 'sniffle gear' seemed to strengthen the credibility of the pessimists.

The truth was that most American journalists had a considerably more discriminating view of the dangers inherent in the approaching conflict than reports on this side of the Atlantic suggested. Even the élite members of the press corps publicly expressed their concerns. Veteran CBS anchor Dan Rather observed that 'there's a pretty fine line between being embedded and being entombed', while the former *New York Times* correspondent Sydney Schanberg warned: 'embedded means "You're there". It also means "You're stuck".'

To lower the risk of being stuck, some American media organisations decided to avoid those Pentagon courses or supplement them with training from British companies such as Pilgrims. CNN alone spent about €1 million supplying independent training to seven hundred staff members in the months leading to war (far more than RTÉ would spend on its entire war coverage). The vast majority of American journalists would work entirely outside the embed process, and many would show great courage as 'unilaterals'. And even among those members of the American media destined to report as embeds, there was a fair proportion of hard-headed realists.

The complexities of the debate inside the American media seemed to pass over the heads of its European critics, who instead focused on the antics of fringe characters such as Geraldo Rivera, the Fox News correspondent who had turned up in Afghanistan with a pair of pearl-handled pistols. In Ireland, in the months leading to war, the working assumption was that America's gung-ho media were helping that 'idiot' Bush lead his 'hysterical' people into war. By constant repetition, the critics successfully shaped the conventional wisdom, but as they remained vigilant for any sign of bias or warmongering on the part of others, they were becoming blind to the impact of their own prejudices on the quality of the dialogue about the approaching conflict.

On the other side of the Atlantic, on the fringes of the mainstream media, a dangerous momentum was building. Even as the prospective embeds and their editors were debating the ethical challenges of the oncoming war, a loose network of conservative commentators had emerged with an 'enemies list' and a deep well of prejudice from which to draw. This militant tendency of the American media was feeding off the resentment felt by many ordinary citizens, who were listening with growing exasperation to the rising chorus of complaint from abroad. In response, these conservative commentators used existing prejudices about 'Yurp' as a means of undermining broader strategic arguments from the other side of the Atlantic. Culture had become war by other means.

The militant tendency came to prominence soon after September 11, when assorted foreigners began casting doubt on the conduct of the US-led war on terror. But as the countdown to war in Iraq reached its final stages, it levelled its vitriol almost exclusively at the easiest target: the French. In the pantheon of American comedy, the French play the role that mothers-in-law play in British humour. There is perhaps no major character on prime-time television that has not had a go at the French at some point. From the lower end of the TV food chain, where super-slob Al Bundy in *Married with Children* tells his audience 'It's good to hate the French,' to the lofty heights of *The West Wing*, where President Bartlett is advised that he should thank the French for helping to resolve a foreign crisis: 'I would,' he responds, 'but I'm worried they would surrender.'

One of the leaders of the militant tendency was Jonah Goldberg of the *National Review*. He warned that 'when one froggy intellectual after another starts lecturing the United States on how to do things when so many of the world's problems can be laid at unwashed French feet – well that's when frog-bashing is going to become an American pastime again'. The militant tendency could not have cared less whether the French were actually listening to this invective; their primary objective was to create a space for a virulent brand of loaded rhetoric inside American society. In the supercharged atmosphere that preceded war, they were at least temporarily successful. 'We don't know much about wine,' said respected foreign-policy expert Walter Russell Mead, 'and they don't know nearly enough about Colonel Sanders.'

The tide of vitriol reached its high point in the first weeks of February 2003, as France's diplomatic campaign against war in Iraq reached its climax. French resistance at the United Nations Security Council gave rise to unprecedented attacks in the US media. On its front page, the *New York Post* published a photograph of an American graveyard in Normandy under the banner headline 'SACRIFICE'. Below the headline was this question: 'They died for France but has France forgotten?' On one of the inside pages was a cartoon depicting an ostrich with its head buried beneath the sand. The words above read: 'The national bird of France.' The insults were spread across the pages of other American newspapers: France had become a 'petulant prima donna of *realpolitik*' leading an 'axis of weasels' or 'a chorus of cowards' or an alliance of 'wimps', depending on which commentator you were reading.

By mid-February, a campaign begun by a media élite had filtered down through the more conservative strata in American society to affect daily life in some very strange ways. In New Orleans, local politicians talked of changing the name of the French Quarter, while somebody in Louisiana's state capital, Baton Rouge, floated the idea of renaming the city 'Red Stick'. Some French restaurants in New York complained of a 20 per cent drop in business, Montana's state pension fund discussed plans to sell its French shares and in Kansas City there were complaints about French onion soup. 'Francophobia' also invaded the corridors of power, with Air Force One serving 'freedom toast' to its passengers instead of French toast. Perhaps the high point, or low point, depending on your outlook, came when Representative Bob Ney successfully fought to rename French fries in Congressional restaurants as 'freedom fries'.

With every backlash in the United States, there is bound to be a counter-backlash. As the campaign of 'defrench-ification' reached critical mass, voices of moderation began to join the debate. At first, they used irony to make their point. Why stop at 'freedom fries'? asked a *Los Angeles Times* columnist. Why not write legislation changing a French maid's outfit to a 'freedom frock', the French horn to the 'victory trumpet' and the French kiss to the 'liberty lip lock'? Even some conservative commentators tried to introduce a sense of historical perspective. In his regular column in the *New York Times*, William Safire reminded Americans that they had been here before. During the First World War, he said, sauerkraut was temporarily renamed 'liberty cabbage'. Hamburger had become 'Salisbury steak' and Dachshunds 'liberty pups'. About the only term in common usage during the Great War that retained the name of the enemy was German measles. *Plus ça change*, as the 'weasels' might say.

If there was an unintended benefit from all the anti-French nonsense, it was the reminder that the United States is a wondrous mixture of foreign influences: what you think is foreign is actually American, and what you think of as American is probably imported. So consumers found out that the famous French mineral water Evian was distributed by Coca-Cola, while a company from neutral Switzerland bottled the American alternative, Poland Springs. The bakery chain Au Bon Pain started handing out flyers reminding customers that it was actually an American company, while it emerged that a rival brand, Vie de France, was owned by the Japanese. French's Mustard is British, while the American tobacco giant Philip Morris owned the very Gallic-sounding competitor, Grey Poupon mustard. To make things all the more confusing, that famous line from *The Simpsons* about the French being 'cheese-eating surrender monkeys' did not come from Bart or Homer but from Groundskeeper Willie, a Scotsman.

As the militant tendency looked for ways to destroy connections between France and the United Sates, it was forced to confront an uncomfortable reality about the power of the American economy: it has a lot to do with foreigners. The US Congress found out that the company making meals for the US Marine Corps was a subsidiary of a French conglomerate. Fifty-one members of the House of Representatives signed a letter asking the defence secretary to withdraw the contract from the company, Sodexho. The congressman responsible said getting members to sign the letter was 'easier than giving away money'. There was one small problem: Sodexho employed 110,000 people in the United States. As it turned out, French firms were the fifth largest foreign investors in the US, employing 649,000 workers. How's that for a kick in the teeth?

As the anti-war movement in Europe gained momentum, it began to throw up groups and individuals who resembled their worst enemies in the United States. Just like the militant tendency, they decided the best form of defence was to attack cultural symbols. A German group called Sprache in der Politik (Language in Politics) called on concerned citizens to replace English words in daily use with their French equivalents. So, for example, 'OK' would become *d'accord* and *bon vivant* would replace 'playboy'. According to Armin Burkhardt, professor of German at the University of Magdeburg, it was both a peaceful demonstration of German–French solidarity and a protest at Anglo-American influence. 'He who pursues unlawful and, in part, even immoral policies cannot be a role model.'

The pre-war cultural backlash seemed particularly strong in Germany, where some bakers renamed the round iced cake formerly known as the Amerikaner (in some places, they added a chocolate peace symbol to the cake). A skin and venereal-disease doctor in the town of Rendsburg placed a notice outside his door saying he would not treat British or American patients 'or their sympathisers'. Web sites cropped up offering lists of American and British products that should be boycotted and European options that could be bought. Germany may have led the way in cultural protest, but the contagion spread across Europe like an untreated rash.

All this suggests that the transatlantic culture war that broke out in early 2003 was finely balanced between rival forces of equal intensity. That is not completely true. When you put the phrase 'anti-Americanism in Europe' into Google, the popular Internet search engine, you get 35,000 responses. 'Anti-Europeanism in the United States' will return 944 entries. Most Americans did not define themselves in opposition to European values, but the opposite was increasingly the case in Europe. Americans might have resented French criticism, but a growing number could not be bothered listening to what Europeans were saying; in Europe, we do not have the luxury of ignoring Washington's rhetoric. The American militant tendency might have been loud, but it represented a fringe in America; by contrast, what inspired some Germans to boycott the word 'playboy' is a form of hostility to American dominance that has deepened and widened during Zulu Time.

In March 2003, just weeks before the outbreak of war in Iraq, the Pew Global Attitudes Project published a survey showing the depth of European disillusionment with America. In the summer of 2002, 75 per cent of British people had expressed a favourable view of the United States. This fell to 48 per cent in March 2003. In France in summer 2002, 63 per cent thought highly of the US. The figure was halved by the outbreak of war. The survey recorded an even greater degree of disillusionment among Germans. The remarkable thing about this pre-war shift against the United States was that it seemed to extend right across Europe. The people of nations with their own historic rivalries were united by their growing hostility to the American role in the world. The European Union could not agree a common foreign policy, but its people seemed to have decided an agreed message to the United States: we don't like you any more.

That Pew Global Attitudes Project did not publish findings about Ireland, but I assumed that the Irish public were just as jaded with the United States as the rest of Europe was, possibly even more. And yet in spring 2003, Eurobarometer conducted a survey that seemed to show that Ireland retained a positive view of America relative to other member states of the EU. The poll found that a slim majority of Irish people believed the US was a positive force when it came to the fight against terrorism (just one in ten Greeks believed the same thing), and when asked whether or not the US was a force for peace in the world, the Irish gave the third most optimistic response of all.

Commentators greeted the results with a positive spin about the 'pragmatic' Irish, but a closer look at the trends revealed that Ireland was growing increasingly suspicious of the United States. Between autumn 2002 and spring 2003, there was a 14 per cent drop in the number of Irish people who believed the US was a force for good in the fight against terrorism. In fact, we were growing cynical on that score at a faster pace than some of our European partners. And what about that finding that we still felt better about the US contribution to world peace than most Europeans? The reality was that the proportion of Irish people who thought the Americans were a positive force for peace was just 37 per cent; across Europe the average was 23 per cent. In other words, support for America had become a minority view in Ireland. It's just that the minority was not yet as small as it was in other European countries.

While the polls clearly showed increasing suspicion, we remained Europe's most fervent admirer of the United

States on at least one issue. When asked if the US was a force for good in the growth of the world economy, 53 per cent of those surveyed in Ireland said yes. In this finding was the hint of an underlying duplicity in our attitude. Given Ireland's traditional economic relationship with the United States, you could argue that we do not feel as bad about America as other Europeans because we still have our bread buttered by Uncle Sam. As we struggle to keep those American factories on the outskirts of Irish towns, perhaps we tend to be more circumspect in our view of the Yanks than the French or the Germans. Or maybe we are just that little bit cuter in how we express our growing disenchantment with the USA.

The more I listen to Irish conversation about America, the more I am convinced that we have the ability to hold two contradictory impressions of the United States at the same time. Maybe it is a trick handed down from the past, when we were forced to look upon our rich patron across the Atlantic with a respectful smile while quietly cursing our dependence through clenched teeth. There is also the possibility that our schizophrenic take on America is a reflection of divisions among us. I bet that your feelings towards the United States have a lot to do with your age and the era you grew up in. You could go as far as to say that Ireland is divided between an ageing minority who look at America and think Kennedy, and a rising cohort who can visualise nothing but Bush.

There are signs of this split personality even when it seems Ireland is speaking as one. In the immediate aftermath of the attacks of September 11, this country provided comfort in a way few nations did. There was sincerity in the emotions spilling over on radio and television, outside the American Embassy, in the personal messages that poured across the Atlantic by phone or Internet. Still, this venting of emotion was never an act of political solidarity: it was simply a human response to the stomach-churning awfulness of the scenes in New York. And side by side with the desire to reach out and comfort, there was also a chilling fascination with the endless looping images of the planes and those buildings, a combination of what French philosopher Jean Baudrillard called the 'two elements that fascinate 20th century masses: the white magic of movies and the black magic of terrorism'.

In Ireland, we knew in some intellectual sense that the world had changed, but September 11 was largely played out in our lives as a television spectacle. To Americans, it was the mass murder of people just like them: anonymous office workers and air travellers who should have had nothing to fear on a sunny Tuesday morning besides the hassle of a big-city rush hour. When they turned off their televisions, the horrors of that day were still a reality. As they returned to their offices, their public buildings, their schools and their airports, the images still haunted them. Outsiders called it paranoia, but to most Americans it was searing vulnerability. It was the discovery of a hidden threat in the mundane routine of any average day, in the anonymity of any big American city. No matter how much genuine emotion we felt after September 11, we were never going to arrive at the same conclusions as the Americans.

Before long, our sympathy for the United States existed side by side with a rising disdain. It emerged slowly from the talk shows and the editorial pages and was encouraged by stalwart critics who had bided their time and waited for the images from New York to loosen their visceral hold on our consciousness. The brutal realities of war in Afghanistan helped speed that process, and by the first anniversary of September 11, Irish priorities in a changed world were very different from those of the American people. In America, the objective was to punish the guilty and prevent the wrongdoing from happening again. In Ireland, we wanted the United States to understand the causes and to constrain its desire for vengeance. While they were obsessed with the event, we could not see beyond the response.

In the months before war in Iraq, sympathy slipped off the list of dominant Irish emotions towards the United States. It never disappeared entirely, but it had no active role in the harsh climate of pre-war debate. While the new mood was publicly defined by fear of war, globalisation and the prospect of American empire, it was being shaped by less obvious emotions and instincts. It was as much about gut feeling as conscious political choice. It could be gauged more accurately in pub chatter than in the high-minded debate about the use of Shannon airport. It was still about politics but went hand in hand with a powerful cultural critique. In one incarnation it was subtle; in another it was savage. One moment it was a phobia; the next it was an addiction. Whatever it was, it had arrived, and it was about the hit the streets of Dublin.

3

The March

By the end of the first week of February 2003, countless
international journalists were trapped in the painfully
complicated process of securing visas for Iraq. Those of us
who wanted to get into the autonomous Kurdish enclave
in Northern Iraq had to deal with the Iranian authorities.
We only needed to stay in Tehran as long as it took to
secure safe passage across the border, but to the powers
that be in the Iranian capital, it was not that simple; it is
never that simple. Everything pointed towards a US-led
invasion of Iraq in early March, and there was a growing
risk the Iranians would seal their border with Iraq before
our transit visas had been approved.

At least the anxious wait for that visa would give us a
chance to stop obsessing about the petty details of
personal circumstances and look at the deeply disturbing
bigger picture. The newspapers were full of rage from all

quarters, and while there was some wishful thinking about the unstoppable momentum of the anti-war movement, there was confident talk of the absolute inevitability of war. With the clock ticking ever louder, protest groups chose February 15 to make their defining stand, and as the date approached, it was clear that while their movement might not be unstoppable it certainly was unprecedented.

On the Sunday before the planned demonstration, my wife and I took a walk along the south Dublin coast between Dalkey and Killiney. The winter sunshine transformed the gloomy grey of the ocean into a slightly more hopeful dirty green and lit up the long arc of shingle beach in the distance. In that place, it was easy to forget about the uncertainty of the coming weeks. As we followed the rough path from the Vico Road to the obelisk on the top of Killiney Hill, the quiet voice in my brain kept repeating, 'Don't mention the war.'

We had just started back towards Dalkey along the wooded lane that runs beside the main road when I saw a mother and her young child. We had come upon them suddenly, and they were oblivious to us. They skipped along the pathway, and it seemed the mother was singing a nursery rhyme to her child. As we came closer, the rhyme turned out to be a chant. 'One, two, three, four, we don't want Bush's war.'

I assume that woman and child were among the estimated 100,000 people who flooded the streets of Dublin in protest the following Saturday. 'This was not a demonstration,' wrote Deaglán de Bréadún in *The Irish Times*, 'it was a population movement.' The sheer scale of the turnout did not surprise me given what I had seen on Killiney Hill the previous Sunday. Lives normally untouched by politics were being changed by the prospect of war in Iraq. The change was perhaps temporary, but it was change nonetheless, and it was reflected in the complexion of the massed ranks of the anti-war movement. In my experience of street protest in Dublin, there are usually only a small collection of words you can use to describe those who turn up, such as active, committed, angry, passionate. On February 15, the people who turned up to protest were, by and large, nice.

In every account of the event in Dublin were the single-transferable quotes, 'I haven't really taken part in marches like this before' and 'We wouldn't normally come to things like this.' The event reminded me of the St Patrick's Days of my childhood, when suburban parents dragged their kids into town to watch the parade of cheap corporate floats and American high-school bands make fitful progress through the city streets. Those kids had grown up and were taking over the streets with their help of their own children. On the train into Dublin that day were young boys and girls with peace symbols painted on their faces. In one newspaper report, a nine-year-old child told a reporter that she had skipped her gymnastics class to protest. 'War is just nasty,' she offered in explanation. Another newspaper published a photograph of a young girl with a hand-made placard that read: 'George Bush, you are bold.'

Many of the protestors had an affluent air that seemed out of place beneath the forest of *Socialist Worker* posters. This was especially true of those I saw taking a shortcut up Grafton Street. With cute kids in one hand and takeaway cappuccinos in the other, they marched forward towards a world without war. The slow pace of progress gave some of them time to nip into their favourite shops; I passed one woman in the make-up department of Brown

Thomas who was still holding her anti-war placard. The revolutionaries of 1968 used to say they would hang the last capitalist with the guts of the last bureaucrat. In 2003, the warmongers would be finished off with a nice pashmina from BTs.

The same hugely expanded constituency of angry but nice people turned out in all corners of the globe that Saturday. A journalist covering the march in London for *The Observer* said he had received a call from a friend who had never taken part in a demonstration in her life: 'You wouldn't believe it,' she said; 'there are girls here with good nails and really nice bags.' In describing the 'nice' factor, you could easily slip into cynicism about the nature of the gathering, but that would miss the point. The relative innocence of that huge crowd amplified its voice and underlined the success of the organisers. The protests were the work of a dedicated core of activists, but most of them were mature enough to realise this was not a popular endorsement of any one of their diverse philosophies. Their talent had been to identify what the anthropologists call a 'symbolic consensus' – a slogan or an image that 100,000 people could rally around without having to agree on what it really means. On that day in February, the consensus had formed around three words: stop the war.

While they marched, I was preparing to leave for Iraq and feeling very much out of place each time I passed within sight of the demonstration. My shopping bags were full of water-purification tablets, first-aid supplies, emergency food rations and heavy-duty boots. In my world, war was already a reality, and preparing for that conflict had overtaken any personal feelings about its morality. The families passing by me occupied a very different reality. To some degree, this day would insulate them from the approaching war and protect them from future conflicts. No one could claim that the assault on Saddam had been waged in the name of the parents filling those city streets, or the future generations who walked beside them. Never again would a politician underestimate the capacity of these ordinary people to express their anger as a collective. In their reflections on February 15, philosophers Jacques Derrida and Jurgen Habermas talked of the demonstrations as the beginning of a European public consciousness that transcended national boundaries. They also suggested that these protests, the largest seen in Europe since the end of the Second World War, were a profound rejection of the 'declaration of loyalty' to Washington by some European political leaders.

In Ireland, the scale of the protests implied a sense of unprecedented fear about the direction of American foreign policy. It also had something to do with the perception that our own leaders were complicit in Washington's war on Saddam, and the continued use of Shannon airport by the US military made Bertie Ahern and his government prime targets for abuse. The depth of the passion that day had much to do with the clarity of the issues at stake. In purely domestic terms, it was hard to remember a time when the perennial debate about neutrality had such a clear focus. In the faces of US troops in transit at Shannon was the physical evidence of compromise in our foreign policy. Right or wrong, their presence could not be ignored.

Still, whatever Bertie was allowing to happen at Shannon, there could be only one real enemy that Saturday and it was, without doubt, George W. Bush. Perversely, he had been a central player in the emerging European consciousness, because you might not be able to say exactly what that consciousness stood for, but you could say what it was against: it was against that place called Bush's America.

As I watched the crowds pass the Department of Foreign Affairs on Dublin's St Stephen's Green, I saw a group of young people carrying posters adorned with images downloaded from a web site called 'bushorchimp'. On one side of the poster was a series of photographs of George Bush with various different expressions on his face. On the other side were the faces of chimpanzees striking the same poses. Among the other Bushphobes on the march was a County Westmeath farmer who had carried a furze bush to Dublin. 'The bush represents President Bush,' he told a reporter from *Ireland on Sunday*, 'who is the most evil person in the world.' Singer Mary Coughlan echoed the theme when she declared, 'Saddam and Bush are both bad bastards.'

If the crowds really did endorse a comprehensive philosophy that day, beyond the basic anti-war message, it was opposition to George Bush. To some extent, the prevailing Irish loathing of Bush had a sharper edge because we had been closer to his predecessor than most other European nations. Bill Clinton was a man of obvious complications, intellectual depth and with a hint of cool, while Bush represented an unthinkable degree of simplicity. It had reached the point that when Bush appeared on television he was nothing more than a collection of personality traits that irritated the Irish psyche like an unreachable itch: the redneck drawl, the ostentatious devotion to God, the cowboy clichés, the indelible smirk, the relentless optimism, the overpowering patriotism, the appearance of arrogance and the assumed stupidity. Coincidentally, they are the biting generalities that pepper our national conversation about Americans.

Loathing Bush was a game the whole family could play, but it was the kids who seemed to be the most enthusiastic players. Not since the 1980s, when Ronald Reagan invaded Grenada, bombed Tripoli, armed the Contras and generally screwed up Latin America, has there been such hatred of a US president among the young Irish. But twenty years earlier, American foreign policy was just one of many issues that brought people out onto the street. It was, after all, the era of hunger strikes, apartheid, emigration, unemployment and so much more.

These days, it could be argued that hatred of George Bush, and the vision of America he conjures up, is the only political issue that provides common purpose in a youth culture defined by affluence and success. Whether you are a street-fighting idealist who thinks US corporations rule the world, or a teenage fashion victim who feels sorry for all those fat Americans, there is something mad, bad and dangerous about Bush's America.

Finding a cause with such mass appeal is tough in a chilled-out age like this. A few months before the war, I returned to Trinity College Dublin to research an article about campus life for the *Irish Independent*. My first stop was House 6 on Front Square: the nerve centre of student activities. The most productive days of my college years were spent in this building, and it was my base as president of the Students' Union in 1989. In 2002, the president was an impressive European Studies graduate called Will Priestley.

When Will opened the door of his office on the first floor of House 6, I was pleased to see posters and placards laid out on the floor. The fine tradition of student protest lived on, but with a slickness that was notably absent in my day. Back then, we relied on a creaky old Gestetner machine and a photocopier that kept breaking down. As I listened to Will's laptop beep with incoming e-mails, I realised how much things had changed.

Predictably, the big issue for Will was money: tuition fees were threatening a comeback, student rents were rising and more students were working longer hours in part-time jobs. It all sounded very familiar, but the difference between past and present was that in the new student reality there were few *other* reasons to be angry. 'Apathy is still the biggest problem,' Will told me. 'But when you look back, you also realise how much things have changed and how many of those old issues just are not there any more.'

He had a point. When I think about the slogans of the late eighties, I get an eerie feeling. Free the Birmingham Six, Nelson Mandela and the Guildford Four. Legalise divorce, homosexuality and abortion information. Pardon Nicky Kelly. Liberate East Timor. Bring peace to Northern Ireland. Stop emigration. End unemployment. Even the condom dispenser in the toilet of the student bar required a titanic struggle.

On issue after issue, we achieved all or part of what we wanted. I felt like apologising to Will Priestley for using up all the good causes. Of course, some causes still existed, but it was almost as if they had to be depoliticised before they appealed to the wider student body. Will was proud that the Students' Union had extended its range of activities to charity work, including a ten-kilometre walk for the children of Chernobyl. In the old days, charity was for wimps. For Will Priestley, it was a sign of commitment: 'People say all students do is moan and booze and that's just not true.'

On my way across TCD's Front Square, every face I saw exuded a laid-back confidence. In fact, as I took a closer look at my surroundings, I detected a right-on serenity about the campus. It had the feel of some stylised New Age retreat, populated with hip and good-looking young people in search of enlightenment and self-awareness. What really fascinated me was the number of students who simply took a year off after they left college. Almost one out of every ten graduates was listed as not available for employment or further study, and many of them set out to see the world. My generation travelled for work; this generation travelled to find themselves.

Of course, there is a fine line between a voyage of self-discovery and an exercise in self-indulgence, and the line is getting increasingly hard to locate. Shortly after my visit to Trinity, I came across research carried out by the Amárach consulting group. Its Guinness UDV Quality of Life survey asked people in Ireland aged between eighteen and twenty-four what they would do if they came into some extra cash. Back in 1989, 48 per cent said they would use the money to help a good cause. In 2001, only 25 per cent of young people gave the same answer (57 per cent said they would spend the money enjoying themselves).

You could argue that this survey proves that my generation were better at self-conscious righteousness than young people today – had we been completely honest, the results might have been different. However, other research seems to prove that the young Irish are moving away from activities that benefit society as a whole towards behaviour that could charitably be described as 'self-fulfilment'. The trend is most pronounced when it comes to political activity. In another Amárach study, people aged between eighteen and twenty-four were presented with nine different activities and asked which they were likely to do in the next five years. The thing they were least likely to do was be a member of a political party.

In fact, they were far more likely to bungee jump or sky-dive (7 per cent said political party, 27 per cent said bungee jump or sky-dive). When a generation would rather fling themselves out of a plane than be involved in party politics, you know something is up.

Rather than thinking about this purely as an expression of one generation's psyche, it is more useful to look at these shifting priorities as part of a broader trend within Irish life, a trend that has positive as well as negative effects. In post-Tiger Ireland, traditional moral standards often seem less influential than lifestyle trends, and familiar badges of identity no longer accurately reflect divisions in Irish life: whether you choose *Pop Idol* over *The Week in Politics* says a lot more about you than whether you vote Fine Gael or Fianna Fáil. Our society is more open to the rest of the world than at any time in our history (although that does not necessarily mean we are any better equipped to understand it). The relentless drive to enhance our lifestyles has brought with it an appetite for symbols of diversity. It seems to have made our children more grounded and mature, and at an earlier age. Risk-taking is increasingly celebrated, and honesty has ceased to be a sure sign of mental illness. Public declarations of happiness are no longer greeted with an embarrassed cough, and whingeing is not the valued art form it once was. Optimism is the new black.

Whether this is a process of liberation or the victory of style over substance, the growing emphasis on personal fulfilment means that our society is being shaped as much by cultural influences as by political ideas, if not more. The process by which we filter those influences is perhaps the least understood aspect of modern Irish society, particularly the subconscious mechanisms we use to relate to the dominant culture in the world today: American culture. We may have picked up a couple of hints from Berlin, but Boston did most of the work on the design of our new house. Once again, those below the age of forty best illustrate the struggle of coping with an enhanced US role in our daily lives. In everything from accent to body shape, trends perceived to be American have made their mark on the young Irish. Yet among this age-group are perhaps the most strident critics of the perceived cultural excess and political mistakes of Bush's America.

In November 2003, I was invited to chair a debate on the approaching war in Iraq by the UCD Literary and Historical society (L&H). It was a Friday night, yet the lecture hall was packed when the debate began. Three hours later, most of the audience was still there, enjoying the entertaining self-indulgence of the speakers. The most difficult task I had all night was finding students prepared to argue in favour of a US-led war. Aside from a few hard-core conservatives, only a handful of speakers would take the pro-war side, and I got the feeling that most of them were doing it for intellectual sport rather than out of conviction. If I needed proof of the prevailing campus consensus, it came shortly after the debate when the L&H presented an honorary fellowship of the society to Noam Chomsky, the veteran intellectual powerhouse behind the American anti-war movement. In perhaps one of the most telling declarations of the pre-war period, the L&H auditor said: 'There were no dissenting voices over this choice.'

As the anti-war movement developed in early 2003, the *Irish Times*' education editor, Sean Flynn, took a critical look at the student *Zeitgeist*. 'So what exactly is it that angers and excites our student population ...' he asked, 'the big hate figure is now George Bush and his nasty designs on Iraq.' He pointed out that the big hit on campuses was *Stupid White Men*, Michael Moore's easy-reading diatribe against modern America: 'Students apparently love the sassy way it satires George Dubya and his generals.'

Of course, it is not just what Moore says about the United States that is interesting, but also what his appeal says about Ireland. The undeniable reality is that his criticism of George Bush ('an idiot leader for an idiot nation') would never have become a populist rallying call in Ireland unless it was wrapped up in a blistering cultural attack on America. In *Stupid White Men* we find the mission statement of the campaign against Bush's America: 'A nation that not only churns out illiterate students BUT GOES OUT OF ITS WAY TO REMAIN IGNORANT AND STUPID is a nation that should not be running the world.' The capital letters are Moore's, but the sentiment is increasingly ours.

How do you put a name on all this? When you find a phrase that captures the schizoid relationship we seem to have with the United States, you simultaneously find a thousand reasons why it is inappropriate. Just take a look at the student experience. In that report by Sean Flynn, a UCD academic dismisses the campus hostility to the United States: 'This is trendy, chic stuff. Most of these students are desperate to get the J1 [a working visa for the United States] and they wear the Nike runners and the Reebok sweatshirts. Anti-American? Are you joking?' This is a view that is as illuminating as it is irritating. It comes up with exactly the right answer to exactly the wrong question.

It has been virtually impossible to engage in a serious

debate about our attitudes to the United States thanks to the ridiculous obsession with that single phrase: anti-American. During the debate over the war in Iraq, it was used so much it nauseated me just to see it in print. America's admirers introduced it as a lazy smear against George Bush's critics, but it became meaningless through over-use. It might even have disappeared from the debate were it not for the injured innocence of the critics. With mind-numbing regularity, they emerged to say how outraged they were that anyone would think they were anti-American. Everybody was so busy telling you that they loved America but hated George Bush that no one seemed to know whether you could actually be anti-American or not.

Of course, in theory, you can. There can be little doubt you are anti-American if you agree with any one of the following statements.

- Americans are inferior.
- Americans, because they are Americans, deserve contempt.
- The world would be a better place if America did not exist.

Using this definition, my guess is that there are no more than a handful of people in Ireland who are truly anti-American. Even the most ardent critics of the United States as a political entity will find something they admire about the US as an ideal. And, just because you hate American foreign policy, it does not necessarily mean that you hate the American way of life (although, as we have seen, the two views are certainly not incompatible). For these and many other reasons, the phrase anti-American should never be uttered again in sensible conversation about the United States. Of course, that leaves us with a problem: how do we explain our feelings towards the Yanks?

4

THE USEFUL PARODY

'Young man, there is America, which at this day
serves for little more than to amuse you with
stories of savage men and uncouth manners.'
Edmund Burke, House of Commons,
March 22, 1775

As millions of Europeans joined the anti-war protests,
American commentators sought new phrases to describe
the growing frustration with their nation. Every writer
with an interest in foreign affairs had a theory about the
complicated emotions being expressed by foreigners,
although none of them ever did justice to the views of the
average Irish young person. The crudest ideas came from
the militant tendency of the American media, who
believed America was under attack because it is great and
its enemies cannot stand that fact. This is what President
Bush seemed to have in mind after September 11 when he
said, 'They hate our freedoms.'

The 'hate principle' makes sense when it is applied to
societies in which the information age has spread a limited

vision of the American dream but delivered no tangible means of attaining it. Look at the young people who live in authoritarian Arab nations such as Egypt and Saudi Arabia. Not only is the United States synonymous with failed Western solutions to their problems, but also it has propped up the regimes that deny them the very democracy that US politicians preach. Meanwhile, these young Arabs are bombarded with sensational and seductive images of an America they will never get to experience, even if it existed in reality. In this thwarted fantasy there is humiliation and anger, and this heightens the attraction of radical interpretations of old truths. Along with this radicalism comes blind hatred of the West and its dominant force, the United States.

None of this explains why people in societies with thriving liberal democracies and high standards of living would resent the United States to the degree they now do. In an attempt to solve the puzzle, US conservatives have come up with a variety of theories based on the 'jealousy principle'. The most eloquent formulation comes from writer David Brooks, who has described 'erudite Europeans' as bourgeoisophobes 'who burn with humiliation because they know, deep down, that both America and Israel possess a vitality and heroism that their nations once had but no longer do.' Brooks argues that Europeans have seen their ideals and aspirations put into practice by a society they regard as naïve and unworthy of respect. There is nothing as humiliating as being forced to buy your recycled dreams from the vulgar supermarket of imitation that is the United States.

The jealousy principle has some credibility when you apply it to the élite groups in Europe who resent US domination of global politics. But does it really explain why mocking America has become such a popular pastime among ordinary citizens? Do the Irish really feel the Americans have stolen from them? Quite the opposite: we seem to feel we have taken all we need from them, now that we are affluent and self-fulfilled. Jealousy implies there is something we still have to learn from the United States, and that is not something we will contemplate as long as Bush is in the White House and super-sized meals are being served at McDonald's.

Take a moment to consider another possibility, which you could call the 'resentment principle'. Now that our focus is on lifestyle and not politics, cultural trends are more important in shaping our world-view than political ideas. Because the United States dominates global culture, its influence extends to more aspects of Irish life than ever before. As the extent of this Americanisation becomes apparent, there is a rising level of resentment.

Once people look for ways to express this resentment, their feelings about America's cultural dominance make them far more receptive to arguments about US political and military dominance. Now throw George Bush into the mix. As soon as he was transformed into a collection of cultural defects, loathing of 'his' America became a truly national, cross-party and intergenerational movement. The rise in hostility cannot be explained simply as a response to a shift in US politics. It is also about recent changes in Irish political culture or, more accurately, the politics of Irish culture.

I think the resentment principle goes some way towards explaining the Irish condition. The creeping American feel to our way of life has led some people to conclude that we are losing control of our identity, while others may see it as part of a broader dilution of our Irishness. If this Americanisation was bringing positive change to Irish society, then it might not be resented so much, but on a landscape shaped by Michael Moore and Noam Chomsky, there are few American virtues and many vices.

There is a flaw in the resentment principle. Campus life shows us the extent to which students are deeply hostile to the symbols of American power and yet subconsciously embrace the dominant trends of the American lifestyle. Of course, there are the politically conscious among them who reject brand culture, but what about the apolitical majority? What of the broad mass of young consumers whose world-view is shaped more by tastes and trends than by political philosophy? Since there is no trace of resentment in their intimate relationship with America's best-known cultural exports, how come they generally end up hating the source of the things they love?

The answer lies in the separation of American symbols from American identity. In the schools, pubs and clubs, amid the raised inflections and the baseball caps, there is no fear of 'cultural imperialism'. US sports franchises and fashion houses provide a popular look, but that does not necessarily mean they provide the dominant sensibility. 'Just do it' is no longer a statement of the American imperative in the mind of your average Irish kid, any more than *Riverdance* is an accurate reflection of their sense of identity. This is what US media critic Todd Gitlin calls a 'limited-liability connection' to American culture. Wearing an American brand does not make you feel American: it makes you feel global. It is a marker of membership, says Gitlin, that allows the wearer to 'express some worldwide connection with unknown peers'.

People from a fairly wide range of age-groups, from teenagers to thirty-somethings, have confidence in their ability to pick and choose from the cultural package they are being offered, partly because they have a highly developed sense of irony. The Irish band The Thrills provided a practical instance of this with their acclaimed debut album, *So Much for the City*. The band emerged from the coastal suburbs of South Dublin but quoted lyrics from The Monkees, borrowed an occasional guitar riff from Gene Pitney and sang about the joys of life in Big Sur and San Diego. They told us Santa Cruz was 'not that far', and we all sang along, even as we listened in rain-soaked traffic jams in faceless Irish suburbs.

I loved the album because it made me feel like I was hearing a really good inside joke (although the joke soon became a little worn through overplay). It is the feeling I get when I hear friends quoting lines from *Scarface* or my teenage daughter imitating a Hispanic New Yorker. These are moments when you are tempted to believe American culture is like Guinness: so much better when consumed in Ireland. We get to pick and choose what we like and make it our own, while laughing at all the associated bad taste and self-indulgence. Another Amárach survey provided an insight into this balancing act, as it applied to branded products. A little more than half of the eighteen to twenty-four-year-olds said they always tried to buy a branded product, yet when asked if people their age paid too much attention to brands, 59 per cent said yes. The moral of the story is you can love the America that produced Tommy Hilfiger and hate the America that produced George Bush. Indeed, fashion requires it.

None of this actually contradicts the central core of the resentment principle: the loathing of Bush's America may be explicitly political, but it owes its mass appeal to an underlying popular hostility to perceived American cultural vices. The only doubt surrounds the process by which Irish people of different life experiences come to the same negative conclusions about Americans and their behaviour. Perhaps the missing link can be found in the evolution principle: we disdain America's current incarnation because we in Ireland, and Europe generally, believe we have reached a higher stage of human development. This is a principle described by the American conservative Robert Kagan in his book *Paradise and Power*. He argued that Europe believes it is entering 'a post-historical paradise of peace and prosperity' while the United States 'remains mired in history'. Such a perspective would explain the scale of those anti-war demonstrations. They were both a declaration of our commitment to the absolute primacy of international rules and institutions, and a challenge to the perceived underdeveloped consciousness of those who would challenge them.

What about the vital cultural dimension? Take a look at the way young people express themselves when it comes to the United States. Their disdain does not involve fear or jealousy: it is commonly expressed as mockery. They may blame Americans for electing a government that pollutes and bullies, but they also pity them for having to live in a society that lends itself to self-indulgence and inequality. Their critique of the US now comes with a ring of superiority, and in Ireland today you hear as much amused pity as angry denunciation when the United States is discussed. In all this is the cultural benefit of the evolution principle: as long as Americans are square and dysfunctional, we get to feel even more hip and happy.

Under the evolution principle, we do not dislike America in its present state because we are motivated by spite or jealousy; we are driven by a desire to preserve our superior way of life. We feel we have an obligation to protect the world from a nation that is out of control in both a political and a cultural sense. We may sound hostile right now, but Americans should understand that they would benefit in the long term if they just listened to us about George Bush, Kyoto, Iraq and fast food. They think we do not understand them, but we understand them in a more profound way than they could imagine. Above all, the evolution principle depends on the belief that our judgements about the United States are based on the best available facts and not deep-seated prejudice. Put simply, we are convinced that we 'know America'. This is where we run into trouble.

Let us imagine for a moment that we are almost right about America, but not quite. Just say that, as well as New York liberals, Washington neo-conservatives, Midwest Republicans, war junkies, gun nuts, bible thumpers, white rappers, Fox News, Homer Simpson, Michael Moore, Arnold Schwarzenegger, Carrie Bradshaw, Beyoncé Knowles, MTV *Cribs*, Prozac, the Atkins diet and Botox, there was something else that defined the United States. What would happen if lodged in the gaps in our knowledge were vital strands of America's DNA? Let us consider the possibility that in the things we overlooked were realities that contradicted our existing vision of America. For argument's sake, think about three images: an enormous pudding-faced woman with a double cheeseburger in one hand and a Diet Coke in the other; a tightly packed Manhattan party girl with fake boobs pounding away on the Stairmaster; and the happy face of a California teenager encircled by the traditional Islamic *hijab*. Which of these images correspond to our preconceptions, and which one represents the reality of a rapidly evolving America?

The clue is in the question.

It seems to me that our subconscious has evolved a filter to cope with the torrential flood of images of America. The filter generally blocks those things that do not correspond with our existing assessment of the United States and lets in those that serve to strengthen it. From the resulting pool of facts, we make logical judgements which eventually produce a broad vision of the United States that we believe to be reality. The fact that it is only a partial reality does not detract from its power. The process is like building a home. Equipped with a design, we find the facts that become the frame, which holds up the assumptions that support the walls and ceiling. Whether we became hostile to the United States because of cultural resentment, political awakening or prevailing trends, we all live in the same house, and the sign on the wall reads: 'We are better than the Yanks.'

What we are left with is a prevailing vision of America that you could call the 'useful parody': it bears more than a striking resemblance to the real thing, but we have made structural changes to suit our tastes. The useful parody is inspired by two subconscious desires: to reconcile our faith in ugly America with the facts and to establish that we are superior to a society that increasingly dominates our culture. It is the result of a complex process that begins with the need to establish 'good America' and 'bad America'.

For the last couple of years, bad America has been interchangeable with Bush's America or, in its most crude formulation, 'Texas'. Different people put different things in bad America. For people motivated solely by political animosity, bad America is Bush (Junior and Senior),

Reagan, Nixon, Watergate, Irangate, the military-industrial complex, Donald Rumsfeld, Henry Kissinger, Oliver North, the Ku-Klux Klan, the Florida recount, Kenneth Starr, all aspects of the 'vast right-wing conspiracy' and anyone connected with the invasion, oppression or exploitation of other countries. For people who are solely concerned with culture and society, bad America is pious, intolerant, dumb, small-minded, self-indulgent and childish. It lives out its dreams through shallow Hollywood spectacle and its nightmares through dysfunctional heroes such as Jerry Springer and Oprah Winfrey. Arrogance, selfishness and jingoism define its relations with others. Throw in the death penalty, inequality and racism and you have the basic model of bad America.

In a sense, it is like Orwell's Room 101, providing a shared repository for our personalised fears. The current European vision of bad America is overtly political, even though it is fundamentally cultural. 'I detest Disney-fication, I detest Coca-Cola, I detest burgers,' wrote novelist Margaret Drabble in a *Daily Telegraph* article about the US campaign in Iraq. 'I detest sentimental and violent Hollywood movies that tell lies about history.' Conjuring up bad America is a bit like publishing pictures along with words: if we provide our audience with a stark image of shared prejudice, they are more likely to accept our version of the objective truth.

Bad America is the concentrated version of the America we believe exists right now. It works most effectively when it is invoked alongside good America, or 'real America' as some people have taken to calling it. Perhaps the best expression of this came from Danish director Lars von

Trier at the Cannes film festival in 2003. He had never been to the USA, but he told a press conference he 'felt like an American'. He had travelled to Cannes to promote his film *Dogville*, the first in a series of three damning parables of life in the United States. 'I am sure it is a beautiful country,' he told journalists at a press conference. 'I would love to go there, but I am afraid to go. It could be a wonderful place, but I can't go there right now because America is not how it should be.'

Good America is how America should be. In the political sphere, it embodies the values of freedom, free speech, tolerance, JFK, Bill and Hillary Clinton, Mother Jones, Jesse Jackson, Martin Luther King, civil rights, the Declaration of Independence, the Normandy landings and the Marshall Plan. For those who think the Marshall Plan is a high-protein diet, there is also a cultural vision of good America (or what some Irish people might refer to as 'New York'). Good America has given us Charlie Parker and the White Stripes, *The Godfather* and *Some Like it Hot*, Marilyn Monroe and Humphrey Bogart, Ernest Hemingway and Henry Miller, *Cheers* and *The West Wing*. Boil it down to its essence and good America is, in the words of American philosopher George Santayana, 'football, kindness and jazz bands'.

The dual purpose of good America is to prove just how terrible bad America is and to make us feel that our hostility is not rooted in prejudice or, worse, anti-Americanism. *The West Wing* is a good example of how this works. US television critics had said all they needed to say about *The West Wing* when they observed that this was the story of the Clinton White House without Bill Clinton. It showed us what could have happened if only Clinton had a little bit of discipline and a Hollywood scriptwriter. *The West Wing* allowed us to indulge ourselves in a dream version of American democracy, but it was less a vision of what could actually have been and more a reminder of just how bad things actually were. The fictional President Bartlett was the anti-Bush, and by loving him we were reminded of how much we actually hated the reality, or the reality that we had chosen to believe in. Ironically, the perk of loving *The West Wing* was that it made our disdain feel less sharp than it actually was. 'What do you mean I'm anti-American?' we could tell our friends. 'Sure don't I love your man from *The West Wing* and he's American.'

One of the big problems with the concepts of good America and bad America is that there is no recognition of the relationship between the two. There would have been no *Godfather* without organised crime, no Woodward and Bernstein without Nixon, no *West Side Story* without ghetto violence and no Kenneth Starr without Bill Clinton. The United States is the struggle between good and evil, a compelling spectacle of extremes. Perhaps that is why we tend to overlook the middle, home of the endless shades of good and bad that really define America. Too many journeys in search of America's soul start in New York and end in Los Angeles without ever passing through the small towns in between. It is like a search for Ireland that begins at the Guinness Brewery and ends in Jurys Cabaret. Just imagine if there were only good Ireland and bad Ireland. Overnight we would be reduced to James Joyce and a drunken teenager with vomit on his shirt.

Building the useful parody is so much easier in the age of information overload because we have an unlimited range of sources to choose from. But without some class of screening, we would be swamped by as many good images of the United States as bad. If that happened, our subconscious prejudice would be exposed because we would be forced to make at least some conscious choices between good and bad. Luckily, most of those choices are made for us by the gatekeepers of the information age. Never before have all media outlets been so intimately aware of the personality of their audiences. Fierce competition has led to an unprecedented scrutiny of the changing tastes and trends of the audience, and the vague hint of a developing consensus will unleash a wave of comment and analysis seeking to define and reflect that consensus. There really is no margin in bucking the developing trend.

I am not suggesting some elaborate anti-American conspiracy in the Irish media. In my experience, few journalists consciously set out to pander to the prevailing loathing of Bush's America. However, you cannot ignore the deepening addiction to images that prove our existing thesis about America. Just listen to the murmurs of approval that greet every critical look at US foreign policy or the silence that follows an explanation of George Bush's political appeal in the United States. Similarly, you do not hear many applause lines in articles about the superior quality of American television drama, but a good line about the neurosis of the average American will have your readers laughing into their Corn Flakes. The seductive appeal of your audience's preconceptions is intense.

The burden of proof for any judgement or assumption is lower in the case of the USA than it is for any other topic. And if you do not have all the facts, you can always rely on the established prejudices of your readers and viewers. That is not to say populist judgements cannot have a ring of truth about them, especially if they are based on the known facts about George W. Bush. By writing about Bush as the sum of the things we mock in

American life, it is so much easier to win the argument against his political philosophy. To hammer home the factual political analysis, it becomes necessary to summon up a mental image, a signifier, that is drawn from Ireland's imagined America.

In Bush's case, the list of signifiers includes cowboys, Texas, the TV series *Dallas*, guns and any aspect of fundamentalist Christianity. The images turn up with boring regularity in editorial cartoons, but they have also become an accepted feature of heavyweight commentary. In *The Irish Times*, the weekend before the anti-war protests, a columnist wrote about the bonds that unite *Dallas*, Texas and George Bush: 'The real oil addicts were far more power-crazy than smiling, scheming, lecherous J.R. Ewing ever was.' In the space of a few hundred words, Texas and George Bush were reduced to one-dimensional caricatures that were instantly recognisable to anyone who consumed America through television: 'George Bush and his Texan cabals have the power ... to do more or less as they please. They have realised the dream of J.R. Ewing.'

This is all legitimate comment, as the columnist is employed to deliver subjective analysis of events. But the useful parody takes on an insidious character when it appears amid the hard facts of news coverage. Take this headline in the foreign-news pages of *The Irish Times* from June 2003: 'Texas-style diplomacy runs into trouble.' Here is a phrase that has no meaning except as a trigger for our subjective prejudice: 'Texas-style'. I defy any Irish person to run that through their mind and end up with anything but images of swaggering cowboys and dodgy dealings. The danger here is that the line between factual reporting and editorial comment is disappearing without reporter or audience being aware it is happening. This applies to the characterisation of George W. Bush and his administration, but it also applies to the reporting of other aspects of life and politics in America.

The simple fact is that it is virtually impossible to find a positive image of America amid all the dead bodies, cruelty and Hollywood excess. The torrent of sin and indulgence never lets up, and it flows from every section of every newspaper, from news coverage to lifestyle journalism. In a book review in *Ireland on Sunday*, we find: 'the average American is far closer in appearance to Roseanne Barr and a real life *Baywatch* would be populated with 20 stone tubs of lard, barely able to lift a lilo without stopping for a breather.' To explain why David and Victoria Beckham have failed to click with Americans, a columnist in the *Sunday Tribune* tells us, 'their sheer tackiness, their love of designer clothes, their abundance of money and their penchant for spending in the silliest, most conspicuous manner, their dimness, their absolute lack of any sense of irony or self-awareness – are all commodities that are in abundant supply in the USA.'

If these were isolated examples, they would not matter, but they are not. Pick up the Sunday newspapers any weekend and look for a positive reference to American politics or culture. There is the odd kind word from a business leader and complaints about anti-American bias in *The Irish Times* and RTÉ. But besides all that, there is nothing but an occasional reference to 'how America should be' as proof of how bad America actually is. At this moment in history, if we formed our opinions solely on the basis of the media consensus in Ireland, there is only one conclusion we could reach about the United States: we are superior. If we begin to suspect that our prevailing view of America is tainted by prejudice, we can always turn to our American friends to prove we are on the side of the angels.

5

WHEN GOOD AMERICANS GO BAD

'You know, the enemy, when they hit us on 9/11, really didn't understand America. They thought we were soft. I guess they were watching too much TV!'

George W. Bush, Charleston, West Virginia, January 22, 2002

If George Bush did not exist, we would have to invent him. In almost everything the US president does, and almost everything he says, are little nuggets of proof that reinforce our assumptions about *his* America. When the White House declared its war on terror, we looked for restraint along with the vengeance, and all we heard were spaghetti-western promises: the enemy was 'wanted: dead or alive'; the United States would 'smoke 'em out of their caves'. When we came looking for signs of creative thinking, we saw unintended comedy. 'We are resolved to rout out terror wherever it exists,' Bush said in January 2002, 'to save the world from freedom.' If you made this stuff up, no one would believe it.

Bush has been prone to off-the-cuff blundering since he emerged as a candidate for the White House. The first time I saw him deliver an unscripted campaign speech, in South Carolina, the impression he conveyed was not of stupidity but panic. When he began his address, he seemed confident that he had all the pieces of the jigsaw, but then he quickly forgot how to put them together. The speech degenerated into a series of loud, shouted promises to 'touch every willing heart' and be 'a reformer with results', punctuated with manic pauses. As the audience struggled to keep up, the candidate searched for an appropriate exit line. Winston Churchill once said the secret of a good speech was to sit down the first time you came to a sentence with a grammatical ending. This was never really an option for George Bush. The only apparent limit on his speechmaking was exhaustion.

Over the course of the campaign, the standard of Bush's speechifying rose considerably as he got used to fitting all the pieces together. But occasionally he would discover that a piece of the puzzle was missing, and instead of stepping over the gap in his knowledge, he would dive straight in. The tendency was most pronounced on foreign affairs, where he talked about the 'Grecians' and the 'Kosovians'; spoke of a 'world of madmen and uncertainty and potential mential losses [sic]'; and promised 'a foreign-handed foreign policy'. In hindsight, some of the ad-lib gaffes appear to be a little more calculating than they did at the time. In November 1999, the BBC interviewed then Governor Bush about his presidential aspirations. He talked tough on Iraq (even though 'shock and awe' was still nothing more than a glint in the eye of some hopeful neo-conservative): 'No one had envisioned Saddam, at least that point in history, no one had envisioned him still standing – it's time to finish the task.'

Aside from the occasional portentous declaration, it was impossible to say there was a Bush doctrine buried under all the mangled metaphors. In fact, the candidate seemed quite proud of his lack of a foreign policy 'vision thing', as his father might have put it. 'Nobody needs to tell me what I believe,' he said in September 1999. 'But I do need somebody to tell me where Kosovo is.' In making a virtue out of his vices, Bush was paving the way for his eventual success. He had made the calculation that many Americans wanted a complete change from the Clinton administration, which had developed a reputation for slavish devotion to the polls and chronic indecision. 'I know what I believe in, and I know where I want to lead the country,' Bush told a home-town crowd in Crawford, Texas. 'And most of the decisions come pretty easily for me, to be frank with you.'

There was nothing particularly American about Bush's anti-intellectual approach to power. Some of the most successful Irish politicians of the last ten or fifteen years had traded heavily on their obvious lack of pretension. Albert Reynolds was the self-declared 'one-page man' who could make big decisions without getting mired in detail, while Bertie Ahern's little character flaws made him so much more human. In fact, the comparison between Dubya and Bertie is particularly revealing. As Ahern drifted towards centre stage, there were sniggers about his anorak, his mispronunciations and his struggle with words ending in 'th'. But those who 'misunderestimated' him (to use a Bushism) lived to regret it.

Dubya and Bertie were the kings of lowered expectations, and both exploited their enemies' complacency with the help of ruthlessly efficient political machines. Yet they were also 'uniters not dividers', who rose to prominence by forging unlikely alliances: Bertie settled strikes and forged social partnership in Ireland; Dubya love-bombed Texas Democrats into supporting his brand of 'compassionate conservativism'. The two men also seemed to have similar interests outside politics: Dubya had baseball; Bertie had the Dubs. Clearly, there are a great many differences between these two men, including the blindingly obvious (Bush does not drink Bass and Bertie has not invaded Iraq). However, the bottom line is they share an ability to confound critics and turn apparent flaws into political virtues. Even if you have grown tired of the man, you can still appreciate the story of Bertie's rise to power. In a similar way, you might hate Bush's America, but it's not hard to understand the core of his appeal.

Some of us seem happy to write Bush off as an expression of temporary insanity on the part of the American people. But it is worth taking a close look at his political skills, if only to understand the mind-set of the voters who choose the leader of the free world. Despite his obvious limitations, Bush has what they call in the business emotional intelligence. At close quarters, it comes across as intimate charm; on a bigger stage, it is understanding what your audience feels and the ability to turn that to your political advantage. Bush knows that dogma is a big turn-off for the American electorate, so he presents it as moral certainty, which is a definite vote-winner after the ambiguity of the Clinton years. Bush has also moved quickly to exploit the shifting allegiances associated with historically high levels of immigration. Stupid White Men are not the only people who vote Republican these days. Believe it or not, more than a few Smart Asian Women, Hip Indian Students and Aspiring Latino Tycoons will cast their ballots for Bush in the 2004 presidential election.

There is a danger that our desire to see the back of George Bush will blind us to significant changes in American political culture. Even worse, our hatred for the current president could lead us to misjudge the character of the American people. Just as we have created good and bad visions of the United States, we may be tempted to separate the people who live there into those who revere George Bush (let's call them 'hyper-Americans') and those who are convinced he is Satan (the 'good Americans'). The problem is that many millions of Americans do not feel such clear emotions about George Bush or his political vision. Among those who supported his decision to go to war in Iraq were people with very deep reservations about his administration's neo-conservative foreign-policy doctrine. Among those who admire his moral certainty on terrorism are people who strongly oppose his hardline on abortion and the death penalty. These are the people who can tell us how the United States got where it is today and where it is heading. But these days, we seem to hear only the loudest American voices, the ones that shout the clichés that support our useful parody.

First, let's take a look at the voices of the resistance, the voices of the good Americans. There is nothing more satisfying than hearing the United States criticised with an American accent. Every person I know who feels strongly about the US has an American they will point to and say: 'If only the American people would listen to this person, they wouldn't be so bad.' Of course, the best of all good Americans is the ubiquitous Michael Moore. I first saw him in action at about the same time as George Bush was making those manic election speeches. During the opening round of the 2000 presidential election, Moore transformed a flat-bed truck into a mobile mosh-pit full of teenagers and drove it around the icy roads of Iowa. He turned up at campaign events and invited candidates to stage-dive into the crowd of teenagers as an act of faith in the young people of America. A candidate from the rightward fringe of the Republican Party, Alan Keyes, accepted the invitation and enjoyed a brief bounce in the polls.

Part of Moore's appeal was that he was a regular working-class boy from the decaying heart of the industrial Midwest. He traded on satire instead of high-flown rhetoric and proved that loud Americans with big bellies and baseball caps could still be right, at least some of the time. When millions of progressive Americans went looking for a populist voice to right the oppressive tilt of the Bush administration, they found a grounded yet charismatic hero in Moore. The fact that millions of Americans bought Moore's books and paid to see his documentary *Bowling for Columbine* helped to make him a Yankee messiah on this side of the Atlantic.

'Moore is mild-mannered, yet fearlessly direct,' wrote an Irish film critic when Moore visited Ireland in November 2002, 'a straight man prepared to venture anywhere for answers.' Yet, as we got to know Moore, he began to display a simplistic anger that really was not what we expected from our good Americans. A reporter who interviewed him for the *Sunday Tribune* at about the same time seemed a little taken aback: 'There is an arrogance to Moore,' he wrote, 'which is quite unattractive.' In the interview, Moore criticised the US police for not being assertive enough in responding to the Columbine High School shooting tragedy in 1998: 'There's just two punks in there, who aren't very good shots. Nine hundred rounds, 37 hits, that's pretty bad. That's the new British Olympic shooting team.' Having met family and friends of the Columbine victims in the immediate aftermath of the tragedy, I wondered what they would think of this interpretation of events.

Aside from the nauseating reference to 'hits', Moore's comments display that trademark simplicity of judgement. There is also an important omission in what he serves up as comprehensive truth. The two young gunmen littered Columbine High School with home-made booby-trap bombs, which made the police's job far more difficult. This was not mentioned in the interview with Moore, but you suspect he was banking on our inclination to believe the worst about any American institution. You have to hand it to the man: he understands his audience.

If you removed good-American voices from our intellectual life, then we would have almost no Americans left. We no longer consume a variety of ideas from the United States, and if you do not believe me, then go to your local bookshop and count the number of books that are critical of the United States. In the summer of 2003, I tried this out in the politics and history section of one of Dublin's best bookshops. The new international titles were piled on two tables. There was a total of seventeen books, and fourteen said something significant about the United States. Besides apparently neutral biographies of JFK and Dwight Eisenhower, and a book on the exploration of North America, everything else was written by good Americans or those who agreed with them. Hilary Clinton's autobiography sat beside *The Clinton Wars*, written by a former Clinton adviser. There were three books by Noam Chomsky. Will Hutton's exposé of conservatism in America from a British perspective, *The World We're In*, sat beside a highly critical examination of globalisation (by coincidence, the cover of that book featured a complimentary quote from Will Hutton). Of course, Michael Moore's *Stupid White Men* was there along with Greg Palast's investigation of corruption in the US political system, *The Best Money Can Buy* (by coincidence, the cover of that book featured a warm endorsement from Michael Moore). The final book was entitled *The Great Sedition Is Silence*, another critical look at four years in Bush's America.

Around the same time, I looked up the book *Fast Food Nation* on the Amazon web site that serves Britain and Ireland. There is a section entitled 'Customers who bought this item also bought ...' At the top of that list was Michael Moore's *Stupid White Men*. I checked the entry for *Stupid White Men* and saw that customers who bought that book also bought books by Noam Chomsky and John Pilger and a title called *Why Do People Hate America?* Guess what customers who bought *Why Do People Hate America?* also bought? At the top of the list was *Stupid White Men*.

There is no conspiracy here, just the law of supply and demand and a useful parody. The same good Americans (or Europeans who share their views) now provide the sum total of our intellectual understanding of the most powerful nation in the world. It is perhaps one of the most depressing aspects of life in Ireland that the US provokes so much anger and so little original thought. It is quite possible that the good Americans are right about the United States, but how do we know if we do not read anyone else? If the only people we are prepared to listen to are dissidents, then very soon there is no dissent, just the same overworked clichés.

Let us look beyond the good Americans for a moment. Besides sound-bites from right-wing politicians and the people at those Washington think-thanks, do we really get a sense of what the average patriotic American is thinking?

Unless you bypass the usual filters, you will rarely find
voices that plough the wide expanse of middle ground in
America's national discourse. Here's a useful test: for one
week, ignore all coverage of the United States in the Irish
media. Instead, plug directly into the *New York Times* on the
Internet (and check out the *Dallas Morning News*, the
Weekly Standard and the *New Republic* while you're there);
watch the CBS evening news in its late-night slot on Sky
News; and then pick up *USA Today* from any big
newsagent. On Sunday, revert to Irish coverage and
compare and contrast. You will probably feel a little
relieved at getting back to the ingrained scepticism after a
week of slick sincerity, but you will also notice that
something is missing from the United States as represented
in our media. It is like a doughnut: there is no middle.

There are so many influential US voices that rarely
make it through the filters of the useful parody that it
would be impossible to list them all. For the sake of
consistency, let's take a brief look at someone I have
already mentioned: *New York Times* foreign-affairs
columnist Thomas Friedman. He is a powerful voice for
that huge slice of American citizenry that desperately
wants its country to be safe while also doing the right
thing. In his book *Longitudes and Attitudes*, Friedman
complained that American intellectuals are expected to
play along with the notion that their nation is to blame for
all the world's problems. 'When you refuse to do this in
mixed company,' he wrote, 'it's as if you had unleashed a
huge fart at a cocktail party – people look at you funny
and just start to back away.' Yet, at the same time, he has
been a passionate critic of the shortcomings of US policy
towards the Middle East. 'For too many years,' he wrote in
the summer of 2002, 'we've treated the Arab world as just
a big dumb gas station, and as long as the top leader kept

the oil flowing, or was nice to Israel, we didn't really care what was happening to the women and children out back ... It's time to stop kidding ourselves.'

You can buy Thomas Friedman's books here in Ireland (behind the multiple piles of *Stupid White Men*), and his column is occasionally reprinted on this side of the Atlantic (when it is anti-Bush enough), but his distinctive voice is drowned out by the noise of construction work on our useful parody. That does not mean we do not hear pro-American Americans; it's just that they tend to be chosen because they reinforce our stereotypes about the United States rather than challenge them.

A regular player in Irish discussions about the US is the hyper-American. A good example of the hyper-American is Richard Perle, a former assistant US defence secretary and adviser to the Pentagon. His uncompromising views of world affairs and his intimidating visage have earned him the nickname 'Prince of Darkness'. Like the classic hyper-American, he is the personification of what we fear about the current mood in America.

Another hyper-American is writer and commentator Anne Coulter, the self-appointed scourge of liberals and foreigners. In response to scenes of Arab celebrations after the attacks of September 11, she wrote of 'the ones cheering and dancing right now' that 'we should invade their countries, kill their leaders and convert them to Christianity.' Coulter is one of the star performers of the American militant tendency and was profiled in *The Guardian* one Saturday in spring 2003. On the letters page of the same newspaper the following weekend, she got just the reaction she wanted from British readers. 'Manifest fascism' is how one letter writer described her views and those of her fellow hyper-Americans. 'We believe in freedom and they absolutely do not,' said another. This is the purpose of hyper-Americans: they transform hatred of the Yanks from a prejudice into a mission.

In the coverage of American culture in the weeks before the first anniversary of September 11, Irish journalists paid a lot of attention to American country-music singer Toby Keith. There were numerous references to his song 'Courtesy of the Red, White and Blue', which warned America's enemies they would get a boot in their ass. After all, it was the American way. Various writers cited Toby Keith as proof that the United States was in the grip of a dangerous form of paranoid patriotism. There was hardly any mention of the fact that Bruce Springsteen far outsold Keith when he released *The Rising* at around the same time. This was an album filled with sensitive and reflective songs about the impact of September 11. In the lyrics of one song, 'Paradise', he conjures up the last moments of a young suicide bomber while also expressing the suicidal despair of the lover of a victim of September 11.

It was testament to the profound misunderstanding of the American psyche today that many British and Irish opinion formers looked to Toby Keith as a mirror of the American *Zeitgeist* instead of to Bruce Springsteen. To be fair, the critics did eventually lavish attention on Springsteen, but only when he publicly criticised President Bush and joined the ranks of the good Americans. It brought to mind something an old friend once told me: 'The Irish love Bruce Springsteen. They just don't like the people he sings about.' Maybe we just assume that the trucker on the New Jersey turnpike or the waitress in the suburban diner are under the spell of Toby Keith and his hyper-American friends.

Perhaps it's more complicated than that. Could it be that we find it hard to come up with an objective assessment because our perspective is warped by self-interest? This is, after all, a *useful* parody. As long as the United States is reduced to its lowest common denominator, we get to feel superior. As long as George Bush is a dumb Texan, we can treat his foreign policy with contempt. As long as Americans are killing each other with guns, we are obviously more civilised. Believe it or not, it was a French intellectual, Jean-François Revel, who described the useful parody best: '[America] consoles us for our failures by supporting the fable that it's doing even worse than we are and that what goes wrong here comes from there.'

Europeans are compelled to focus on the ugliness of American life for the same reason millions of people find satisfaction in the *Jerry Springer Show*. It is a morality play that provides us with clear evidence that our lives are relatively clean and uncomplicated. It is what American critic Michael Medved calls the '*National Enquirer* appeal'. Foreigners consume stories of American excess in much the same way that we lap up tabloid revelations about the rich and famous. 'Like the *Enquirer* approach to the private peccadilloes of world-striding celebrities, you are supposed to feel fascinated by their profligate squandering of opportunity and power,' says Medved. 'The violence, cruelty, injustice, corruption, arrogance and degeneracy so regularly included in depictions of American life allow viewers abroad to feel fortunate by comparison.'

In some ways, Americans have only themselves to blame. So few influential Americans seem to realise that there is a link between the crap they send across the Atlantic and the self-serving caricature Europeans have constructed. There are a few conservative politicians in Washington who seem to understand this. As chairman of the House

International Relations Committee, Congressman Henry Hyde once summed up the problem like this: 'How is it that the country that invented Hollywood and Madison Avenue has allowed such a destructive and parodied image of itself to become the intellectual coin of the realm overseas?' The answer is right there in the question: it is precisely because America invented Hollywood and Madison Avenue that its global currency has been devalued.

The corporate empires that dominate American popular culture know what sells to a foreign audience, and nothing succeeds like excess. US movie and TV exports often purport to be 'gritty and real' when in fact they are the fairground mirror, twisting and contorting reality to raise a laugh or elicit a groan. Still, the fairground reflection makes more money than the real thing. Hollywood is giving the market what it wants, and in the case of European consumers, the market wants tales from the frayed edge of American life. Of the three hundred Hollywood movies released in 2001, 65 per cent were rated R, or adults only. If you think this trend towards commercial excess is merely a passing phenomenon, then think again. The proportion of Hollywood profits that come from foreign audiences has risen dramatically; it was 30 per cent in 1980 and 50 per cent by the year 2000. This is the worst possible news for anyone who cares about how Europeans and Americans see each other. The more Hollywood panders to foreign stereotypes, the stronger those stereotypes will become, and the harder it will be for America to liberate itself from the grip of the useful parody.

Here is where I should make a distinction between culture and mindless fun. A few months after that media conference, *The Irish Times* devoted a big spread in its weekend magazine to the rise of American television programmes such as *Jackass*. In keeping with the useful parody, the article found evidence in this cultural trend that bolstered the broader conventional wisdom about America. Under the title 'It's like totally excrement', the article summoned an image of television executives devising 'increasingly outlandish ways of attracting the most coveted species currently roaming television's vast wasteland: the young American (or Americanised) male'. What followed was a description of that young American male and an illuminating reflection of broader Irish attitudes: 'Millions of dollars are dedicated to gaining the attention of slack-jawed youth shuffling around in gargantuan cargo pants and turned-around baseball cap, permanently shell-shocked by the concussions delivered to his brain from his personal sound system.' A generation had been consigned to the scrap heap of history with a few strokes of a keyboard. Once again, in an Irish newspaper, a breathtaking assumption about the general was derived from a partial manifestation of the particular. It seems to come to us as easy as breathing.

The article showed how much bad American television needs cultural snobbery in places like Ireland. I am sure the makers of *Jackass* would have been thrilled by the cultural significance accorded to their show, but unlike Hollywood caricatures, this is a TV programme with absolutely no power to change our perceptions. There is nothing subliminal here, no moral imperative, no hidden values buried in the depiction of senseless self-abuse. There is not even a plot, for God's sake. I have watched the stars of *Jackass* getting the cheeks of their buttocks pierced together, and while it makes no sense to me, it does not come across as innately American. I walk away from the spectacle unchanged, undamaged, having learned no lesson, just like the overwhelming majority of

Irish viewers. Perhaps I will be proved wrong by an orgy of arse-piercing among slack-jawed Irish teenagers, but I don't think so.

Even where American culture has some meaning, we should be careful about how we interpret the word American. It is just possible that those US imports are a reflection of a European collective fantasy almost as much as an American one. The more those Hollywood bosses rely on profits from foreign moviegoers, the more their movies will reflect the demons that lurk in the global subconscious. To some extent, they are already stripped of national characteristics because those characteristics tend to get in the way of the main purpose of American culture, which is to entertain. When Disney's European theme park near Paris opened in 1992, it was described as a 'cultural Chernobyl'. In response, a Disney official dryly observed: 'It's not America, it's Disney ... we're not trying to sell anything but fun, entertainment.'

What is America anyway, if it is not a place that stole every other country's little indulgences and moulded them into a way of life? The US cannot be the same today as it will be tomorrow because of its insatiable hunger for fresh visions of the good life. It is what John Updike once called 'a vast conspiracy to make you happy'. Ideas and innovations will be robbed, adapted, perfected, corrupted, offered for sale and eventually bought back under a new label. American rhythm and blues influenced Jamaican ska, which sparked a British music movement in the 1980s that influenced a whole wave of California bands in the 1990s. There is nothing innately American in this process except for the relentless pursuit of pleasure without the constant need for significance. In fact, in a much more profound sense, there is hardly any human virtue or vice that can be safely called American. Not any more.

Possibly the most dangerous element of the useful parody is the belief that American flaws are exceptional. Books such as *Stupid White Men* describe trends that are increasingly universal, but that is not why they are bestsellers in Ireland. If we thought we were reading about our own developing problems, then we might not like these books so much. In reality, there is no such thing as a uniquely American problem, only a problem that first became apparent in the United States. The forces that spawned developing epidemics such as obesity respect no natural boundaries and will eventually take on the national characteristics of the society they invade. We look and say, 'That is so American,' unconscious of the fact that it is so increasingly Irish.

Sometimes it is hard to see why we should give up our myths about America. For all the negative energy invested in the useful parody, there is also an element of simple fantasy. Our limitless consumption of stories from the American fringe satisfies our appetite for black and white in a world of grey. Tales from the United States are modern fairy stories, providing a glimpse of a dangerous and fantastical world in which there is none of the ambiguity of real life. It is a world that is based in fact but shaped by our love of fiction. With the help of mass media, we will make constant visits to this world, and each time we leave, we will smile and thank God we don't have to live there. But this is Zulu Time. We all have to live there.

PART TWO

DURING

6

LEARNING TO LOVE
THE GREAT SATAN

'We believe such an empire would empty the
future of all that humanity holds decent and dear.'
                      Tehran Times on US imperial ambitions,
                                              February 22, 2003

'Dallas Halts San Antonio's Streak at 9.'
                      Tehran Times on US basketball,
                                              February 22, 2003

The movie on the flight out of Frankfurt was called *Life or
Something like It*. It featured Angelina Jolie as a young and
ambitious American television reporter and Ed Burns as
the cameraman she loves to hate, or hates to love, or some
other murky mixture of the two. After a series of highly
charged confrontations, Jolie finally challenged Burns with
a pout: 'Are you trying to have sex with me?' Both
characters repeated the line several times before they
finally consummated their troubled relationship. There is
nothing like a little light Western titillation to prepare you
for arrival in the Islamic Republic of Iran.

As the final scenes played out, the public address system cut in, and the sexual tension that filled the headset was replaced with Teutonic briskness. The Lufthansa flight attendant had interrupted the movie to tell passengers that the plane was about to begin its descent into Tehran. Along with the usual reminders about seat-belts and customs was a warning of an imminent shift in civilisation. With the fuzzy image of Jolie and Burns frozen on the screen, the voice on the PA advised women passengers to cover their heads in accordance with Iranian law. The movie resumed, and without any apparent fuss, countless headscarves were produced from bags and overhead compartments. As the naked head of Angelina Jolie faded under the credits, and the last alcoholic sips were drained from plastic glasses, I turned towards the window. At first, there was nothing but darkness. Eventually, the lights of Tehran's sprawling suburbs started to shine through the breaks in the clouds, offering an ambiguous welcome to the House of Islam.

Tehran is one of those places that repels you and fascinates you at the very same moment. The suffocating mix of obvious devotion and lurking repression is matched by the physical risks that are everywhere in Iran's capital city. They say one person dies in a car accident in Iran every twenty-six minutes, and that seems like a hopeless underestimate, given the lethal anarchy on the roads and highways that criss-cross the Iranian capital. If other drivers do not get you, the pollution will. The most common car on the roads is the locally made Paykan, which is based on the design of the old Hillman Hunter. It pumps out untreated fumes from low-grade, high-sulphur Iranian petrol, and even on a relatively fresh winter day, a dirty pall hangs over Tehran as a reminder of what uncontrolled growth looks like.

The permanent manky feeling you get travelling around the city becomes easier to bear as you discover the addictive side to Iranian life. There is an intellectual vibrancy you do not find in other Middle Eastern countries, a tradition of poetry, music and film that has survived years of theocracy and a complicated elegance in the way people relate to each other. Iranians have an ostentatious devotion to etiquette, which they comm-unicate through a code of words and gestures known as Ta'rouf. It stresses the need to be humble in your dealings with others without being taken advantage of. Saving face is paramount, and while rudeness is not uncommon, public displays of anger are. Islamic custom and Persian culture add layers of sophistication to Iranian society, making it puzzling and absorbing in equal measures.

I made my first visit to Tehran in 2001, soon after the events of September 11. Like your typical insecure Paddy, I tried to find connections between Ireland and Iran as a means of currying favour with my hosts, but I soon realised the two societies do not have a lot in common. Alcohol is banned, so Tehran is one of the few remaining cities in the world that has no Irish pub, and while the Mullahs had named the street beside the British Embassy after Bobby Sands, the gesture had lost its meaning with the passage of time. In fact, so degraded was Iran's memory of the late hunger-striker that a Tehran business-man had apparently named his burger shop after him. The Irish soccer team was due to play Iran in a World Cup qualifier the month after my visit, but that prospect would produce two words of useful conversation – Roy Keane – before the glaze would return to the eyes of my partner in conversation. The only other evident link to Ireland I could find was a single word of graffiti sprayed on the side of a wall in the centre of Tehran: Boyzone.

To most Iranians, I was just another Ferangi – a Westerner. In fact, being Irish was far less interesting than being British or American. There was something unexpectedly refreshing about being from a place that has no meaning. You do not have to live up to a set of false preconceptions about where you come from, and best of all, the unforeseen sense of dislocation forces you to take a look at your own received notions about the people around you and the society that has shaped them.

Friday prayers at Tehran University are a weekly show of strength by hard-liners in the Iranian leadership, and while the event has faded in importance in recent years, it is still an impressive sight through the eyes of the newly arrived Ferangi. Friday prayers are an exercise in choreography as much as in religious devotion. Different people have different places in the prayer hall, with the military men gathered together in a rough square in the centre, the older men closer to the front and the rows of clerics arranged in three or four neat lines at the front. Sprinkled among the Mullahs were the distinctive black turbans of the Sayyed, the direct descendants of the prophet Mohammed. All sections of the crowd rose to their feet and fell to their knees in perfect democratic harmony, and when Ayatollah Ahmad Jannati rose to deliver the sermon, each person appeared to know the role he was expected to play.

Among the several thousand men listening to the sermon were many veterans of the war with Iraq, or 'the imposed war' as some refer to it. Estimates vary, but as many as half a million Iranians died during that pointless conflict at a time when Iran's population was sixty million people. No one here would shed a tear at the prospect of Saddam's imminent removal from power. 'We are thirsty for the blood of Saddam Hussein,' the Ayatollah told the crowd, although it turned out they were not that thirsty if the Americans were the ones shedding Saddam's blood. 'The US seeks to break out a war to exert its hegemony in the region, in order to strengthen its grip over the oil reserves of the region,' thundered Ayatollah Jannati, a key ally of the ultra-conservative Supreme Leader Ayatollah Ali Khamenei. The audience responded with a chorus of '*Marg bar Amrika*' ('Death to America'), which was particularly loud from the old men near the front. All this made perfect sense against the backdrop of the power struggle that now defines Iranian politics. To keep the reformers in check, the hard-liners needed an external threat to rally the faithful, and George Bush, not Saddam, was the most potent bogeyman available to them.

Despite the brutal certainties of Friday prayers, there were also inconsistencies. Among the clerics at the front of the crowd was Ayatollah Mohammad Baqer al-Hakim, the leader of Iraq's largest Shi'ite opposition group, SCIRI. After long years of exile, he would benefit directly from the imminent American invasion. A couple of months before I saw him at Friday prayers, he told the *New York Times*, 'It is very important that there be an understanding between the Iraqi opposition and the United States.' I could not see his face when the crowd chanted 'Death to America', but he might have allowed a little ironic smile to crease his lips. He must have known he was on his way home to Iraq, thanks to the help of the Great Satan. He could not have known he would be dead within seven months, killed on his return to Najaf by a suicide bomber.

When the prayers were over, I started to canvass the departing worshippers about their views on George Bush.

One man began quoting poetry before eventually breaking into song. When the singing was done, he demanded my phone number in Ireland so he could keep in contact. I shrugged and laughed nervously, but that seemed to make him angry. The crowd around us had closed in with menacing speed at the first sign of agitation, so I scribbled down my mobile-phone number, making sure to get one digit wrong. When I handed over the scrap of paper, the man exploded with lunatic joy and leaned in and kissed me with great passion on both cheeks. Stunned and unsettled, I could feel beard rash sting my face.

On the drive across Tehran, I sat silently in the back of the car, unable to get the images of angry Mullahs and deranged zealots out of my brain. You could not find a better explanation of Iran's enduring image problem than Friday prayers. If you were only interested in the prevailing thesis about Iran, you could stop there, just after the cries of 'Death to America' and the inappropriate kissing. But if you wanted something more than half-truth, you could take a deep breath, forget Friday prayers and go skiing.

The Elburz Mountains provide a stunning backdrop to the Iranian capital, at least when the smog thins out. They begin just where the affluent northern suburbs of Tehran come to an end, and at the meeting point are the ski runs of Mount Tochal. This is not the best ski-resort in Iran, but for Tehran's cool kids, it is the closest. When we pulled up at the base of the mountain, it looked as if we had stumbled across the first showing of a winter fashion collection. Teenage boys with snowboards and slicked-back hair lolled about at strategic intervals along the road leading to the first ski-lift. The lucky ones were paired off with teenage girls, each one better dressed and more beautiful than the next. Under a billboard advertising expensive watches, the boys eyed the girls and the girls eyed each other, competing for attention as much as for love.

While the fashion was up-to-the-very-minute Western, an Iranian touch made these young women look mature beyond their years. The law requires them to observe Hijab and cover their heads, but the women at Tochal interpreted the rule with creative disdain. Their dark features were elegantly framed by fashionable headscarves pushed back to reveal their hairline. From behind designer sunglasses and carefully applied make-up, they were a little bit Audrey Hepburn and a little bit Penelope Cruz.

The Tochal ski scene represents a small but significant public challenge to the power of the clerical establishment. The lax attitude to Hijab and the whiff of romance exposes these teenagers to the risk of harassment or arrest by the Morals Police, or Komiteh. But the level of repression varies according to the prevailing political climate: if the conservatives feel the need to remind people that they are the boss, then the teenage rebels can expect close attention from the roving patrols of Komiteh, although it is hardly worth the effort. Everyone knows Tochal is just a small taste of a broader youth culture that is flourishing behind the closed doors of Northern Tehran.

My first day in the Iranian capital began with the chants of Friday prayers and ended with the sound of an Iranian garage band. The 'garage' was actually a soundproofed attic in a sturdy middle-class apartment-building a few miles from Tochal. I was told the band played 'progressive Eastern metal', which might as well have been a phrase from an advert for power tools for all it meant to me. It turned out to be a big, pacey, doom-laden guitar sound that gets much of its Eastern flavour from the *daf*, an Iranian musical instrument that looks like the bastard child of the *bodhrán* and tambourine.

The band was founded by a politically savvy twenty-four-year-old called Amir Tehrani. When we sat down to talk, there was something quite intense about him, despite the unrelenting stream of jokes and one-liners. Before he answered each question, he would pause, and occasionally tug on his neat goatee beard, before launching into elegant English. He said that the name of the band, The Mine, was an expression of his feelings about the Iran–Iraq War. Most of his contemporaries could not remember what it was like to live in Tehran in the last days of the conflict as Saddam's missiles rained down on the city, but Amir had soaked it all up. 'I was born in 1980,' he told me; 'when I came to know myself, I knew war.'

Amir and the other band members were cautious rebels. They said they wanted nothing to do with the illicit drinking and drug-taking that have become increasingly common in recent years. Although they have adopted a lifestyle that puts them in conflict with the clerical establishment, they shy away from unnecessary confrontation with Ershad, the state agency that controls all forms of cultural expression. They need permission for their rare appearances in public, they cannot get their music published and they cannot write lyrics. Despite this, Amir said that some inside the vast Iranian bureaucracy were trying to make life easier for young people. He was a loyal supporter of the Iranian president, Mohamad Khatami, who was elected in 1997 on a platform of reform. Although Khatami has been frustrated at every turn by the conservatives, Amir said things had changed for the better since his election, albeit in small ways. 'At least I can carry this in public,' he said, reaching for his guitar. 'That wasn't possible before Khatami.'

Not everyone thinks like Amir and his affluent friends in North Tehran. The hard-liners have always actively courted the poorest Iranians, and some of their most devoted followers come from the depressed suburbs of South Tehran and the underdeveloped regional cities. In recent years, the conservatives have increasingly delegated their battle against civil dissent to the Basij, a militia force made up of young Islamist militants. It was originally set up to entice poor kids into the service of the Islamic revolution back in 1979, and during the Iran–Iraq War it provided a steady stream of martyrs on the front-line. Today, the Basijis look more like a biker gang than a paramilitary force, and they turn up looking for trouble wherever there is a chance to crack a dissident's head.

For all their obvious menace, the Basijis are a throwback to the past rather than the shape of things to come. They make life hard for the young reformers, but they can do nothing to stop the rolling wave of dis-enchantment with Iran's ruling class. At least two-thirds of the country's seventy million people are under thirty and half are under twenty. They are the product of a baby boom instigated by the Mullahs right after the revolution, a population spurt that might well prove to be the undoing of the Islamic Republic.

Iran's young adults now represent a 'third generation', a vast but formless political force that has no institutional memory of either the Islamic revolution or the Iran–Iraq war and so has no basis for blind loyalty to the ruling clerical élite. In the words of one top reformer, 'wherever this generation decides to go is where Iran will go in the next decade'. The tragedy of the third generation is that many of its members are deeply confused about where they go next. Members of the post-revolution generation are growing up to find that their economic prospects are bleak and are rapidly losing faith in the political system, including reform-minded elements. A study leaked from the Interior Ministry shortly before my visit to Iran showed that just a little more than one in ten Iranians were satisfied with the status quo, and some private polls indicate greater disillusionment.

For the moment, the Mullahs have managed to keep a lid on this alienation through carefully calibrated repression. They are also blessed by the lack of a broad-based opposition. For working-class kids in places such as South Tehran, pro-democracy agitation is a time-consuming luxury they cannot afford. Even among the children of the economic élite, talk of radical change seems increasingly empty, and many have decided that their only hope lies in leaving Iran. The result is a brain drain that puts Ireland's twentieth-century experience of emigration in the ha'penny place.

The night I had my first taste of progressive Eastern metal, Amir Tehrani introduced me to his father, Hossein, a warm and expressive man who was also a well-travelled English-literature graduate with a passion for the work of James Joyce and a great guide to the hidden realities of Iranian society. He was sceptical about the prospects for change in Iran, not because of the staying power of the conservatives, but because Iranians had lost their knack for civil society. 'Just look at the chaos on the roads,' he said. 'People just don't treat each other with respect. How can they expect to create a better society if they don't treat each other with respect?' Hossein also had a rare insight into youth culture because he ran a computer training college in the centre of Tehran. As we said goodnight, he insisted we visit him at work and talk to some of his students.

The next afternoon, I sat with a group of twenty young Iranians listening to the arcane details of computer software being explained through English. Hossein boasted that his students have the highest pass rates for Microsoft-validated courses in the world, even though they are taught through a second language. The sad thing is that few of them will apply their hard-earned skills for the benefit of their homeland.

Almost everyone I talked to in that college seemed destined for further study abroad, and very few expected to make a life for themselves in Iran. By far the most attractive destination was the United States. Every day, these students pass graffiti that rails against the Great Satan, yet when you ask where they see themselves in ten years, many will tell you, 'America'. In the one country where a revolutionary form of Islamic fundamentalism is enshrined in the structure of government, the rising generation is looking to the United States for inspiration. 'In Arab countries, the rulers love America and the people hate America,' Hossein explained, 'but in Iran it is the other way around.'

Iranians like to think they are a race apart, and to some extent they are. They want every visiting foreigner to know they are not Arab, they are Persian. They resent the way Westerners use the terms 'Islam', 'Arab' and 'Middle East' as if they were the same thing (they are not – of the world's 1.2 billion Muslims, only 260 million live in the Arab world). Iranians are also distinct within the House of Islam because most of them are Shi'ites, whereas the majority of the world's Muslims are Sunnis. However, Iranian pride sometimes comes with a trace of superiority. You get the sense that some Iranians look to the United States with admiration because that view distinguishes them from the crude anti-Americanism that is sweeping the Arab world. Perhaps they feel it makes them more civilised.

Snobbery does not fully explain the scale of the change in attitudes to America in recent years. The hard-liners may still chant 'Death to America', but ordinary Iranians held spontaneous candlelit vigils in sympathy with the Americans after September 11. In autumn 2002, a polling institute published a survey that showed three out of four Iranians were in favour of dialogue with the United States, and almost half believed Washington's policy towards Iran was to some extent correct. The results did not go down well with the conservatives. The founder of the institute that published the poll ended up in jail.

In spite of periodic crackdowns, the new mood towards the United States is evident in public life. When you pick up the various English-language publications in Tehran, you are immediately struck by their generally objective treatment of news about America. In fact, aside from a few strongly worded editorials, they project a far more positive view of the US than most newspapers in Ireland. The most bizarre features of these publications are the incredibly detailed reports about American sports.

A couple of days after my arrival, the sports page of *Iran News* led with a report about US basketball star Kobe Bryant. Underneath that story was a photograph of the University of Southern California quarterback Carson Palmer calling a play during the second half of a football game against Arizona State University. Three out of five other articles on the page were about American sports fixtures. You would expect foreign stories to feature prominently in an English-language publication, but given the small number of Americans in Iran, why all the admiring talk about Carson Palmer and Kobe Bryant?

The easy answer is that in the era of globalisation

nowhere is immune to American influence, not even Iran. The Internet, illicit satellite dishes and smuggled CDs, DVDs and videos have clearly changed the tastes and attitudes of Iranian young people. But that is not a good enough explanation for their pro-American tendencies; young Arabs see the same flashy images of America and come to completely different conclusions about the United States. Maybe close ties with the million-plus Iranians who live in the US is a factor, but I don't think that explains it either; Arabs are a growing ethnic minority in the United States, yet they seem incapable of changing the minds of the people they left behind.

Perhaps the most compelling explanation of pro-US sentiment in Iran is also the simplest: America is no longer a threat. If young Iranians see an evil spirit at work, it is not America but a virulent strain of fundamentalism. The Indian-born journalist and writer Fareed Zakaria expressed it best when he said that everywhere else in the Middle East and North Africa fundamentalists 'are the alluring, mythical alternative to the wretched reality in which people live. In Iran fundamentalism *is* the wretched reality in which people live.' In that context, it is not hard to see how American ideals and values might become the 'mythical alternative' for millions of Iranians.

The Iranian students I met in Hossein's college were not naïve. It seemed to me that their perspective was much broader than their average Irish contemporary; although, there were jarring reminders that they still live in a closed society. Almost all the women wore a black veil and *manteau*, a formless coat designed to hide the shape of their bodies.

Hossein introduced twin sisters who he said were

among his star pupils. They looked like the epitome of modest Islamic womanhood, yet there was a touch of American high school about them. One of them showed off a St Valentine's Day present she had just received. That may sound innocuous, but the establishment were working hard to counter the growing popularity of Valentine's Day. The previous week, the Morals Police had raided several shops in North Tehran and ordered them to remove images of couples embracing and other corrupt materials from display windows. The twins seemed oblivious to all this as they discussed the ornate Valentine's present before them. I asked whether the gift-giver was a boyfriend or just an admirer. The twin who received the gift laughed and said he was an *ex*-boyfriend. 'He just wasn't man enough for me,' she said, dropping her tone and raising her manicured eyebrows.

When the other students arrived for our interview, the twins realised there was no male voice in the group, so they went off to find one. They returned with a confident young man called Amir who spoke English with jarring formality and an American twang. He kicked off our discussion by mocking Western stereotypes of Iran: 'We are Persians not Arabs and yet you all seem to think we are riding camels over here.' He seemed more American than any other person I had met in Tehran, yet he was passionately against US interference in Iraq, a view shared by the rest of the group. Each person expressed admiration for American ideals and talked about the need for Western-style reform in Iran, but all of them strongly opposed an American-led war against Saddam. All except one young woman, who believed US intervention would help the entire region.

'Why not?' she asked. 'We need democracy.'

As she spoke, I could see Amir becoming agitated.

'It [America] is bringing technology ... It really can make the region better, I am positive,' the woman said.

'Not by war,' Amir fired back.

'No, but by clearing out those close-minded leaders.'

'Not by force.'

'No,' the woman said quietly.

The same themes were present in almost every conversation with young Iranians. American values were widely praised, American culture was effortlessly adapted, but US political intentions were generally suspect. Some people were clearly desperate for change, but most wanted change on their terms, not George Bush's. The Americans might help, but they could not dictate, not again. These young people knew their history. They looked at United States policy toward Iran and saw self-interest. It was the CIA that helped overthrow Iran's first democratically elected leader, Mohammad Mossadegh, in a coup in 1953. That coup gave absolute power to a pro-American Shah, and his unpopularity paved the way for the fundamentalist revolution of 1979. The message from Iran's reformers was the Great Satan should face up to the Great Responsibility: you need to help Iranian democrats now because you screwed us before.

In the weeks before war in Iraq, those same Iranian democrats were beginning to feel that dark forces in Washington had cooked up another shabby deal under which US pressure for regime change in Tehran would be dropped as long as Iranian hard-liners kept quiet about the imminent regime change in Baghdad. As I prepared to leave for Northern Iraq, the *Tehran Times* published a report that seemed to back up the conspiracy theory. Deputy US Secretary of State Richard Armitage was quoted as saying there were big differences between Iran and other American enemies: 'They are a democracy, so I think you would approach a democracy differently.' Remember, the year before US officials had been telling the world that Iran was at the heart of the 'axis of evil'.

The stakes in all this are enormous. The next decade in Iran will have a profound impact on the entire Muslim world. If things go well, the third generation will build a prototype Islamic society free of pro-Western dictators or medieval fanatics. Given the right conditions, there will be a peaceful transition to a pluralist form of Islamic democracy that will be a model for Muslims across the world. However, this hopeful scenario is just fantasy unless someone, or some movement, defuses the time bomb ticking away inside Iranian society.

The third generation is increasingly restless in the face of economic hardship and repression, while the hard-liners are becoming increasingly desperate in the face of popular discontent. Without meaningful progress, there is the potential for violent upheaval on a scale that is hard to imagine. And if you think that upheaval would be contained within Iran's border, then think again. Iran's alleged attempts to develop a nuclear bomb and its assistance to terrorists down the years should be a warning. If Iran's conservative leadership chooses to lash out, then the rest of the world will have a serious problem.

The young Iranians I met before the war had reached the point where their hope was rapidly turning to cynicism, thanks in part to Western failures. The Americans were trying to bully Iran because they had failed to learn from their history, and ordinary Europeans were ignoring Iran because they had failed to appreciate what was at stake. On issue after issue, in country after country, these are exactly the failures that define Zulu Time.

7

THOSE WHO FACE DEATH

'The Kurds have no friends but the mountains.'
Old Kurdish proverb

'Thailand?'

'No. Not Thailand, Ireland.'

A vague glimmer of recognition flickered in the soldier's eyes, and then it was gone. In fact, all the Iranians at the checkpoint seemed baffled by us. I was Irish, Tom the cameraman was Belgian, Dave the producer was Dutch American and our two drivers were members of the Patriotic Union of Kurdistan (PUK) who lived in Iran. I collected our passports and handed them to the smartest-looking soldier in the bunch. He took them and walked back to the guard hut, with one of his friends slouching a few paces behind.

For the first time since our arrival in Iran, it was warm. Irish-summer warm rather than baking desert hot, but pleasant enough all the same, especially for a late-February morning. We had left Tehran airport at 5.30 that morning in frigid darkness and arrived at Kermanshah just as the first light of dawn peeked out from behind the snow-tipped peaks of the Zagros Mountains. Kermanshah is the last big Iranian city before the Iraqi border, a Kurdish town in a mainly Persian country. In a dingy hotel at the edge of the city, we met our PUK guides, and without a smile or a word of English, they loaded us and our gear into two battered old Peugeots and drove west at high speed. We made better time than we expected and encountered none of the problems we had been warned about until we hit that checkpoint, about an hour beyond Kermanshah.

As we sat silently in the car, the Iranian soldiers looked on with the catatonic stares of bored and slightly hostile teenagers. They posed no imminent threat, but the look on their faces said: 'Come and have a go if you think you're hard enough.' The clever response was to avoid eye contact and enjoy the sunshine pouring through the open windows. After two or three minutes, the soldier returned to the car, handed back the passports and waved us on with a quick flick of his wrist. The cars picked up speed, and within seconds the checkpoint was a shimmering image in the rear-view mirror.

Outsiders are not made to feel welcome on the border between Iran and Iraq. The frontier has been the scene of too much bloodshed over the years to be anything but tense and forbidding. The road we took out of Kermanshah was once the main Baghdad to Tehran highway, before Saddam Hussein used it as an invasion route for his mountain infantry divisions in the first days of the Iran–Iraq war. The carcasses of his tanks were mounted on pedestals along the side of the road as a testament to his failure to hold this land. In his one expressive gesture of the day, the driver of our car pointed to a tank without a turret and said, 'Iraq. Boom, boom.' We nodded sagely and murmured our appreciation, even though we were not quite sure what exactly his point was.

Even now, the frontier zone is a restricted area, and there were working artillery pieces and gun emplacements at regular intervals on the approach to the border town of Qasr-e Shirin. Posters were pasted on every available vertical space. Half of them appeared to be pictures of martyrs from 'the imposed war', and the other half were touched-up portraits of candidates in a forthcoming local election. You could have looked at the contrast between those posters as proof that democracy can overcome violence, or you could have concluded that not a lot separates politics and war in this part of the world.

The actual frontier between Iran and Iraq is surprisingly underwhelming. The final checkpoint looks more like a neglected car-park than the scene of historic drama. The Iranian border guards were friendly and efficient, but only because they were glad to see us go, and with the minimum of hassle we transferred our gear into what looked like a small street-sweeper's van on the other side of the border. Minutes later, we were sipping the first of many strong, sweet teas in the PUK offices in Iraq, or Northern Iraq, or Kurdistan, or Iraqi Kurdistan, or Free Kurdistan, or whatever you wanted to call it (no two people we met ever used the same description). Our escort on the final leg of our journey was a local commander of the Peshmerga. This is the closest thing the Kurds have to a standing army and that word, Peshmerga, means 'those who face death'. The first time you hear the translation, you think there is an un-warranted touch of machismo about it, but once you get to know the Peshmerga and their history your scepticism melts away.

As we drove on, we crossed the valleys that wrap

themselves around the base of the Zagros Mountains. The countryside seemed to change around each sharp corner. During our climb through mountain passes, the land around us was red, rocky and desolate, with only an occasional dusting of greenery to distinguish it from some distant planet. When the roadway dropped sharply into the valleys, the edges of the surrounding hillsides softened until they looked like sleeping bodies, with folds and curves sculpted by waters from unseen sources. Then we climbed again, and the long mountain ridges sharpened once more to the narrow edge of a blade.

The longer we drove, the bigger the passing towns became and the greater the sense of dislocation. The boisterous mix of ancient and modern in Kurdish towns is particularly hard to get used to. Some of the younger women walked by with skirts, make-up and jewellery, but a more common sight was of the full-length *chador* grasped tightly under the chin. The old men with leathery faces still wore their old tribal turbans and the wide, flowing trousers of Kurdish tradition. Some of the young men wore the baggy trousers, but they also tended to have the blow-dried quiffs that were popular among the New Romantics in the early eighties.

Three hours after leaving Iran, we approached the outskirts of our final destination: a city of 600,000 people and almost as many spellings. It was variously Sulamaniyah, Sulaimaniya, Slemani and, in the mouths of lazy foreigners, Sully. I settled on what appeared to be the most prevalent local spelling, Sulaimani, and the most common local pronunciation, 'Sula-man-ee'. I would spend the next seven weeks of my life in this town, but I was never quite sure if I was calling it by the right name. Although it didn't really matter, because there is never just one right answer to any question in Kurdistan.

By the time we arrived in Sulaimani, the only two decent hotels in town were fully booked up. There was one alternative in the city centre, and it smelled of piss and paraffin. Each room had an *en suite* bathroom, but the toilet was a hole in the floor. As night fell, any trace of that earlier warmth was driven away by freezing air sweeping down from the mountains. My first taste of Sulaimani the next morning was the leaden tang of fumes. As in Tehran, the obsession with the internal combustion engine borders on psychosis in the Kurdish enclave of Northern Iraq, but there is an underlying affluence to the traffic chaos of Sulaimani we had not seen in Iran.

As we made our way through the morning traffic towards a new hotel, our car jostled with top of the range BMWs and Mercedes as well as creaky old Datsuns with doors held on by twine. In recent years, the pace of life had quickened in Sulaimani and the other regional capital, Erbil. Many of the Kurdish emigrants who fled Northern Iraq in the years after the first Gulf War had come home with money, ideas and fancy automobiles. Every second car seemed to have a German licence plate underneath the local Iraqi equivalent, and most drivers had mobile phones pressed to their ears.

Cash had filtered down through most layers of Kurdish society, and Sulaimani was one big department store, with each street specialising in an individual product or service. One row of shops advertised nothing but wedding photography, while around the corner all they sold were clocks. In the square by the mosque, street traders called out prices for every conceivable consumer durable, apparently oblivious to the periodic call to prayer.

The Sunni faith plays an important role in life in Northern Iraq, but they say that the Kurds 'hold their Islam lightly'. Light enough to also grasp the godless promise of Western imports. In numerous off-licences, you could buy Dutch beer and Scotch whisky, while mobile phones somehow came with British phone numbers. On the main road into town, you could stop for a burger at MaDonal, which was a few doors away from the golden arches of Matbax. On every roof of every house, there was a satellite dish. On my second day in Sulaimani, I came face to face with the boys from Westlife peering out of a poster in the window of a music shop in the centre of town.

On closer inspection, the influence of foreigners was surprisingly limited. In spite of that Westlife sighting, I never heard a Kurdish person listening to Western pop music. Foreign food was limited to MaDonal, Matbax and the Indian restaurant at Sulaimani's only fancy hotel. As a foreigner, I never felt anyone was greatly impressed by my foreignness, especially when they discovered that I was not British or American. While the US dollar had become the most popular foreign currency in Northern Iraq, the old Swiss-print Iraqi dinar still reigned supreme in the markets of Sulaimani, even though the typical bank note was often held together by sticky tape. The Kurds had waited a long time for their moment. Now they had their autonomy, they were using it to build a society that was truly Kurdish: independent in spirit, if not in name.

Saddam Hussein had been forced to grant self-rule to the four million Kurds of Northern Iraq in 1992. But for another six years, the two rival Kurdish political factions, the PUK and the Kurdish Democratic Party (KDP), kept trying to wipe one another out. They agreed a ceasefire in 1998 and have shared power ever since. Each group has

DURING

administrative control over a part of the Kurdish enclave and their own regional capital. Officially the enclave remained part of Iraq, but in practice it became another country. Together, the two Kurdish factions built a relatively prosperous form of secular democracy at the heart of the Islamic world. Freedom of expression was taken seriously, with as many as 130 media outlets, including thirteen television stations and dozens of newspapers, pumping out all forms of comment and dissent. Women had a far more prominent role than they did in neighbouring states, and the observance of the Islamic code of dress was strictly voluntary.

Some Kurdish political leaders still had the look of military hard-men, but others, such as the PUK regional prime minister, Barham Salih, were every inch modern democrats. What kept them together was the understanding that they had no real friends in the wider world. On one side was Saddam's Iraq, which would like nothing better than to crush the Kurds one more time, and on the other side was Turkey, which saw Kurdish autonomy in Iraq as a long-term threat. The Kurdish enclave was pro-American and secular and therefore would find little support from other Muslim countries. Finally, Kurdish leaders had learned that the US and Western Europe could not be trusted in times of crisis. The only people the Kurds could rely on were themselves.

The real genius of politicians in northern Iraq was in realising that self-reliance required something more than a strong ruler and an independent army: the people needed to see tangible benefits from autonomy and be prepared to fight to the death to defend their big cars and satellite televisions. If the Kurdish enclave had a mission statement, it was expressed through the words of the thirteenth-century Turkish poet Yusuf:

113

To keep the realm needs many soldiers,
horse and foot;
To keep these soldiers needs much money;
To get this money, the people must be rich;
For the people to be rich, the laws must be just.
If one of these is left undone, all four are undone;
If these four are undone, kingship unravels.

Through bitter experience, the Kurds knew there were other reasons kingship unravels, and one of them is war, particularly other people's war. Back in 1920, the Treaty of Sèvres promised the Kurds their own state, but the post-war jockeying of the colonial powers led to betrayal. The Cairo Conference of 1921 saw part of the Kurdish homeland folded into a new artificial entity called Iraq. A couple of years later, the Treaty of Lausanne delivered millions of Kurds into the unwelcome embrace of Turkey. As a consequence, the Kurds became the largest ethnic group in the world without their own homeland.

In recent times, two events have determined the Kurdish outlook on the world. The first is the Anfal offensive of 1988, when Saddam Hussein made a bid to wipe out Kurdish resistance while the international community stood by and did nothing except mouth empty platitudes. Iraqi armed forces killed an estimated 100,000 people by a variety of means, including poison gas. UN agencies estimate that 4,000 villages were destroyed and more than 800,000 Kurds were displaced by the offensive. The second defining event came just after the first Gulf War in 1991, when US president George Bush encouraged Iraqis to rise up against the Iraqi dictator. The Kurds heeded the appeals and launched a rising from the north. But the Americans never delivered the necessary support, and as with the Shi'ite rebels in the south, thousands of Kurds were killed when Saddam counter-attacked.

What the Kurds have learned from history is that they will always be the first to be sacrificed for the greater good of the big powers. They have also learned that the Western world, and Europe in particular, tends to talk a great deal about the suffering of others while doing very little to stop it. The two lessons coalesced in those weeks before the outbreak of the second Gulf War. As Europe and the United States faced off against each other, the Kurds looked on with a mixture of *déjà vu* and desperation.

A few days after arriving in Northern Iraq, we travelled to the Takia refugee camp, pitched on a hill about ten miles from the front-line with Saddam's forces. The four hundred refugees who lived there had fled from the city of Kirkuk, which remained under the control of the Iraqi security services. Kirkuk is the Kurds' spiritual capital, their Jerusalem. It was the primary target of their failed rising in 1991, and regaining control of the city would be their overriding goal if and when Saddam was ousted.

The Takia camp had filled up gradually over a period of years, but with war just around the corner, the trickle of refugees was becoming a flood. In one tent were three generations of the same family who had just crossed into the safety of the Kurdish enclave. All the men had been ordered to join a pro-Saddam militia and renounce their Kurdish heritage, something they were not prepared to do. Resignation was etched on the faces of that family, but there was anger in other parts of the camp. As we walked to the edge of the main compound, I saw three women carrying larges bales of sticks on their backs. A refugee leader called Khalid turned to our translator and said, 'Even with all the oil, we still have to burn wood.'

If there was a moment when the traditional Kurdish

hospitality disappeared, it was when some of the men in the camp began to talk about the anti-war protests in Europe. In Takia, there was no question about the morality of the approaching war, no room for nuance: you were either with Saddam or against him. 'Why are the Europeans doing this?' asked the camp spokesman, Hikmat Mohammed Tawfiq. 'They are cultured people. Why do they defend Saddam and not help us? Saddam is a fascist; he is a bloodsucker.'

I told them that most anti-war Europeans did not feel they were defending Saddam when they took to the streets in protest. But it was much harder to explain why no one had come to the aid of the Kurds as they braced themselves for the approaching conflict. International aid agencies did not want to become part of American war preparations, so they appeared to do nothing to head off the potential humanitarian catastrophe that was facing the Kurds. There were minimal stockpiles of food aid in Northern Iraq, and medical supplies were dangerously scarce. A few weeks before the invasion of Iraq, the local hospital reported that it had sixty-five pints of blood to serve the needs of more than a million people. So what would happen if there were a repeat of 1991, when more than a million Kurdish refugees were forced to flee to the harsh sanctuary of the mountains? What would happen if war spilled over into the Kurdish enclave? Those questions were drowned out by the noise of political bickering in Paris, London, New York and Washington.

The most terrifying prospect for the Kurds was that Saddam would use weapons of mass destruction against the Kurdish enclave, just as he did during the Anfal offensive. UN sanctions against Iraq prevented the importation of anything that could be of use to the military, including gas masks and antidotes, and the ban applied to the entire territory of Iraq, including the Kurdish enclave. So the very people who had suffered most at the hands of Saddam's chemical weapons programme were still the people most at risk.

Four million Kurds lived within range of Iraqi rockets, yet they had access to no more than a handful of effective gas masks. People in big towns such as Sulaimani were forced to rely on home-made masks of pockets of cloth stuffed with charcoal and salt and to construct makeshift bomb shelters by sealing rooms with plastic sheeting. Yet when they watched their satellite televisions, they saw the citizens of Israel and Kuwait being fitted out with state-of-the-art protection against the threat of chemical attack. As one Kurdish politician put it: 'Maybe a Kurdish life is not as important as a Kuwaiti life.'

With the clock ticking inexorably towards war, the massed ranks of the Iraqi opposition arrived in the Kurdish enclave for their first major gathering on Iraqi soil. The politicians met in the town of Salahuddin, named after the most famous Kurd in history. We know him as Saladin, the legendary twelfth-century warrior who drove the Crusaders out of Jerusalem. He had repelled an army of invaders, and now his descendants were willing partners to the invading army. Kurdish history is littered with such contradictions.

In theory, the opposition would decide the shape of the government that would rule Iraq after Saddam. However, the unspoken reality was that the key decisions would not be taken in a conference centre in Salahuddin, but thousands of miles away in the corridors of power in Washington. This was a stage production, not a historic landmark, and it had a slickness more suited to Broadway than a hilltop village in Northern Iraq. The scores of journalists who came to cover the conference were led to a small restaurant that was part press centre, part prison. Access to the main conference centre was restricted, with the big players such as CNN and the BBC getting the first pictures of the opposition leaders in session. Everyone else had to wait inside the media centre, with nothing better to do than glower at each other and watch the sleet splat against the steamed-up windows.

The Arab media were a breed apart: their reporters were dressed in expensive suits, they smoked constantly and they seemed to enjoy each other's company. The Europeans appeared to be in a state of permanent strop, bitching about anybody who might potentially get in their way. The Americans were serious, detached and very cool in their scruffy combat chic. They sported an exotic range of war-zone headgear, including Afghan *chitrali* caps, Palestinian *kaffiyah* scarves and even the odd Soviet-era furry hat. Outside the media centre, an élite squad of Peshmerga braved the wintry showers and biting wind, conscious that we in the media were, for this one day at least, a fifth-column of enemy forces.

The most excitement we had all day was watching the cavalcade of white Land Cruisers ferrying opposition leaders to the conference centre with irresponsible speed. In the lead vehicle of one convoy were the dark glasses and awesome fire-power of a US Special Forces team. Behind them was another jeep containing the sharp suits of an Iraqi exile leader and his entourage. A few minutes later, sirens and screaming engines announced the arrival of a group of Shi'ite clerics, who sped by in a blur of bright lights and brown robes. While George Bush and Tony Blair were struggling to build their 'coalition of the willing', we were trying to make sense of the 'coalition of the confusing'.

The Kurds were perhaps the most clear-headed of all the opposition groups lining up for a slice of power after Saddam. They were unique among the disparate groups gathered in Salahuddin because they had managed to construct a model of what Iraq might look like one day. Paradoxically, they were also the group that had most to lose if the approaching war plunged Iraq into anarchy. Even more than the Monarchists, Communists, Fundamentalists and Pluralists that made up the rest of the Iraqi opposition, the Kurds were vocally loyal to US war aims. At the same time, they were also better prepared for whatever betrayal might be coming their way, mentally if not physically.

As we drove home from the opposition conference that night, there was a banner in a square in the centre of Erbil that read, 'Future Iraq: rule of law, justice and tolerance.' Perhaps destiny would smile on the Kurds and the rest of the Iraqi people and deliver their democratic paradise. But as the opposition graced the stage at Salahuddin, the past was still controlling the present. Whatever the slogans might say, this was still a place of betrayal, indifference and false hope until someone could prove otherwise.

8

The Storm before the Storm

'You know, when I first started in journalism I
thought that foreign correspondents spoke every
language under the sun and spent their lives
studying international conditions. Brother, look
at us!'

Corker of *Universal News*, from *Scoop*,
Evelyn Waugh, 1938

Every war zone has its hotel, a place where the
professional observers of the peep-show of misery go to
feel like decent human beings. In Northern Iraq, the hotel
was the Sulaimani Palace, a high-rise expression of
uncharacteristic optimism on the part of the Patriotic
Union of Kurdistan. The PUK built the Palace to
accommodate the tourists who were certain to flood
Sulaimani once the good news about Iraqi Kurdistan
reached the outside world. While the Palace waited for the
tourist invasion, it would have to make do with journalists.
War is hell, but it is also good business.

Every newly arrived correspondent trooped into the

lobby of the Palace looking for a woman called Dildar, who sat in the café with her spectacles lodged on the end of her nose. She did not seem to have an official title, but she was the PUK official who made things happen. Each morning, Dildar sat in a haze of cigarette smoke, holding court with a scrum of correspondents looking for favours. In return, she might accept a hug, a cigarette or a piece of gossip. She liked to let you know how busy she was, and if you spent a little time consoling her, you became one of her favourites. Dildar's thick black hair and slight frame made her seem almost childlike, although she was probably in her early forties. She had spent years in exile in Britain and 'confided' to me that her son was obsessed with the Irish soccer team. Dildar's particular gift was the ability to create mutual intimacy without ever revealing any meaningful insight into her life. All I knew was that she had some clout with the big boys in the Peshmerga.

By and large, Kurdish political leaders treated the foreign correspondents extremely well, although they had a particular infatuation with the Americans. The NBC network had been given the entire seventh floor of the Palace, and visitors to their makeshift studio had to first pass a uniformed guard armed with a Kalashnikov. The American media were prime targets for Ansar al-Islam, an Islamic group allied with al-Qaeda that was battling the PUK near the border with Iran. Such was the threat of bomb attack that the Peshmerga had mounted a round-the-clock guard on the hotel, posting a machine-gunner on the back of a pick-up truck just outside the lobby.

Two weeks after I arrived in Sulaimani, NBC invited all the journalists in the city to a pre-war party at the Palace; 'the Storm before the Storm' was how they put it on the invitations. It was a suicide bomber's dream. Virtually every foreign correspondent and a good portion of the Peshmerga command structure turned up in the ballroom of the Palace for free food, booze and Kurdish traditional singing and dancing. At each table that night, the big topic of conversation was how to get close to the action once war arrived. The benefits of being in Northern Iraq were that there was no official censorship of our reporting, there was very little control of our movements and there were no embedded correspondents getting preferential treatment. But the drawbacks were that nobody would protect us when the shooting started. For better or for worse, we were on our own.

The NBC producers had obviously worked out a deal with the Kurdish military men about getting access to the front-line when the battle with Saddam actually commenced. As the Americans drank with their new best friends in the Peshmerga, the rest of us checked out potential travelling companions. There were competing theories about the best route into Kirkuk and the most likely invasion route for US forces, but everybody agreed on the need to travel in convoys. Still, we had to avoid travelling with people who might go a little crazy when the going got tough.

There were certain characters that you just knew were certifiably insane the moment you met them. At the NBC party, a French reporter sat down beside me and, without any encouragement, began talking about his war preparations. As he boasted about his secret route into Saddam-controlled Iraq, he was simultaneously stuffing a plateful of food into his mouth. Bits of pitta bread and hummus flew past my ear as he shouted to be heard above the music. Despite his obvious excitement, there was a blank look in his eyes that made me uncomfortable. There and then, I resolved to go in the opposite direction if I ever met him in the field. In fact, I was tempted to draw a bull's-eye on his forehead as a warning sign to anybody who wandered across his path.

There were a few other head-cases loitering around the Palace. One Austrian photographer wore nothing but army surplus khaki fatigues. One moment he would be screaming heavily accented obscenities at junior officials from the PUK, and the next he would be grinning wildly at you from across the room. A Japanese reporter had the unnerving habit of walking around the lobby of the Palace in circles, talking to himself with his head bowed and a cigarette dangling from his lips.

The madness began to infect everybody who spent any time at the Palace, partly because we kept having the same conversation over and over again. As February came to an end, you could not go five minutes without hearing a prediction about exactly when the war would begin. There were various schools of thought, including a group that became known as the 'moonies'. They had an almost religious belief that the timing of the war depended on the cycle of the moon: when the skies are darkest, the Americans will invade.

There was an inverse relationship between the number of confident predictions a correspondent would make and his or her experience of war. The people who came up with the most imperious judgements about the probable course of the approaching conflict had rarely, if ever, heard a shot fired in anger. As the weeks dragged on without an invasion, their predictions became more frequent and less accurate. They were people to be avoided at all costs. In stark contrast were the veterans who appreciated the calm before the storm and spent their evenings drinking beer and eating curry instead of searching the web for insights into Donald Rumsfeld's brain.

Occasionally, the professionals swapped the macho atmosphere of the Palace for the relative quiet of the Ashdi Hotel down the street. The most popular dish in the restaurant there was Chang's Chicken, named after *New York Times* photographer Chang Lee, who had grown so jaded with the food that he hijacked the kitchen one evening and taught the chef to cook a decent stir-fry. Over Chang's Chicken one night, it was decreed that a fine of 10 dinars (about €1) would be applied to anyone who made a prediction about the timing of the war. Privately, I made an additional pledge to avoid those bearing grand philosophical statements about past, present and future wars.

From the strong and silent types, however, you were happy to hear the occasional war stories. Among the friends I made in the Palace was a British cameraman who I will call John (because most of the stories he told me were off the record). He had served with the SAS in the first Gulf War, hunting Scud missiles in the western deserts of Iraq. He told us he was a qualified medic, helicopter pilot and rally driver and could handle every Russian military vehicle ever built. He also spoke French.

'Yeah, but he's a crap cameraman,' said a colleague.

'Tell me that when you're lying on the ground with a sucking chest wound,' John replied.

The collective neurosis of the press corps in Northern Iraq had ratcheted up several notches by the second week of March. We had expected the big questions to be resolved by this stage, yet there was still a depressing level of uncertainty. It was clear that war was inevitable, but was an invasion days, weeks or months away? To add to the confusion, the Turkish parliament had blocked the transit of 64,000 US troops through their territory. What did that mean for the American's much-vaunted 'Northern Front'? If the Americans were still coming, what part of the Kurdish enclave would they land in? Would they bring embedded reporters? Would we go mad before we got the answers?

There were various ways of coping with the continued uncertainty, but one of the most effective was retail therapy. Shopping for provisions gave you the feeling that you were taking the initiative. You were taking steps to guarantee your safety and enhancing your ability to stay the course, no matter what George Bush or Saddam Hussein threw at you. I celebrated St Patrick's Day by buying gas masks for RTÉ's translator, Blnd, and driver, Mustafa. They brought me to the military section of the bazaar, where the narrow alleys were crowded with stalls selling everything from ammunition holders to Iraqi Army memorabilia. As Blnd checked the expiry date on the gas mask's filter, I haggled with a trader over an Iraqi Army-surplus sleeping-bag. It was green and seemed appropriate for the day that was in it.

All over Sulaimani, journalists cruised around in their four-wheel drives searching for supplies for the long days and nights ahead. They were all looking for the same things: generators for television-editing equipment, charge cards for satellite phones, extra petrol and as much food and water as their vehicles would hold. There was something slightly unfair about how well prepared they all were. Ordinary people across the Kurdish enclave were making do with gas masks filled with charcoal and salt, while the foreign press had full chemical suits packed away beside their body armour and helmets. Some of the American networks had even bought canaries in case of chemical attack. If Saddam dropped the bomb, the birds would get it first. Apparently, CNN had two canaries call Diehard 2 and Diehard 3. Unfortunately, Diehard 1 died. The cause of death was boredom, according to a sceptical British broadcaster.

To rationalise the disparity between the foreign press and our Kurdish hosts, I chose to believe that we each had an obligation to prepare for the worst to the best of our ability. If the nightmare scenario did become reality, I would rather feel a little bit guilty for my good fortune instead of be a little bit dead. Every night, I gave thanks to the powers that be in RTÉ for that blue bag in the corner, stuffed with the masks, overalls and boots that would protect me from any 'nasty piece of kit'. There was also some comfort in the knowledge that, throughout history, reporters have tended to overdo their preparations for war. Take the Abyssinia campaign in 1935, as described by Philip Knightley in *The First Casualty*: 'Correspondents with the Italian Army wore heavy woollen belly-bands, on the advice of the Army medical chief, as a means of preventing cholera, while silk pyjamas worn under the clothing were said to prevent typhus ... Laurence Stallings of Fox Movietone took a large Red Indian motorcycle and sidecar. No one knew what to expect.'

We had moved beyond silk pyjamas, but there was still something disconcerting about the conspicuous prepar-edness of the modern foreign press corps. I never actually saw anyone brandishing the atropine injection pens, but some people definitely had them packed away (remember, it fires a needle into your skin at 147 miles per hour). At the very least, there was ciprofloxacin (Cipro), made famous as the antibiotic of choice during America's anthrax scare of 2002. In terms of communications, there had never been a better equipped bunch of reporters. Just a couple of years ago, a satellite phone was a fragile and bulky device you carried in a briefcase. In Northern Iraq, a company called Thuraya was selling satellite phones just slightly larger than your average mobile. If you did not have a Thuraya, then you were strictly amateur. The same went for hand-held Global Positioning System (GPS) devices, which allowed you to plot an exact course through unfamiliar terrain. Even the videophone, which had made its debut in Afghanistan, had become something of a fashion statement. It allowed you to broadcast passable images from the middle of nowhere with the help of a small fold-out satellite dish. RTÉ had supplied me with a videophone and one of those dishes, and I felt very *nouveau* until I was told everyone else was now using two satellite dishes to get a better signal.

You could be forgiven for thinking that all the foreign press did in the weeks before war was compare notes on equipment and moan about the food. However, for most people, these were just welcome distractions from the realities of life outside the doors of the Palace. In fact, the media bubble was never completely sealed from the disconcerting reminders of past, present and future wars. As Dildar escorted our producer, Dave, into the headquarters of the local television station, Kurdsat, she pulled out her pistol and gave it to the security guard.

'Can you use that?' asked Dave.

'I was a Peshmerga,' Dildar replied. 'What do *you* think?'

One night in Erbil, a Kurdsat technician was helping us to send a news report back to Dublin. As he entered the satellite van, he bent over and his gun fell on the floor. Without a word, or any obvious sign of embarrassment, he reached down, picked it up and put it back in his belt.

None of the Kurds we worked with liked to talk very much about their personal experience of conflict, but there were plenty of non-verbal reminders of what they had been through. Our driver, Mustafa, looked to be in his late fifties or early sixties, but on a long drive through the mountains one day, he revealed he had just turned forty-one. After some cajoling from Blnd, Mustafa produced a membership card of the Kurdistan Political Prisoners Association. When he was a Peshmerga, he spent fourteen months in a jail in Baghdad for trying to cross into Iraq from Iran. After that experience, I decided to ask everyone I interviewed what age they were, just to remind myself of the unspoken personal histories that ran parallel to the articulated pain of Northern Iraq. The gap between appearance and reality was most pronounced in a large Kurdish town near the border with Iran.

To the outside world, Halabja has almost ceased to be a real place. It has been added to the list that includes My Lai, Dresden, Srebrenica, Belsen and Guernica. It is a word that cannot be uttered without some reference to war crimes or genocide. It is no longer a point on a map but a landmark in history and a loaded reference in the broader political debate about Saddam Hussein. Halabja ceased to be a real place on the morning of March 16, 1988, when the Iraqi military carried out the most devastating poison-gas attack on a civilian population in history.

Most people in the city had taken shelter that morning, after Iraqi aircraft dropped conventional weapons on the town. The planes returned from their airbases in Kirkuk a second time and dropped innocent-looking streamers. Locals did not know it then, but the Iraqi military was checking wind speed and direction. At 11.35 a.m., the jets came back a third time and dropped several different poison gases on Halabja. The most common memory among survivors is the smell of apples, bananas or garlic, depending on who is telling the story. In the hours after the attack, five thousand people died in the narrow alleyways of the city and ten thousand were injured. To this day, the people of Halabja still suffer from unusually high rates of serious diseases such as cancer.

Some of the victims are buried in the 'Martyrs' Cemetery', and that is where I met Jubreel Omar Rawand. He was part of a group of survivors that had come together to highlight the continuing health crisis caused by the chemical attacks on Halabja and two hundred other Kurdish villages and towns. Their spokesman was a nervous older man, whose left eye looked seriously diseased. He appeared to be at least fifty years old, but when I asked him his age, he told me he was thirty-four. He was two months younger than me. We talked by the gravestones of the 'martyrs', and he seemed deeply uncomfortable with my questions and the setting. As we left, I tried to persuade other members of the group to bring me to their homes and talk to me there. Jubreel eventually agreed.

He lived in one of those narrow alleyways that you see in the footage of the aftermath of the attacks – the video images of countless lifeless bodies of women and children. Jubreel led us through the heavy gate of his house and into a small front room where we sat in a circle. His wife brought us tea while he pulled out a photo album. He spoke quietly about the people in the pictures and, in a barely audible monotone, said thirty-three members of his extended family had been killed that day in 1988. He stopped at a photograph of his youngest brother. I asked what age he had been when he was gassed. Fourteen, said Jubreel, before taking a deep breath. His eighteen-month-old son broke the silence by climbing onto his father's lap and patting his face. The child had a cleft palate, which Jubreel insisted was the result of the 'poison that was inside me'.

The people of Halabja did not mark the fifteenth anniversary of the attack with any major ceremony. All across the Kurdish enclave on March 16, 2003, people observed a minute's silence at 11.35 a.m., but in the town itself, there was almost nothing to indicate this was a significant date in the calendar. The tragedy was that Halabja was still subdued by war. In the mountains overlooking the town, the Peshmerga had stepped up their long, inconclusive battle with Ansar al-Islam, and speculation was growing that US Special Forces were about to join the Kurdish militias for a final showdown with the Islamic group.

On the day of the anniversary, we followed the dirt track leading to the hilltop memorial to the victims of the Halabja attack. It was a beautiful spring day, and at first, we could hear nothing but birdsong and a light wind. As Tom started to film the town below, there was a dull thud from over the ridge, followed by two short bursts of heavy-calibre gunfire. Ansar and the Peshmerga had begun their usual afternoon exchange of mortars and bullets. Later, at the Martyrs' Cemetery, we could still hear the sound of that dirty little war. The mourners, sitting on the graves of their dead, threw an occasional eye towards the hills above, as if they were casually checking for approaching rain.

There were two roads from Halabja to Sulaimani: Ansar controlled one and the Kurdish militias controlled the other. The Kurdish road was safer, but not completely safe; in the last week of February, an Ansar suicide bomber had killed four people at the Peshmerga checkpoint just outside Halabja. As we drove back to

Sulaimaini on March 16, we could see clouds of white smoke rising periodically from the valley to our right. It was clear this sideshow war was coming to an end just as another conflict was about to get underway. Within days, Halabja would be cut off from the outside world by two different battles on two different fronts. Fifteen years on, the town was still a prisoner of history.

Back in Sulaimani, the PUK held a press conference to mark the Halabja anniversary. The real purpose was to show how long Saddam had been killing Kurds. One woman told us that Iraqi soldiers had arrested her husband in June 1963. When she found his body nine months later, it was clear he had been burned alive. He was part of a group of 180 men from Sulaimani that had been arrested and later killed by Iraqi troops. One old man who had survived the massacre was asked to address the press conference. 'If you want to explain the pain of our people,' he said, 'you will have to write a thousand books and then you would know only a quarter of the city's suffering.'

That comment touched upon the most depressing aspect of this pre-war purgatory. Every day in Northern Iraq, there was another reminder of just how much suffering these people had endured. The approaching war could deliver the Kurds into sectarian chaos just as easily as it could give them permanent liberation. But did anybody back home really care?

There was hardly space in the world's newspapers for a few hundred words about the Kurds, let alone a thousand books. The Kurdish enclave was what journalists call a 'side-bar' story. It could not compete with the diplomatic firestorm between Paris and Washington, military preparations in Kuwait or Saddam's fiery rhetoric of resistance, but it did provide a compelling insight into the humanity of war. Not the morality of war, or even the mortality, but the humanity. Would this war make the lives of those who survived better or worse? Would they be freed from suffering on the scale of Halabja or condemned to live out that nightmare for generations to come? No one could deliver definitive answers to those questions, but you were obliged to keep looking, even if it became harder with each passing day.

On March 16, the US-led invasion was just days away. Most reporters in Northern Iraq had been there for at least a month – in some cases, for several months – and no one could say when they were going home. The walls had begun to close in, and time had slowed down, almost stopped. As well as the constant exposure to other people's suffering and the growing sense of isolation and futility, there was the unspoken dread. It seemed almost harder for those who had experience of conflict: they knew what to expect; they wanted to get it done with and go home. Among the others, there were varying combinations of fear and expectation. Most had a healthy respect for their own mortality, but some appeared to have bought the bullshit line that 'war is fun', or in the words of a former British war correspondent, 'there is something fantastically exhilarating about being terrified out of your wits'. The veterans will tell you those moments do exist, but not without moments of soul-destroying tedium. The good reporters find a balance between the two by reminding themselves that their work makes a difference. But when a correspondent begins to lose his or her connection with their audience, then their work starts to become meaningless.

The night we came back from Halabja, Tom and I settled down in my hotel room with a bottle of whiskey.

Our hotel did not have a satellite dish, so we had to make do with the local television channels. On every station, they were broadcasting endless footage of the victims of the attack on Halabja. The video images of corpses and suffering children were played on a loop, over and over again, with morbid mood music in the background. We watched for a few moments before it eventually became too much. Tom began flicking around in the hope of finding some relief. Eventually, we came across an English-language movie with Hebrew and Arabic subtitles. No sooner had we settled back to enjoy it than a young female character was shot in the head. It was a movie about a Nazi concentration camp.

We drained the whiskeys, and Tom said goodnight. I still needed to find something to take my mind off corpses and poison gas, so I fiddled with the radio I had bought the previous day in the bazaar. It was a cheap knock-off made by some outfit called Philibs, but it had looked slightly more attractive than the Panasaunic model beside it. The previous day, Tom and I had been struck dumb when we came across an RTÉ sports announcer on the radio reeling off the day's GAA scores. For a few moments, we listened to this little snippet of home coming out of that cheap black transistor before it was overwhelmed by the crackle of a thousand voices.

In my search for some life-affirming radio, I came across the unmistakable sound of Alistair Cooke on the BBC World Service. In his 'Letter from America', the grand old man of British broadcasting was talking about the conference that drew up the framework of the United Nations before its formal creation in San Francisco. The meeting had taken place at Dumbarton Oaks, an imposing mansion in Washington's most elegant district, Georgetown. I used to walk past Dumbarton Oaks regularly when I lived in Washington, and Cooke vividly described Rock Creek Park, which ran past my old apartment building, and 'the broad river in the centre and its rich wooded slopes descending boldly to it'. For a few moments, war was very far away, and so was Halabja.

At the end of his script, Alistair Cooke wondered aloud why the United Nations has been so powerless in the face of international crises like Iraq. He pointed to the tragic compromises made when the UN was being created and quoted a former British foreign-policy mandarin who believed the international body was 'aborted in Dumbarton Oaks'. Cooke then disappeared into the radio twilight zone and was replaced by a BBC newsreader with news of the war summit in the Azores. Bush, Blair and their 'coalition of the willing' were going to give the UN Security Council one last chance. 'We concluded that tomorrow is a moment of truth,' said the American president. 'Tomorrow is the last day we can determine whether or not diplomacy can work.'

I changed the channel and found Voice of America. It was playing rock classics, which was good. I poured myself a nightcap and turned up the volume. One song ended and another began. The lyrics were very familiar. The sound of U2 was coming through the cheap plastic speakers. History and hopelessness had rhymed. Diplomacy would fail. War was on its way. The world had been here before. The song's chorus echoed around the hotel bedroom with the power of past, present and future nightmares. 'You've got stuck in a moment,' sang Bono, 'and now you can't get out of it.'

9

The Shock and the Awe

'Why? Why do you Americans allow this to
happen? Why doesn't Bush do something? Why?'

Kurdish refugee, quoted in Time magazine,
April 15, 1991

They're nice people, and they're cute, but they're
really just bandits. They spend as much time
fighting each other as central authority. They're
losers.'

US State Department official on the Kurds, quoted in
Newsweek magazine, April 15, 1991

The Peshmerga officer said the Iraqi security services had
once tried to kill him with a booby-trap bomb. The
explosives were packed inside a radio that was packaged
as a gift from a sister who lived across the front-line. The
notion that death could be dressed up as love was no
surprise to the soldier. His job was to root out Saddam's
agents on the Kurdish side of the front-line and coax
secrets from the Iraqi side, so it was logical that someone
would want him dead. In spite of the assassination

attempts, he had made friends in the senior ranks of the Iraqi Army. His best source of intelligence was an Iraqi commander who was looking for a potential escape route when the Americans came with their B-52s.

As the commander talked, he kept glancing towards a long, curved ridge about half a kilometre from the Peshmerga guardhouse. There was movement along the ridge, but in the midday warmth it was slow and irregular. What looked like a small rock formation was an Iraqi gun emplacement, and what appeared to be lazy insects were Iraqi infantrymen. Just beyond the horizon was a big Iraqi military base, and burrowed into that front-line ridge were Iraqi tanks and a missile silo. The commander said the soldiers we could see were conscripts and would not put up a fight against superior American fire-power. But for the moment, he warned, they will shoot you if you get too close. The warning seemed lost on the children who were playing around the perimeter of the cemetery that lay mid-distance between the Iraqi and Kurdish positions.

The front-line ran in a broad arc around three sides of the Kurdish town of Kifri and marked the southernmost point of the Kurdish enclave. The town sat on approximately the same line of latitude as Saddam's hometown of Tikrit, and the drive from Kifri to Sulaimani was only slightly shorter than the drive to Baghdad. It was hard to find a Kurdish community more exposed to retaliation from Saddam than the people of Kifri. Over the years, the townspeople had enjoyed the same broad autonomy from Baghdad as their fellow Kurds farther north, but they also had to put up with sporadic bombardment from across that front-line. Driving around the edge of the city, you passed buildings with chunks missing, vehicles crumpled by the impact of high explosives and dried-mud walls tattooed with bullet holes in neat symmetrical patterns.

The closer war became, the greater the risks for the people of Kifri. Yet they seemed to have reconciled themselves to risk a very long time ago. The centre of the town rang with the sound of frontier anarchy, with just a little more volume and a lot less reserve than most places in the Kurdish enclave. The sight of a foreign-television camera crew provoked a minor riot in the market, and the local police had to step in and slap down the trouble-makers. One toothless old man fought his way through the crowd to tell us how much he wanted the US to kill Saddam, even though 'the Iraqis will take our town within fifteen minutes of the start of an American invasion'.

It was not enough to say that life went on in spite of the close proximity of Iraqi forces: there were aspects of life that existed only because of the front-line. We had heard rumours of a gang of smugglers running nightly raids into Saddam-controlled territory in search of cheap petrol and fighting gun battles with Iraqi soldiers. The stories were confused; the gang were either heroes of the 'Resistance' or a gang of villains from a *Mad Max* movie. The local Peshmerga commander played down rumours of gun battles, and locals seemed uncharacteristically tight-lipped about the gang. But as the sun set over town, it became clear that the truth lived up to the rumours.

In the dusky gloom, the driver was hostile and suspicious. He would not talk about where he was taking his vehicle or whom he was waiting for, but he was clearly a smuggler. As daylight disappeared, another Russian-built truck arrived, and a small crowd gathered. Gradually, the drivers began to enjoy the attention, and they eventually explained the general principles of their operation. The trucks carried empty oil barrels across the frontier, using a dirt track that ran around the back of a nearby mountain. On the other side, they filled up the barrels with fuel and drove them home to Kifri, where they were sold for as much as ten times their original price. Making money was only part of the motivation, the smugglers insisted. They were also patriots, throwing an economic lifeline to the Kurdish enclave by providing a steady supply of fuel.

The men confirmed the reports of gun battles with the Iraqis. Each of the drivers had been fired upon many times, but they claimed they gave as good as they got and carried a variety of weapons, including rocket propelled grenades (RPGs). They also relied on good intelligence about troop movements. One driver said his twelve-year-old brother regularly hid in the long grass on the other side of the mountain and phoned back information. The boy carried a revolver for his own protection.

Despite their precautions, death and injury were as much a part of the business as profit. Since the granting of Kurdish self-rule after the second Gulf War, the drivers claimed that 350 smugglers had been killed on these nightly runs: an average of one dead smuggler every two weeks. The pace of the killings had picked up, with fifty smugglers killed in the previous six months. The Iraqis returned the bodies of the dead only after their families had stumped up a substantial cash payment. The going rate for a corpse was between €50 and €100.

We were invited to follow one of the lorries on the first part of its journey. The cabin smelled of booze, and even in the dark it was clear the smuggler in the passenger seat had reached a state of alcohol-induced calm. Over the sound of rattling beer bottles, he said: 'I drink to forget my family.' All along the territorial boundary between Saddam's army and Kurdish forces, there were plenty of men and women like him. Not all of them had the same daredevil cachet as the Kifri gang, but they were all smugglers. After years of uneasy peace between the Peshmerga and the Iraqi Army, the smugglers had become a subversive vanguard. On a daily basis, they siphoned from Iraq the economic means to support the Kurdish dream of self-rule. Their motives may have been tainted by greed, but in those difficult times material desire was iron in the Kurdish soul. Not surprisingly, Iraqi commanders saw the smugglers as a real threat, and as war approached they fought back hard.

Near the town of Kalak, locals spoke in hushed tones about a local Iraqi commander they called Abdul the Crazy. He controlled the bridge that connected the Kurdish enclave with the rest of Iraq, and each evening, after the bridge closed, he would set fire to all the fuel he had confiscated on his side of the river. It was his way of saying, 'I know where you live.' Further south along the front-line, on the approach to the town of Chamchamal, an Iraqi commander set fire to a woman called Nazifa Namiq with the kerosene she was trying to smuggle into the Kurdish enclave. She would have made the equivalent of €5 for the trip. She lived long enough to get to a hospital, but doctors gave her only a fifty-fifty chance of survival. I do not know if she is alive today.

Clearly, the higher the risk, the greater the profit, and this partly explained the endurance of the smuggling industry. Three weeks before the first American missile hit Baghdad, a smuggler in Chamchamal told me a twenty-litre 'jerry can' of petrol cost 2 dinar (about 20 cent) on the Iraqi side and could be sold in the fuel market at Chamchamal for 40 dinar (about €4). This was at a time when generous estimates put the average weekly wage in the Kurdish enclave at 150 dinar. By the time the Americans crossed into Iraq, the profit from black-market fuel had increased exponentially, and as war progressed, the price began to change by the hour.

Profit alone does not fully explain the mentality of the smugglers. In their minds, death had become a way of life, and that reality influenced all their actions and reactions. They were ordinary people doing extraordinary things for reasons outsiders could never truly understand. There is no point in trying to put yourself in a situation where you hand your twelve-year-old brother a pistol and send him off to spy behind enemy lines: you will never know. How many of us will ever watch kerosene flames spread across our body and hear the sound of another person's laughter?

The fact that we will never experience these things does not mean we cannot appreciate the sheer awfulness involved, but we should think hard before we try to judge the motives of those affected. There is no universal moral code that explains human behaviour, only different circumstances and different reactions. In our value system, idealism and greed are polar opposites. But in a society where death has become a way of life, the heroes are the people whose talent for self-preservation yields benefits for those around them.

Looking at the faces of those drivers in Kifri or the kids carrying jerry cans in Chamchamal, there was no self-pity. These were people who understood there is no nobility in suffering and that poverty and happiness go together only in the mind of someone who is no longer poor. Instead, they have worked out a formula that balances daily brutalities with something they can call 'normal life'. The price of survival varies, but it invariably requires the sacrifice of some part of what we might call 'humanity'. If somebody is prepared to kill you without hesitation, then you must be of the same mind to survive. If somebody forces you to suffer, then it becomes that little bit easier to inflict suffering. The Kurds have always been underdogs, but unlike their admirers in the West, they know the underdog is not always virtuous. Virtue is a luxury that comes with victory.

There was a certain calculated dishonesty in the rhetoric of Kurdish politicians in the weeks before the war, and it had something in common with the lies coming from the supporters of the Baghdad regime. In their public appeals to the world, both sides played to Western definitions of right and wrong. They understood that those who live in civilised and democratic societies tend to place people on either side of a moral dividing line. Like ancient mariners who saw serpents on the unexplored parts of their maps, observers in the Western world will often superimpose their moral code on situations they do not understand. In the weeks before war in Iraq, the people who faced each other across multiple front-lines played to the gallery for sympathy and understanding. Yet, at the same time, they knew that the moral certainties that shaped Western hearts and minds would have no bearing on their lives in the weeks that followed. Maybe when the war was over, but not until then.

There were few places that helped you to understand the pre-war mind-set of the Kurdish enclave better than the front-line town of Chamchamal. From the top of the citadel on the edge of town, you could hear the uncontrollable clatter of border life and see the spider web of alleys and roads pushing perilously close to Iraqi positions dug into the long, fertile ridge that framed the city. Through a hollow in the ridge ran the main road to Kirkuk, a forty-minute drive to the south. In normal circumstances, the road carried a carefully regulated stream of traffic in both directions. Women and children and men who served in the Iraqi Army could travel from the Kurdish side to Kirkuk on family business. In both directions, there was some legitimate commercial traffic. For foreign reporters, that last Kurdish checkpoint outside Chamchamal was a valuable source of intelligence on Iraqi preparations for the approaching war.

On March 18, news came through that the Iraqis had shut down the road, and Chamchamal was bracing itself for an attack by the Iraqi forces. Tom and I set out on the hour-long journey from Sulaimani in a jeep we had just rented. We suspected there would come a time when Blnd and Mustafa would abandon us, so we decided it was best to get some means of independent travel. We paid a bargain-basement price for the vehicle and got exactly what we paid for. While approaching a PUK checkpoint outside Sulaimani, the accelerator pedal jammed, and as I shifted down through the gears, the roar of the engine drowned out Tom's low groan. The guards at the checkpoint were getting closer, very fast, as I struggled to turn off the engine and slow the jeep. With the help of some unseen divinity, we coasted to a halt just short of the guardhouse.

After some quick repairs, we continued to Chamchamal on a road full of refugees. Tractor-trailers laden down with mattresses, kids and the occasional head of livestock were streaming out of town in an orderly flow. As we approached the centre of Chamchamal, I thought back to the boisterous market town I had seen the week before. Now an urban centre of close to 100,000 people resembled a ghost town. We came across Haji Ali Sabir and his wife, Wanawsha, as they prepared to leave their home on the edge of town. The husband stood on top of what looked like a water tanker directing his wife and two of their kids as they tried to lift a mattress onto the shaky mountain of household goods already strapped to the oval surface of the truck.

This was the fifth time the family had been forced on the road. The dates of their previous journeys matched periodic bouts of conflict and repression. Like everyone else we met in Chamchamal, they said this time was different. This time would be the last time. They would put up with a forced holiday in the countryside because when they came home Saddam's reign of terror would be over. Forever.

The confidence in the voices of the parents was in stark contrast to the heartbreaking sadness in the eyes of their seven children. One young woman stood in the corner behind the door, sobbing quietly. I turned to Tom and saw that he was filming her. There was something unbearably voyeuristic about the scene, and I started to walk away. Before I passed through the front door, I instinctively turned to look over my shoulder. The young woman caught my eye and said, 'Sorry,' in English.

The following morning at 4 a.m. there was a trembling roar from the darkness outside our hotel in Sulaimani. The power had gone off, and from across the hills to the south of the city there was a blackness that was scarily inappropriate. The wind had picked up, and heavy drops of rain were falling on the balcony. There were still twenty-four hours before George Bush's deadline to Saddam was due to run out. The noise was just thunder. From the corridor outside the room, there was the sound of a fist on a door and a loud conversation in French. The waiting could go on no longer.

The following night, we returned to Chamchamal. As we stopped the car, two shots rang out, but it was hard to tell whether the gun that fired them was Iraqi or Kurdish. The market square was desolate except for the emaciated dogs searching vainly for food amid the detritus in the gutter. Occasionally, a jeep with the letters 'TV' taped over its windows passed by. Otherwise, the only cars on the street were battered old hatchbacks carrying Peshmerga patrols aimlessly up and down. We drove around for several hours, not really sure what we were looking for. We eventually stopped at the crossroads, just short of the last Kurdish checkpoint, to get a few hours sleep. As we dozed off, four brand-new jeeps emerged from the blackness at high speed and surrounded us. Five, maybe six, militiamen jumped out and ordered us to join their convoy.

After a brisk drive through back alleys, we were deposited at the desk of the local Peshmerga commander, who chastised us for parking in full view of the Iraqi snipers. To make sure we did not wander off again, he told us to bed down for the night on the floor of a local school. In the comfort of my Iraqi Army-surplus sleeping-bag, I looked at my watch. Two hours to go before Bush's deadline. Someone turned off the lights. Would war begin before we woke up? There was the harsh growl of a throat being cleared. What sounds would we hear from over that ridge?

At daybreak, the only sound was the snoring of a sleeping Kurdish cameraman in the corner of our classroom-cum-bedroom. The war had started, just not here in Northern Iraq. We went off in search of refugees along the road between Chamchamal and the town of Sangaw. After about ten miles, there were encampments by the side of the road, pitched by refugees who believed they were outside the range of any possible retaliation by Saddam. The Ahmed family had made a home for themselves in

DURING

the caves and overhangs of a large rock formation near a swollen river. Plastic sheeting and the children's runners were the only concession to the twenty-first century. Everything else was straight out of a biblical storybook.

In one small hollow in the rocks, Parzheen Ahmed was cooking rice and lentils for her five children. They might as well get used to it because that was all they would be eating for a while. The extended family had left Chamchamal two days before. It was not just the possibility that Saddam would unleash weapons of mass destruction that made them run. Like every other ordinary Kurd, their biggest fear was half-measures. If the United States did the job right and protected them from reprisals, then everything would work out fine. 'We're very sad to have to leave our homes,' said Parzheen, 'but once Saddam is removed, we will forget the sadness.'

But what if things went wrong? What if the Americans failed to protect the Kurds this time around? Burned into the consciousness of every Kurdish person is the Anfal offensive and those failed rebellions after the first Gulf War. For the Ahmeds, Anfal is more than just a bad memory. The family matriarch, Fahima, said her sixteen-year-old son was arrested in 1988 and she never saw him again. Parzheen's sister-in-law, Ameena, said her five brothers also disappeared during the Anfal offensive, and she cared for their sons. In the warren of caves were members of the Ahmed clan who had just fled Kirkuk. One man begged for the use of a satellite phone so he could talk to his relatives, still stuck on the wrong side of the front-line. For all their obvious distress, the Ahmeds had hope. They had food supplies for a week, and before they ran out they would be home. *Inshallah.*

The Ahmed's were the very people this war was being fought for, yet they seemed insignificant to the world's

145

political leaders. Even Kurdish politicians downplayed their potential suffering. They feared that the news of a huge movement of refugees inside their territory would give their old enemy, Turkey, the pretext to invade Northern Iraq on 'humanitarian' grounds. So while tens of thousands of Kurds were forced to live in these rudimentary camps, with limited food and no apparent medical supplies, their leaders swore blind that there would be no crisis. Meanwhile, the international aid agencies were notable by their absence. The UN had delayed preparations for a possible refugee crisis, so they would not be seen to be cooperating with American war plans. Of course, that principled stand was sod all good to the people in this part of Iraq. At least there was good news for the anti-war camp: they could point to a potential crisis in the Kurdish enclave and say we told you so.

And what about the Americans? Turkey had held up US plans to bring the big infantry divisions into Northern Iraq, but the Kurds had still expected thousands of US soldiers and a sky full of B-52s to materialise the very second the war began. They had waited for years for this moment, and now they were still waiting. Those refugees would not return to their homes until they saw American boots on their soil and Saddam behind bars or hanging from a lamppost. But things were not going according to plan. The Kurds were beginning to wonder how exactly their loyalty would be repaid, and when.

The day after our encounter with the Ahmeds, our cheap and nasty hired jeep finally went to meet its maker as we battled a relatively gentle hill on the road between Chamchamal and Sulaimani. It made a comic putt-putt farting sound before expiring halfway up the incline. The lorry-load of refugees inching up the hill in front of us was greatly amused by the sight of two Westerners banging the dashboard of their recently deceased vehicle and mouthing obscenities at no one in particular. Once tyres had been kicked and bonnets slammed, an appalling thought entered my mind. What if we were stuck in this desolate corner of the Kurdish enclave while the Americans activated their Northern Front? We would miss the big story because our vehicle had broken down. As an excuse, it would be on a par with 'the dog ate my homework'.

Worry turned to panic when the phone rang and the office back home told me the BBC was reporting that US Special Forces were on the ground fighting for control of the oilfields of Kirkuk. That sounded like the first stage of an American invasion. Those Special Forces teams would not take on the Iraqis in that way unless reinforcements were close behind. Mustafa had already gone to find help, and it would be at least two hours before he got back. The delay would put us on the wrong side of whatever road-blocks the Americans were using to close off access to the battlefield. It was the type of nightmare scenario that had robbed me of sleep over the previous month.

The phone rang and it was the office again. The reports of a battle for the oilfields had been quietly dropped from the bulletins. The BBC had not officially acknowledged that it had made a mistake, but it was pretty clear the story was bogus. It was not the first false alarm of the day. Just a few hours before our breakdown, I had stood on the roof-top of a house in Chamchamal marvelling at the crystalline beauty of the skies above me. The office rang and said there were reports that smoke was rising from Kirkuk. I asked where the report had come from. 'Chamchamal,' was the response. I looked towards the sky over Kirkuk, and there was nothing. Not even the vague hint of an innocent little cumulus nimbus.

These incidents were part of an emerging pattern. As the days went on, the phone would ring and a report would be quoted. It would often sound plausible, but it would be checked out and would eventually prove to be wrong. Yet at the end of the process, the people who had originally filed those reports never seemed to admit their mistake. Such was the pace of the broader war that you could float any story, enjoy a brief moment of glory and then watch that story sweep away on the raging torrent of events. By the time it became apparent that your story was wrong, nobody could remember what you had actually said in the first place.

It was Friday night, the night of 'shock and awe', and we were back in Mustafa's jeep on the mountain road to Erbil. We sat silently listening to the BBC World Service describe the destructive power of the most powerful military machine the world has ever seen. At each Peshmerga checkpoint, the soldiers set aside their usual detachment and crowded round the windows of the vehicle. 'Any news?' was the greeting at each stop. We could tell them nothing they did not already know: Baghdad was being pulverised.

As we passed into territory controlled by the second Kurdish faction, the KDP, there was a brief flicker in the night sky to our left, but our attention was distracted by a fast-approaching checkpoint. As we chatted with one Peshmerga, another ran out of the darkness. 'Look around,' he shouted. 'Kirkuk's being hit!' We leapt out of the car and stood watching tracer fire chase an invisible enemy into the sky. We stared at the soundless spectacle for a few moments before deciding to drive to the next hilltop, a mile or so away. From there we could see the tell-tale white flicker of impact in the centre of the orange glow. A dull rumble followed a second or two later, just as the tracer fire thickened in the skies over Kirkuk.

The Kurdish militiamen showed no signs of joy, even though the war was coming closer. They also showed no signs of preparation for the next logical step, a US-led invasion from the north. In Erbil the day after the bombing of Kirkuk, a KDP spokesman confidently predicted that the Americans would arrive 'very soon', but out at the front-line checkpoints, the Peshmerga sat in pitifully small groups twiddling their Kalashnikovs and grumbling under their breath. They had just heard reports that Turkish commandos had entered the Kurdish enclave that morning, and this raised the nightmare scenario that Turkey would use the war as a pretext to wipe out the Kurdish experiment in self-rule. What really puzzled them was why the Americans were not taking that threat seriously. The Turks would be stopped in their tracks even if there were only a thousand GIs on Kurdish soil.

Few of the Peshmerga would express their doubts publicly, but on the streets of Erbil there was less restraint. In a crowded market under the shadow of the city's famous old citadel, we met two Kurdish students who spoke perfect English. Like everyone we ever met in these settings, the two young men were four-square behind George Bush and his vision of 'Iraqi freedom', but they were beginning to detect the unmistakable odour of another betrayal. 'America is like a fox,' said one of the young men: 'no friends forever, no enemies forever, just benefits forever. That's the Americans.'

These young men did not know it, but they had exposed the curious shortcomings of Zulu Time. As two young Muslims who were inspired by the United States and who supported the invasion of Iraq, they seemed to be missing from the dominant European perspective of the war. In fact, the criteria we used to judge the motives of the Kurds had no relationship with life as it was lived in the shadow of Saddam's forces. Ironically, the United States also seemed to have a hard time getting its head around the fact that it had friends in places it had trouble pronouncing. When Americans looked towards the Muslim world, perhaps they were so used to seeing faces warped by hate they could not imagine anything else.

As they marched America to war, the neo-conservatives in the White House had no problem finding enemies but seemed incapable of recognising friendship. The generals and the neo-cons were so focused on the removal of an unreconstructed villain in Iraq that they appeared to forget the Iraqis who were actually serious about freedom and democracy. In their makeshift headquarters in Northern Iraq, the exiles of the Iraqi National Congress complained that the Americans were cutting them out of the war and preparing to cut them out of the aftermath. One of the bravest voices of the Iraqi opposition, Kanan Makiya, accused the bureaucrats in Washington of coming up with a post-war plan that would sell out American values. 'The government of the United States is about to betray, as it has done so many times in the past, those core values of self-determination and individual liberty.'

And among those who feared betrayal most were the millions of Kurds who supported Bush's war in the name of liberation. They only had to look at their history to see Washington's definition of liberation has a habit of changing at the very worst moment. But they hoped there was still a chance to avoid the mistakes of history, even if they knew that time was running out.

10

The House of War

> 'All Men dream: but not equally. Those who dream by night in the dusty recesses of their minds wake in the day to find that it was vanity: but the dreamers of the day are dangerous men, for they may act out their dream with open eyes, to make it possible.'
>
> T. E. Lawrence, *Seven Pillars of Wisdom*, 1926

Something was not quite right. There was too much activity at the checkpoint for a routine Sunday night and too many high-ranking Peshmerga milling about in the darkness. As the guards surrounded our jeep, Blnd the translator tried to explain we had been on the road for two days and just wanted to get back to our hotel in Sulaimani, a few miles beyond the checkpoint. A senior Peshmerga pushed through his subordinates to deliver a sharp, furious lecture that Blnd seemed too embarrassed to translate in detail. All we needed to know was that we would be arrested if we did not turn our jeep around and make ourselves scarce.

Beyond the checkpoint was the Bakrajo airstrip, which

151

the Kurds had repaired and extended in preparation for super-sized US Army transport planes. At long last, the airborne cavalry was coming, and the Peshmerga had no intention of letting journalists near the airfield when the first big contingent of Americans touched down on Kurdish soil. We drove back the way we had come, but instead of taking the turn for Erbil we drove straight on, stopping only when the lights of the checkpoint had disappeared. We pulled to the side of the road, wrapped ourselves in blankets, sat on the grass and waited.

Tom and I heard the noise at the same time. Back home, the dull hum of airplane engines is nothing more than background ambience, but in the Northern no-fly zone, it heralded the arrival of war. The noise came from beyond the hill that separated us from the end of the Bakrajo airfield. The monotonous drone gradually rose in volume and then trailed off suddenly, suggesting that the plane had dropped below the summit of the hills surrounding the landing field. The next sound we heard was a chainsaw roar as the aircraft executed a swift turn at the end of the truncated runway before dropping off its cargo. In the twenty minutes that followed, at least two more aircraft executed the same manoeuvre before the hills fell silent once more.

Back at the checkpoint, the Peshmerga were trying to contain a small convoy of journalists that had stumbled across this semi-covert operation. The senior officers had slipped into the night, leaving their underlings to argue with the translators. There always comes a moment during this kind of confrontation when one correspondent will announce his or her intention to defy the men with guns. In all but the most extreme situations, group dynamics will force the rest of the press pack to reluctantly follow suit. The fear of missing something is acute, whereas the fear of being shot recedes in the presence of so many other targets.

Our vehicles had 'TV' taped to every flat surface. It was a gesture intended as 'we come in peace', but beyond that checkpoint it spelt trouble. The lower ranks of the Peshmerga had decided to let the convoy through, but a few hundred yards up the road, the lead vehicle was stopped by what appeared to be two snipers with war-paint on their faces and high-velocity rifles cradled in their arms. They spoke to the drivers in Kurdish, ordering them to kill the headlights on their vehicles. Before the last set of lights was extinguished, five or six soldiers stepped from the gloom to join the snipers.

They were clearly not from around these parts. The microphones on their black headsets and the short-barrelled weapons were not Peshmerga issue, and the colour of their hair and skin suggested that it was far from Kurdistan they had been reared. When one of the men barked an order back into the darkness, it was delivered in American English. This was our first glimpse of US Special Forces. Our encounter with them was over in seconds. In the imposed darkness, they melted away, leaving the snipers to prevent us from moving on. After a few minutes, they too drifted away. We were free to go.

We had been away from Sulaimani for just over forty-eight hours, yet it felt like a different city on our return. Our new hotel, the Abu Sana, had tape plastered across its front door to stop glass spraying the lobby if there was a bomb attack. In the hotel car-park, drivers were removing the letters 'TV' from their jeeps on the assumption that the signs made them an easy mark. In the words of one British colleague: 'TV now stands for Target Vehicle.'

The heightened paranoia had nothing to do with the battles raging hundreds of miles away in Umm Qasr and Basra and all to do with the dirty little war that was about to reach a bloody climax just up the road. The planes we had heard landing at Bakrajo had not come to activate the Northern Front against Saddam, as we had first assumed, but to wipe out the Islamic militants of Ansar al-Islam. They had brought reinforcements and supplies for the US commandos who would coordinate the final offensive against Ansar bases near the town of Halabja. Even before their arrival, US warplanes had begun bombing runs against the group's mountain strongholds. In response, the militants had made every foreigner in Northern Iraq a potential target. The day before our return to Sulaimani, an Australian cameraman called Paul Moran had left the Abu Sana to film villagers fleeing American bombing runs. He was taking some final shots of the refugees passing through a Kurdish checkpoint when an old Toyota pulled up. As a guard leaned in to talk to the driver, the car exploded with the force of more than 200 kilos of TNT. Moran and six other people were killed, and twenty-four others were injured.

Moran's photocopied resemblance was taped to the back door of the Sulaimani Palace Hotel over a message of sympathy from the Kurdish political leadership. Inside, the same Kurdish politicians were telling foreign journalists that they could not go to Halabja because it was too dangerous. Their concern might have been genuine, but so was their relief at finding a pretext to keep the world's media away from their vicious grudge match with Ansar. Some reporters eventually got close to the front-line, but most were turned back at the last big town before Halabja by Peshmerga who displayed a cockiness we had not seen before. For weeks, the foreign media had been their best friends, but now they no longer needed us: they had the Americans and their very big guns.

Over the next five days, the Americans sent B-52s, F-14s, F-16s and AC-130 gunships to 'soften up' Ansar al-Islam before launching a final ground assault. Around 100 US Special Forces soldiers led as many as 10,000 men from the PUK into battle against a fighting force of between 750 and 1,000 Ansar fighters, including more than 100 Islamic militants who had fled Afghanistan after the fall of the Taliban. The Kurdish and American forces made their way rapidly through the string of towns that Ansar controlled, driving the surviving fighters higher into the snow-capped mountains that separated Iraq from Iran. Finally, they took Biyara, the *de facto* capital of the Ansar mini-state. Along the way, the Americans made a couple of deadly errors, including the bombing of a relatively moderate Islamic group based in the village of Khurmal; this left sixty people dead.

Still, the Kurds were not going to let a mistake like that spoil the celebration of a 'historic victory'. When they finally reopened the road to Halabja, there were Peshmerga at each major crossroads posing happily beside what passed for heavy armour in their limited arsenal: flat-bed trucks with Dushka cannons mounted precariously on the back. From the narrow mountain passes in the distance, there were explosions, and occasionally a puff of white smoke would drift out of a rocky ravine. A PUK commander said this was the sight and sound of a mine-clearing exercise, not a last-ditch stand by Ansar. As we made our way towards the source of the explosions, we stopped to ask directions from a militia unit in the village of Zardahar. In a casual tone, one young gunman told Tom and me to follow him into a nearby field where he had something interesting to show us.

The Peshmerga pointed to a pile of rags in the corner of the field and then picked up his pace, as if anxious to show us something he was proud of. We caught up with him just as he pulled back a blanket to reveal the waxen face of a dead man. The hair was thick and healthy, the beard well tended and the left side of the face seemed impassive, as if the man had died peacefully in his sleep. But on his right cheek was a bullet hole, perhaps two or three inches beneath the eye. It would have looked like a rather large mole were it not for the raised purple welt of congealed blood that encircled it. There was more blood on the dead man's chest and another neat circle on his exposed shin. Successive acts of violence had punched holes in this man's body, but now he was in a state of absolute calm.

The entire Peshmerga unit silently gathered around the body in a semi-circle. Their commander said the dead man was a member of Ansar al-Islam. He had been killed while trying to surrender. He had approached their position with his hands up, but as he came closer he dropped his hands momentarily and was shot by one of the youngest members of the patrol. Once the story was told, there was a moment of quiet. It could have been a mark of respect to the dead man, or just as easily an expression of grim satisfaction. You never knew with the Peshmerga. Sharing feelings was never their strong point.

The Kurdish political leadership claimed that as many as 250 Islamic militants had been killed during that 'final' offensive, but that meant that the bulk of Ansar's members had fled to Iran or had dispersed back into Kurdish society. That last prospect really set teeth on edge. What if the zealots had shaved their beards and slipped back into the big cities of the Kurdish enclave? What destruction could they bring with them? And as for the Americans, the flight of the Islamic militants would have deadly consequences in the difficult months ahead. Just as al-Qaeda had eluded the US assault on its Afghan stronghold of Tora Bora, Ansar had lived to fight again, at a time and a place of its own choosing. War with Saddam would be over in days, but war with Iraq's domestic and imported fanatics had only just begun.

Qais Ibrahim Khadir was one of three members of Ansar al-Islam sent to kill Kurdish regional Prime Minister Barham Salih in April 2002. Khadir and his comrades attacked Salih's home in Sulaimani with Kalashnikovs and grenades. They killed five of his bodyguards, but the Prime Minister survived; he had stepped back into his home to take a phone call moments before the shooting started. Khadir said he personally fired 140 shots and killed two of the guards. He was shot twice in the leg but managed to escape to a safe house where he was eventually arrested. His fellow assassins were killed at the scene.

In Sulaimani's main jail, Khadir told me the assassination attempt was one of the great things he had done in his life. 'If God helped me to get out of prison, I would do the same thing,' he said. Khadir was defiant in his words but insecure in his body language. He made it clear on arrival that he would not shake my hand at any point and did not want prison staff near us as we talked. As he listened to an explanation about RTÉ and Ireland, his facial expression was beatific, but there was a flicker of anxiety in his dark eyes. He was twenty-six, yet he had a teenage complexion and long eyelashes that made his full beard look comical. To ward off any visible sign of amusement, you only had to remind yourself that this young man's proudest moment was an attempted assassination. 'In our view, Dr Salih was not from the Islamic group. We call him a *kaafir*, an infidel.' As well as being *kaafirs*, Salih and other pro-Western leaders in the Islamic world were also *murtad*: people who leave Islam and become traitors to it through their beliefs or actions. The penalty for this is death, Khadir explained.

My purpose in meeting Khadir was to find out if Ansar al-Islam and al-Qaeda really did have something in common besides the same radical Salafi/Wahhabi tradition of Islam. Ansar al-Islam (or Jund al-Islam, as it was originally called) came into being when two radical Kurdish Islamic groups merged, just ten days before the attacks of September 11. The groups had sent a delegation to meet bin Laden's top deputies in Afghanistan in the months before their merger. After September 11, the new group welcomed members of al-Qaeda fleeing the US invasion of Afghanistan. Kurdish politicians claimed that Osama bin Laden had helped to create Ansar as an alternative base of operations for his followers. It was all very compelling, although initially Khadir seemed to reject that theory out of hand.

'We have a religious relationship and brotherhood with the al-Qaeda network. No more than that.'

However, as he talked, Khadir confirmed there was a lot more than mere spiritual connections between Ansar and bin Laden. He said some of his friends had received training at camps in Afghanistan, and the group as a whole had got financial support from bin Laden and his network.

'We support all that al-Qaeda has done and all it will do. Ansar al-Islam is not afraid of our relationship with al-Qaeda and what will happen in the future. If America chooses war against al-Qaeda – whoever chooses a war against al-Qaeda – they choose a war with us.'

What Khadir was describing was the *modus operandi* of a network of Islamic militant groups in the wake of September 11. Al-Qaeda should be thought of not as a unitary group with a central command, but as a loose alliance of forces. One way of understanding al-Qaeda, according to British journalist Jason Burke, is to think of it 'as a venture capitalist firm, sponsoring projects submitted by a variety of groups or individuals in the hope that they will be profitable'. It is a structure designed to frustrate a war fought on conventional terms, as Khadir explained. He talked to me a few weeks before the US-led assault on Ansar, and while he knew his comrades would be driven out of their mountain statelet, he also predicted that members of the group would survive the offensive, return to Iraq and join up with other Islamic militants to wage holy war on the American occupiers.

'They will attack us from the air, so we will come to them from the ground. We will come to the cities to make our fight. We will kill all *kaafirs*. He might have ten children or one hundred children. We kill him and his children if he is a *kaafir*.'

In profiles of Qais Ibrahim Khadir, some journalists concluded there was nothing in this young man's life story to suggest he would some day embrace holy war. But the more you learned about his background, and the more you read about Islamic militancy, the more logic there was in the eventual outcome of his personal journey. We got some sense of that journey from Blnd. He had told us that he had family business to take care of on the morning of our meeting with Khadir, so he sent a friend to accompany us to the prison. When we met up later, he admitted he did not want to be with us that morning because he had gone to school with Khadir and would be uncomfortable meeting him again.

Blnd and Khadir grew up in Erbil and were children of the Kurdish élite. Both their families were heavily involved in politics, although Blnd's clan sided with one faction and Khadir's family with the other. What they shared was a thoroughly modern, secular and middle-class education. Blnd said his young classmate had always been a bit intense, but he was also very popular. In retrospect, he believed Khadir had started to go off the rails after falling in love with a girl called Dahlia. In a newspaper interview, Khadir's mother said her son had been so infatuated with her that he would use only a soap called 'Dahlia' and spent all his money getting taxis to meet her after school. In the end, the romance went nowhere.

Khadir did not show any interest in radical ideas until 1996, when he was twenty and began listening to discussions about Islam in a local barber's shop in Erbil. At around this time, he abandoned secular politics and began preaching to his family about Islamic tradition. On one occasion, he tore every image of himself out of his family's photo albums. Eventually, he left Iraq and travelled to Jordan and, later, Yemen to pursue his studies under militant Islamic scholars.

Khadir was no ghetto kid looking for liberation from poverty and oppression. He was a young man given an exceptionally good start in life who became disillusioned with secular answers to his problems. In many ways, he was just like the hijackers who sent those planes crashing into the Twin Towers. They were, by and large, middle-class drifters who embraced the certainties of Islam when their dreams failed to deliver realities. Like Khadir, they were normal kids from good families who remained hidden to the world until it was too late to save them.

In the brutal way he used the word *kaafir*, Khadir revealed the influence of the radical scholars who have tried to steer Muslims towards an apocalyptic version of their faith. *Kaafir* is derived from the term *Kufr*. It simply means 'non-believer', a person who is not a Muslim, and should be understood in the context of classical Islamic notions of religious diversity. The sacred texts describe Jews and Christians as 'people of the book', and the Qur'an explicitly states that they are as much a part of God's plan as Muslims: 'O humankind, God has created you male and female and made you into diverse nations and tribes so that you may come to know each other.'

However, to radical Islamists notions of tolerance and diversity are inconsistent with the war on the secular democracies of the world. Words such as *kaafir* must be drained of neutrality and turned into weapons. Their world is divided between the House of Islam and the House of War (the world of the *kaafirs*), and so Islam's complex moral code must be rounded down to a handful of hostile truths. The radicals say the Prophet urged Muslims to wage *jihad*, or righteous war, and God decreed that martyrs in this war would be rewarded with eternal bliss. But mainstream Islamic scholars point out that the Qur'an defines *jihad* as 'striving in the path of God' and applies to personal moral dilemmas as well as armed struggle. Even when *jihad* relates to war, it is spoken about in terms of self-defence. Suicide is a mortal sin, and both the Qur'an and Hadith (the words and deeds of the prophet) explicitly rule out attacks on innocents, particularly woman and children.

Young men such as Khadir represent a wake-up call for those of us in the West who struggle to understand the rise of al-Qaeda. Osama bin Laden is no more the legitimate face of Islam in the twenty-first century than clerical abuse is the defining condition of the Roman Catholic Church. These radical Islamists represent a 'fundamental' understanding of Islam, but that does not mean they represent the 'true' voice of Islam. Just like Christianity, Islam's central truths are everlasting, but most Muslims have learned to apply those core principles to the reality of an ever-changing world. The next time you hear an Islamic radical quote the Qur'an to justify murder, just ask yourself what would happen if Christians followed a literal interpretation of the Bible. As religious scholar Karen Armstrong points out, the answer is that we would be eating kosher meat (Acts 15:20) and stoning our disobedient sons to death (Deuteronomy 21:18–21).

Just as he is not a spokesman for the faith of more than a billion Muslims, bin Laden is not a creature of oppression. He may be a hero to many in the Islamic world, but that does not mean he has any rightful claim to be a standard bearer for the poor and dispossessed. He and his most active supporters are middle-class militants from ostensibly pro-Western countries, privileged kids like Qais Ibrahim Khadir who lost their way amid broken dreams and unfulfilled promises. We should understand them and the conditions that helped to shape them, but never make the mistake of believing they are the legitimate voice of the oppressed of the world.

If there is one person who understands the threat posed by Islamic militants, it is the man Khadir tried to kill. As the prime minister of one-half of the Kurdish enclave, Dr Barham Salih was a potent symbol of change in the Islamic world. He was a Western-educated technocrat who had shown it was possible to balance Islamic tradition with liberal democracy. That pluralist model may not be right for every Muslim nation, but the very fact that it worked in Iraqi Kurdistan was bad news for Ansar and like-minded groups. 'Terrorism is not just a Western problem; they are also trying to undermine our notion of democracy,' Salih told RTÉ. 'In fact, they probably find us more of a threat because we are in the heart of Islam.' Salih was so serious about maintaining a good example in the face of the militant assault that he refused to sign any of the death warrants that ended up on his desk, including one authorising the execution of the man who tried to kill him, Qais Ibrahim Khadir. Despite intense pressure for Khadir's execution from Kurdish security chiefs, Salih was determined not to make him a martyr. Yet at the same time, he was not squeamish about the battle against Ansar. 'These people are hardcore terrorists,' he said without emotion. 'They will be taken care of.'

The United States was certainly anxious to 'take care' of Ansar al-Islam, but their motives were more complicated than those of their Kurdish allies. Making Kurdistan safe for democracy was a nice bonus, but disrupting al-Qaeda and justifying the wider war were always the big prizes for the Americans. The battle against Ansar helped Washington to persuade the American public that the war in Iraq was making them more secure and protecting their interests around the world. But while there was some logic to that particular claim, US rhetoric about Ansar also contained elements of fiction.

Successive opinion polls published in the weeks before the war showed that a majority of Americans believed that Saddam Hussein had played a direct role in the attacks of September 11. The same polls showed this was one of the main reasons Americans supported the imminent war. People did not come to this conclusion on their own: at the press conference in early March 2003 in which he outlined his case for war, President Bush mentioned al-Qaeda or the attacks of September 11 fourteen times in fifty-two minutes. Meanwhile, the President's top officials were pushing allegations that al-Qaeda, Saddam and

Ansar al-Islam were all linked in some way. In a pre-war presentation to the United Nations, US Secretary of State Colin Powell said a top al-Qaeda operative, Abu Musab al-Zarqawi, had recruited terrorists in Baghdad before joining up with Ansar and establishing a 'poison and explosive training centre camp' in Northern Iraq. He also said that Saddam's intelligence services had 'an agent in the most senior levels' of Ansar.

These claims were a key element in Bush's case for war, but even his most enthusiastic supporters inside Iraq were deeply sceptical of that last allegation. There were few doubts in Northern Iraq that al-Zarqawi was linked to al-Qaeda (he escaped the US assault on Ansar and in February 2004 the Americans offered $10 million for his capture, declaring him 'the most capable terrorist in Iraq'). However, I never met one Kurdish politician who seriously believed Ansar and Saddam were working together. For what it is worth, our Ansar friend Khadir strenuously denied the links with Baghdad, insisting that Saddam was just another *murtad*, a traitor to his faith. None of the foreign press corps in Northern Iraq found credible evidence of these links, except one German reporter who had his stories about Ansar and Saddam spiked by sceptical editors back home. 'They just cannot accept that this fucking stupid cowboy from Texas might have a point,' he declared over dinner at the Palace one night.

George Bush and his Kurdish supporters did have a point about the dangers posed by those Islamic militants in the mountains of Northern Iraq. But the case for wiping out Ansar al-Islam would have stood on its own merits had it not been for Washington's desperate need to justify the wider war. By making allegations about Ansar it could not prove, the Bush administration was snatching defeat from the jaws of victory.

Theodore Roosevelt once said the people who count in life are not the 'cold and timid souls who know neither victory nor defeat' but the person who is actually in the arena, 'whose face is marred by dust and sweat and blood'. When the US Special Forces emerged from their battle with Ansar, they had cleaned away the physical evidence of battle, but they still had the overbearing righteousness of men who are used to winning by all means necessary.

When they invited journalists to a post-battle press conference, their commander was the epitome of that Teddy Roosevelt hero. He stood bolt upright, his elbows bent behind his back at a neat forty-five-degree angle, and delivered a staccato burst of inappropriate phrases to describe deadly realities. He talked about the Ansar 'folks', and when asked about reports that some of them were executed, he said: 'I have no visibility on that.' What caught my eye during the press conference were the Special Forces members who did not speak. There was one man buried deep in the crowd of camouflaged Americans and Kurds who had the inflated body and shaven head of a pro-wrestler: more WWF than Special Forces. The others looked strangely out of place, like a collection of slightly unkempt business executives at the end of an adventure weekend.

Later in the day, we travelled to the former Ansar stronghold of Biyara and came across a Special Forces patrol making its way down the main street. The soldiers walked through the town with exaggerated care, taking turns to stop and stare at the bemused locals through the lenses of their wrap-around shades. My understanding was that some of these men were reservists who held down regular jobs back in the States. It certainly looked that way as a slightly overweight soldier jogged awkwardly towards the rented jeep he was travelling in. Back home, on the highways of northern Virginia, or Orange County, or Long Island, he was just another faceless commuter; in Northern Iraq, he was James Bond.

The myth-making surrounding US Special Forces threatened to obscure the true significance of Biyara. In the courtyard of the town's 250-year-old mosque, local men prayed in the bright sunshine under a powder-blue dome pockmarked by bomb damage. Large parts of the mosque complex had been reduced to rubble, but there was an air of grim satisfaction among the faithful. Ansar had used the mosque as a centre for its extreme brand of Islam, but now the town's true spiritual leader, Sheikh Malik Osman Sirajadin, had returned from exile to preach the mystic pluralism of the Sufi Islamic tradition. More importantly, the town was free of the Taliban-style edicts introduced by Ansar and the threat of physical violence used to enforce them. Liberation had come at a price, as the bomb-damaged mosque testified, but it was still liberation.

If the Americans had been thinking straight, they would have ensured that the lasting image of the assault on Ansar al-Islam was the smiling face of Sheikh Malik. Instead, because they needed propaganda victories, they decided that the important issue at the end of this battle was weapons of mass destruction (WMD). At that press conference, the Special Forces commander said they had found evidence that indicated the presence of chemical and biological weapons at an Ansar base in Zargat, a small mountain hamlet close to the border with Iran.

At the base, the full destructive power of the US bombing campaign became apparent. What had been a sprawling complex of buildings was now a mammoth pile of rubble. But in the shape of the perimeter of the complex, there was an immediate resemblance to satellite photographs Colin Powell had produced in his pre-war presentation to the UN. This was the supposed chemical-weapons factory that Powell claimed had been created by al-Zarqawi and his Ansar buddies.

By the time we got there, British and American chemical experts had already combed the ruins for evidence, and according to locals, soldiers had removed the bodies of about forty Islamic militants. There were explosives in haphazard piles in almost every part of the complex but very little hard evidence of WMD. An empty birdcage lay on its side near the entrance to a cave at the edge of the complex, which indicated that canaries had been used to warn of possible chemical contamination, and there were a few suspect barrels lying around. I came across a laminated page with chemical equations written all over it, but Blnd told me it had been taken from a school textbook. If this really was a chemical-weapons factory, then the Americans must have recovered the proof before we arrived.

Maybe some day that evidence will be made public, but at the time of writing Washington has still not produced facts to back up Colin Powell's assertions about Ansar and al-Qaeda's supposed arsenal of WMD. Likewise, we are still waiting for solid proof that this group really was the missing link between Baghdad and Osama bin Laden. That absence of proof raises a number of obvious questions. Could it be that the American government misled its people in a desperate attempt to connect Saddam Hussein and the atrocities of September 11? And looking back on the American-led assault on Ansar, you have to ask what those Special Forces were fighting for. Was it to deliver a short-term publicity boost for the spin-doctors back in Washington, or to help create long-term stability for the Iraqi people? It might have been one, but it is hard to see how it could have been both. The campaign against Ansar al-Islam should have been a test case in America's war on terror, proof that military action is sometimes the only way of defending pluralism and democracy. Instead, it may well have turned out to be a self-inflicted wound.

Even in the imperial era of Zulu Time, the Bush administration can play a muscular role on the world stage only as long as it has the support of middle America. So to justify successive military adventures, it has been obsessed with scary stories that appeal to deep-seated fears at home but obscure long-term realities abroad. It used Ansar as another bogeyman to scare the American people into supporting war against Saddam, but it left them unprepared for what would happen to Iraq once that war was over. Ansar al-Islam survived and prospered under the shadow of American occupation, becoming a key component of the Iraqi insurgency, and just as Qais Ibrahim Khadir had predicted, the group brought its *jihad* to the cities of Iraq. The pre-war nightmare conjured up by the spin-doctors had turned into a post-war reality. 'By pretending Iraq was crawling with al-Qaeda,' wrote Maureen Dowd of the *New York Times*, 'they've created an Iraq crawling with al-Qaeda.'

The battle against Ansar really should have been a lesson in the enlightened use of American muscle, but instead it has become another parable of American self-delusion that serves only to amuse smug Europeans and strengthen the day-dreamers on the fringes of radical Islam. Thank you, George and friends. We have more than enough of those already.

11

Death as a Way of Life

'Life levels all men. Death reveals the eminent.'
George Bernard Shaw, *Man and Superman*, 1903

The fires burned for centuries before Saddam Hussein, and they will burn long after. While natural gas continues to seep from the earth's pores, flames will rise from Baba Gurgur, Iraq's single richest oilfield. The Turkmen of Kirkuk came up with the name by connecting their word for father with a phrase describing the sound of fire, and local legend has it that Baba Gurgur was the inspiration for the 'burning fiery furnace' in the Bible's Book of Daniel.

For centuries, the gas fires of Baba Gurgur were simply a freak of nature, but then, in the early hours of October 15, 1927, a fountain of oil burst into the air with such force that it took hundreds of local tribesmen eight days to stem the flood. Outsiders regard this as the official birth of the Iraqi oil industry, but many Kurds see it as the source of a lasting curse. The oil-soaked earth beneath Baba Gurgur has delivered tremendous wealth but not for local

169

people. For them, oil has brought foreign interference, repression and war.

On the last Friday of March 2003, the curse was lifted temporarily, and the sight of Baba Gurgur sent a ripple of excitement through a group of Kurdish militiamen on a hillside a few miles outside Chamchamal. Their expectant gaze reached beyond the smoke of the gas fires to the outer suburbs of Kirkuk, the alpha and omega of Kurdish aspirations. Neither journalist nor Peshmerga had expected to get so close to Kirkuk without a shot being fired in anger, but in the early hours of that morning, the Iraqi Army had quietly withdrawn from its bases overlooking Chamchamal and a number of other Kurdish front-line towns. The troops had pulled back to defend a ten-kilometre perimeter around Kirkuk, apparently in preparation for some last stand against the Kurdish militias and the American invaders. As Saddam's forces retreated, the Peshmerga pushed forward to get their first, tantalising glance of the flames of Baba Gurgur and their spiritual capital.

For some of the militiamen, this was a commercial opportunity as well as a moment in history. As we stood on that hillside gazing into the distance, men with guns and broad smiles were stripping the Iraqi bunkers around us of everything of value. They carried sheets of corr-ugated metal, copper wire, clothing and bedding to waiting vehicles. One man went about his work wearing a newly acquired gas mask. They seemed wilfully ignorant of the risks they were taking. For weeks, the Iraqi Army had been laying land-mines all around their front-line positions, and Kurdish military commanders had ordered a thorough mine-clearance operation before they went anywhere near the vacant Iraqi bunkers along the main road to Kirkuk. However, as we had already found out, personal enrichment always trumps personal safety in Northern Iraq.

The surprise Iraqi withdrawal had sent a sudden reckless rush of blood to everyone's brain. We got a glimpse of Baba Gurgur as we drove along a back road used by smugglers from Chamchamal. Every few kilometres, the Iraqi military had dug earthworks into the rough dirt track, presumably to frustrate the smugglers as much as to block advancing American armour. A sturdy four-wheel drive would get you across the ditches, but not even a tank could protect you if you were unlucky enough to hit a land-mine. On balance, the risk seemed worth it; there was an Iraqi garrison town at the end of the road, and not even the Peshmerga had reached it yet.

Qarahanjeer looked as if it had once been a busy little town, but its Kurdish inhabitants had long gone, and the Iraqi Army had erased the physical evidence of their presence. On the walls of the military buildings were Arabic slogans praising Saddam and abusing America and one that urged soldiers to keep active: 'The sweat of training is like the blood of battle.' Inside a building at the side of the main street were documents connected with the Eighth Infantry Division Chemical Warfare Unit. In one room, the components of a gas mask were glued onto a wooden display board, which suggested that this unit was focused more on defence than attack. That did not make for a great story, but it was somehow reassuring.

An imposing tiled portrait of Saddam Hussein was mounted on a stone plinth in the centre of town. The Iraqi dictator looked youthful but slightly dated. He wore a double-breasted navy-blue suit with a dark grey tie, and the pointed tip of a white handkerchief poked out of his breast pocket. Under the shadow of Saddam, a handful of

reporters compared notes about the liberation of
Qarahanjeer. It had all been an anti-climax, although the
deathly silence was still a little unnerving. No one was
quite sure when exactly the Iraqis had left or how long we
would have to wait for the Peshmerga. The answer to that
last question was 'not very long at all'. There were about
ten or twelve gunmen in the battered jeeps that came
speeding past Saddam's smiling face. Their leader was a
stocky man with a chrome-plated Kalashnikov that was all
spit and polish. Just two weeks before, he had left his job
as a mechanic in the German town of Augsburg and
returned to Northern Iraq to fight for the liberation of his
homeland. Initially, he and his comrades seemed a little bit
put out that a gaggle of reporters were already in
Qarahanjeer, but they also sensed an approaching photo
opportunity.

One of the gunmen began to sprinkle Saddam's
portrait with iodine in the manner of a priest before
communion. As the face of the 'Butcher of Baghdad'
turned a dark shade of orange, my satellite phone rang. It
was an old friend and fellow Dubliner, Sean Swan, who
was working for ITV News in Northern Iraq. I had just
started to describe the peace and quiet of Qarahanjeer to
him when a volley of automatic gunfire shattered the
pretence of tranquillity and sent me sprawling on the
roadway. The mechanic had decided to use Saddam for
target practice, and after spraying the portrait with a
random burst of rapid fire, he began to shoot single
rounds, holding the shiny chrome rifle above his head
with his left hand. Before long, Saddam had lost the left
side of his face and a substantial portion of one shoulder,
but his smile was still inscrutably intact. When the firing
subsided, the mechanic gathered his friends in front of
the portrait and ordered us to take his photograph. We

did so without argument. You can reason with men with guns, but men who fire guns are a different proposition entirely.

When I finally reestablished contact with Sean Swan, we arranged to meet for dinner the following night at the Abu Sana Hotel. He brought the crew from ITV and Channel Four News, including Gaby Rado. I knew Gaby by reputation long before coming to Northern Iraq. As far back as the early 1990s, his reporting from the Balkans had made a big impression on me, particularly his exposure of Serb atrocities in Bosnia. Over the years, I had followed him on his travels for Channel Four, from Russia to Afghanistan, and if I was honest with myself, I envied him as much as I admired him.

We had met for the first time in early March in the mountain resort of Dukan, where the leaders of the main Kurdish factions were due to give a press conference. With characteristic arrogance, they summoned foreign reporters to meet them and then left us waiting for close to six hours inside a sealed compound. Gaby and his producer, Sophie, managed to get a delivery of food past the guards at the gate, and they called everyone over to a small garden overlooking the deep-blue stillness of Dukan's reservoir, where they shared out kebabs and warm Pepsi to friends and strangers alike. 'Plenty for everyone,' Gaby said. After lunch, there was still no sign of the Kurdish politicians, so Gaby organised a walk-out. He called on everyone to follow him out of the compound in protest at the way the media were being treated. He took off up the hill with a few proud souls trailing behind him, but most of us sat looking at our feet, embarrassed by our desperate need for some small nugget of news on a slow Sunday.

If Gaby was disappointed in me and the other hacks, then he did not show it the night we gathered for dinner at the Abu Sana. He joined me, Sean and another Irishman from ITV, Mark Davies, at the loud end of the dinner table, where the flow of nonsense conversations matched the apparently endless supply of Turkish beer. I had not enjoyed myself so much in the six-odd weeks I had been in Northern Iraq, and I could feel the soul-destroying tedium of life in our little corner of the war seep away, at least for one night. The entire group retired to someone's hotel room where there was the rare sound of Western chart music and more animated conversation about nothing in particular. I said good-night to Gaby shortly after two in the morning. Seven hours later, as I left my room for breakfast, he fell off the roof of our hotel and died.

I have repeatedly gone over the conversations we had that night, and what really sticks in my brain is Gaby's humility. He was the polar opposite of the self-promoting war heroes who tend to suck the oxygen out of media social gatherings. In a business in which the loudest tend to get the most attention, Gaby was the exception: a man whose understated strength and engaging modesty gave him the authority that other reporters merely dream of. His Channel Four colleague Jon Snow would later write that 'he brought a dependable, engaged and humane quality to his reports that eschewed the flash or the immodest'. That was how I found him in real life as well. When I said good-night to Gaby Rado, there was no reason to believe I would not see him again. Perhaps I looked forward to meeting him again for selfish reasons. There is so much to learn in this business yet so few people who are capable of teaching by example. Gaby Rado was one of them, one of the really good guys.

After Gaby died, it became much harder to deal with the shameless dramatists and self-promoters. On the morning of his death, I watched a television report by a journalist who was staying in Sulaimani. He had travelled to Qarahanjeer the day after our visit, and while he was there, the Iraqi Army had shelled the town. He brought back fifteen seconds of video that showed him scrambling into a ditch, but that was pretty much all he had. He borrowed video footage from several other reporters, including our pictures of the mechanic shooting up Saddam's portrait, and cobbled together a report. But the report was still all about him scrambling into a ditch. To millions of viewers around the world, he must have looked like a war hero. However, that's not how he seemed to the jaded eyes watching him in the Abu Sana.

To some extent, anger at this kind of person became an energy in those moments when you could see no point in carrying on with a story that was so mired in false expectations and spin. A famous British broadcaster once said that every time he interviewed a politician he asked himself, 'Why is this bastard lying to me?' These were words to live by for any reporter covering the war, but what was worse in Northern Iraq was that the lies would regularly come from the people for whom you had some admiration.

Anyone who spent time with Kurdish politicians and military commanders had learned that a straight answer to a straight question was only half an answer. Along with the spoken word, there was sometimes the hint of a smile or a slight movement of the eye, and in that tiny gesture was the hidden truth. After a while, I decided that the various gestures translated into a single universal statement: 'What I am saying is not true, but I know that you know that I am telling a lie, so I am actually not telling a lie because you know the truth is the opposite of what I am saying.' Once you make peace with this form of non-verbal communication, life becomes a lot easier.

In contrast, the growing number of Americans that were crossing my path showed nothing but absolute sincerity. The week the Iraqis withdrew from front-line positions, a thousand paratroopers of the US Army's 172nd Airborne Brigade jumped out of their C-17 transporters onto an airfield near Erbil. Before they set out on their mission from an American airbase in Italy, Colonel William Mayville had given them a pep talk. 'Americans are asking you to make the world a better place by jumping into the unknown for the benefit of others,' he told the men. 'Paratroopers, our cause is just and victory is certain. I want you to join me tonight on an airborne assault.'

Of course, the paratroopers were dropping into the friendliest territory a US serviceman could find in this increasingly hostile world. The troops were being sent to the Kurdish enclave, not to join the main battle against Saddam's forces, but to reassure the Kurds and dissuade the neighbouring Turks from invading Northern Iraq. However, the pretence of imminent threat had to be maintained, so CNN reported that the soldiers had quickly 'secured' the airstrip where they had landed. Secured it from what – an ecstatic gang of Kurdish militiamen? The truth was the paratroopers would have been in as much danger dropping into a cornfield in Kansas. Aside from the obvious exaggeration, there were latent risks in the attitude of the new arrivals. They seemed ill-equipped to distinguish between friend and enemy or to appreciate the nature of the threat that lay ahead. Whether or not truth and justice would play a part in Iraq's future, those soldiers would eventually have to face

up to a world of deceit and death, a world in which
Colonel Mayville's moral absolutes would be of little use.

As the American military machine raced towards
Baghdad, the embedded journalists raced along with them,
visibly straining under the pressure of being impartial in a
partial reality. A few of their faces were familiar to me from
previous assignments, although I was a bit surprised to see
David Bloom's face appear on CNN one night. He was a
big star on NBC News, potentially one of their biggest,
and was embedded with the US Army's 3rd Infantry
Division. Just outside Baghdad, he fell ill with a brain
embolism and died. He was a former White House
correspondent, and I had bumped into him a few times on
the road with Bill Clinton, including one lost night we
shared in the Purple Martini bar in Denver during a G-8
summit in 1997. That was the unbidden memory that
popped into my head as I watched his obituary.

Three days before, Michael Kelly's picture had
appeared in a similar spot on the television screen. He had
died on April 3 in a road accident while also travelling with
the 3rd Infantry Division. He was an outspoken columnist
with the *Washington Post* and had been a fierce critic of Bill
Clinton during the Monica Lewinsky scandal. While his
columns were occasionally vicious, they were also
beautifully crafted and often very funny. Before leaving
for Iraq, I had filed away a piece he had written about the
challenges facing ordinary Americans. 'We are now
entering into a serious time, a time of protracted conflict,'
he wrote. 'And with the sure knowledge of further dead,
people come to terms with things again.'

I could not imagine what the embeds or the reporters
holed up in the Palestine Hotel in Baghdad were trying to

come to terms with. Our lives in Northern Iraq were so far removed from the total war *they* were facing. What we had come to fear were the unexpected risks that lurked in the shadows of our daily routine. There were fewer apparent dangers in our work because the Kurdish enclave was still teetering between skirmish and outright conflict. American air strikes continued along the front-line, and joint teams of US Special Forces and Peshmerga were coming under occasional Iraqi bombardment, but it appeared that the Americans were no longer interested in a full-scale assault on Saddam's forces in the north.

New words were creeping into our lexicon, with people no longer talking of the Northern Front, but the 'Northern Rear'. In the faces of friends and colleagues, you could see the effects of this paralysing ambiguity, and the long separation from reality was also having a visible impact on our collective mental health. In his weblog, BBC producer Stuart Hughes said members of the press pack had lost girlfriends because they had been away for so long; one person he knew was so desperate to get home, he was taken out by 'medivac'. 'Other colleagues are pondering possible escape routes,' he wrote, 'either because they have had enough or because the Northern Front is shaping up to be a mere shadow of what we originally expected.'

The search for original material in this twilight zone had become physically and mentally exhausting. The sheer distances involved in travelling from one flashpoint to another and the dispiriting number of false leads were taking a heavy toll. Then there were the extra risks involved in the increasingly desperate battle to justify our presence there.

The news of what happened to the BBC team filtered through to the rest of us in Sulaimani late on April 2. Stuart Hughes had travelled to Kifri with correspondent

Jim Muir and cameraman Kaveh Golestan. The Iraqi Army had just abandoned their positions outside town after sustained bombing by US aircraft. Among the positions they had abandoned was a citadel on a small hill to the south-west of Kifri. The BBC team drove their jeep up the main road to the fort and parked in a grassy dip to the left of the building. When they got out of the vehicle, there was an explosion, and as they raced for cover there were two more. The team had stumbled into a minefield. Stuart Hughes stepped on one mine and his right heel was blown off. Despite expert treatment from a US Special Forces surgeon, his foot was eventually amputated.

When Kaveh Golestan jumped for cover, he fell on a mine. He was dead by the time his colleagues got to him. Once more, the person who least deserved to suffer was the one who had paid the ultimate price. Kaveh lived in Tehran and was internationally renowned for his work as a photojournalist, documentary maker and champion of press freedom in Iran. He was an inspiration to a generation of Iranian journalists, and one American reporter said in tribute, 'when Kaveh was some place you knew that's where you wanted to be'.

Kaveh had a reputation as the least cynical member of the press corps in Sulaimani, and he seemed immune to its prevailing desperation. Jim Muir later wrote a moving account of that journey to Kifri, recalling that when they had stopped for lunch at the side of the road, Kaveh had said: 'When I'm in situations like these, I feel I am me.' Maybe he was right, and the rest of us were wrong.

Kaveh Golestan was probably killed by a Valmara 69, a land-mine originally produced in Italy, copied by the Iraqis and sometimes known by the nickname 'Black

Betty'. It is a bounding fragmentation mine, which means it is designed to pop out of the ground and explode at waist level, spraying red-hot shrapnel in a lethal radius of twenty-seven metres. It is likely that Stuart Hughes was injured by a PMN anti-personnel mine, nicknamed the 'Black Widow', which has probably killed and maimed more people than any other land-mine. It is designed to drive plastic, dirt and bone into the upper regions of the body. 'The fact that I escaped with my right knee intact', wrote Stuart in his weblog, 'could be regarded as "lucky".'

Tom and I travelled to Kifri the day after Kaveh Golestan died. For several days, we had been planning to make the trip, and despite the accident, Kifri was still as safe as any of the other front-line destinations we had been considering. We arrived early in the morning and followed a convoy of Peshmerga towards the front-line, turning left at the entrance to the citadel and stopping short of the grassy dip where the tragedy had happened.

We climbed to the highest point on the fort and watched the militiamen scatter across the long, dusty plain that stretched out before us. A small white cloud rose from the middle of the plain, and moments later we heard a low thud. Then came another cloud and another thud. The Iraqis were shelling something, but at first we could not make out what. When Tom looked through his camera lens, he saw a motorbike speeding along a dirt track under the noses of the Iraqis. It was a Peshmerga, and he seemed to be playing a game of 'kill me if you can'. Was this kind of suicidal bravery admirable or repulsive? A few weeks before, it might have been the former, but on this day it turned my stomach.

A few yards from the citadel, a group of teenage boys danced through the abandoned Iraqi bunkers, picking up every loose object in their path. The night before, within yards of those bunkers, someone had been blown apart by a mine. Two weeks later, a team of international experts inspected the minefield in front of the citadel and found tripwires connected to explosive charges attached to twenty-five-litre canisters of napalm. The sick thing is that even if those boys had known what was buried beneath their playground, I am not sure they would have stopped playing.

Iraq is among the most heavily mined countries in the world. The international consensus is that between eight and twelve million mines have been laid in the front-line areas of the country, and it will take between thirty-five and seventy-five years to clear them. Over the years, the Kurdish enclave has arguably suffered most from the scourge of these hidden killers. Even before the last war, an average of one person was killed or injured by a mine or unexploded bomb in Northern Iraq every day. The mines kept killing even as Saddam's grip on power was being loosened. During one week in April 2003, a single hospital in Kirkuk reported fifty-two people killed and sixty-three injured by mines and explosive devices.

Like the fires of Baba Gurgur, the killing will go on, even when Saddam is a historical footnote. The great pity is that the broader political significance of Iraq's land-mine problem barely registers in post-war debate. Saddam's enthusiastic use of land-mines was yet another example of his disregard for human life, but he would never have been able to inflict such lasting damage on his country without the active collaboration of the international community, including the Western powers who eventually plotted his demise.

The scale of hypocrisy was evident in the ruins of a town called Kadir Karam. It had been a thriving community of three thousand Kurds until the Iraqi Army came calling during the Anfal offensive of 1988. Many townspeople were killed, and the rest were forced to flee while a large minefield was laid around the southern half of the village. The Iraqis used the town's mosque as a storehouse for their mines and a barracks for their troops, even though the building contained the tombs of two revered Kurdish clerics.

At the end of March, Saddam withdrew his troops, leaving behind the mines. The local Peshmerga brought us inside the mosque to see the damage the Iraqis had caused; then, with a casual warning, they led us to the tombs of the two clerics. Inside one of the tombs was a haphazard pile of sandbags. When our eyes adjusted to the gloom, we could see the short, stumpy prongs of fragmentation mines poking through rough holes in the sandbags. They were V-69s, similar to the device that killed Kaveh Golestan, and they were stacked from floor to ceiling inside the relatively cramped space of the tomb. The day after our visit, the Mines Advisory Group (MAG) arrived to defuse the devices and posted this report on the Internet: 'Pressure of a few kilograms on them will cause the mine to detonate. MAG technicians had to carefully cut open the sandbags using secateurs and disarm the mines one at a time. Just one of these mines detonating in the small rooms of the mosque would mean almost certain death. Due to this danger, the MAG technicians worked individually, one person per room.'

The disposal crew dismantled more than 150 mines inside the Kadir Karam mosque, and news of their discovery sparked international condemnation. Human Rights Watch said Iraq had violated international humanitarian law by storing these explosive devices inside a place of worship. The unresolved question was where did the Iraqis get their hands on all those mines?

After subsequent investigation by land-mine activists, it emerged that the V-69s discovered in the mosque at Kadir Karam were part of a shipment of nine million anti-personnel mines sold to Iraq by the Italian weapons manufacturer Valsella in the 1980s. The deal was in clear violation of UN sanctions, but the company made so much money from its sales to Saddam that it became a takeover target and was eventually purchased by Fiat. Valsella was forced to end its trade with Iraq when factory workers in northern Italy staged a protest strike, and the subsequent controversy led to the arrest of seven company executives. In 1994, the Italian government ordered a halt to all land-mine production. It completed the destruction of its remaining stockpile of the weapon in November 2002, just as the Italian prime minister, Silvio Berlusconi, was pledging support for US efforts to oust Saddam Hussein. Of course, that task would be made more difficult by the presence of millions of Italian mines.

To be fair, Italy had no monopoly on hypocrisy. After the Islamic revolution in Iran in 1979, the United States backed Saddam Hussein as the least worst option in the region. The Reagan administration had close diplomatic and economic ties with Baghdad, even supplying crucial intelligence information to Saddam during the last years of his war with Tehran. In 1983, President Reagan sent his Middle East envoy to Baghdad offering help. The envoy's name was Donald Rumsfeld. There is also evidence that in the late 1980s, when George Bush senior was president, US companies legally exported equipment used in Saddam's nuclear programme.

Of course, the French also wanted a piece of the action. Back in 1975, they sold the Iraqi dictator a nuclear reactor. In Iraq it was officially known as Osirak, but in France it was referred to as Ochirac, in honour of the close ties between Prime Minister Jacques Chirac and the regime in Baghdad. In his defence, Chirac would later claim that everyone was doing business with Saddam in those days, even if that meant exporting weapons. When CNN asked him to name names, he said: 'All the major democracies. Each and every one of them.'

The list of countries that supplied weaponry to the Iraqi military does read like a who's who of the so-called civilised world and includes France, Britain, the Netherlands, Germany, Italy, Japan and Switzerland. In addition, Brazil, Argentina and Egypt helped to supply technology for Saddam's missile programme. Land-mine activists say they have found mines in Iraq that came from Belgium, Canada, Egypt, Romania, Singapore, the former Soviet Union and the United States.

And before we in Ireland pass judgement, we should do some historical soul-searching. In July 1987, the UN Security Council passed a resolution on the Iran–Iraq war, instructing member states to 'refrain from any act which may lead to a further escalation and widening of the conflict'. That did not stop then Taoiseach Charles Haughey from helping out his old friends in Baghdad. He had worked hard to cultivate the trade relationship with Iraq, so even as Saddam was gassing the Kurds and dropping rockets on Iranian civilians in the late 1980s, the Irish government was feeding Iraq with all the beef we could slaughter, insure and then export. In 1989, Haughey sent Saddam a letter saying he was 'very pleased that the friendly and sympathetic relations between our two countries continue to develop ...' Despite what some perennial activists will tell you, there were no mass protests in Dublin when all this was happening.

In time of war, there are those who die, those who kill and those who allow it all to happen, either by supplying weapons or by maintaining silence. Too often we are the silent partners to slaughter.

It is all very well making these judgements with the benefit of hindsight, but such moral clarity was in short supply in Northern Iraq by the end of that first week in April. Innocent people were dying on a daily basis on the frontline, and it was not just Iraqi mines that were doing the killing. On April 6, John Simpson of the BBC narrowly avoided death when a US warplane mistakenly dropped a bomb on the Kurdish military convoy with which he was travelling. Among the eighteen people killed were a senior Kurdish official and a BBC translator, Kamaran Abdul Razak. I listened to Simpson telling the studio back in London that this was 'a really bad own goal by the Americans'. As he spoke blood trickled from his ear.

I watched the attack on that convoy from my sick bed. After almost two months of good health, I had picked up some parasite and was suffering the symptoms of a bad gastric flu. The worst part of being ill was having nothing to do but watch war coverage and think. When John Simpson described that 'scene from hell', one obvious danger presented itself: we seek out human suffering to convince our audiences back home that they should care, but perhaps the more we provide scenes of horror, the less people feel they can do anything to stop it. As images of death and destruction become increasingly graphic, the more they lose their shock value and the less they have the power to create the outrage that leads to action.

Watching the pieces of dismembered Peshmerga on the BBC, there was an even more frightening possibility: that when we present images of the unthinkable through the neat frame of the camera lens, we make them almost logical. The novelist John Banville once said of combat photography that it 'works an opposite magic, making the world's essential strangeness seem familiar, graspable, immanent with meaning'. The same could be said of the rapid response medium of television news: viewers are now used to seeing human destruction as it happens. Whether it was September 11 or 'shock and awe', the unthinkable became conceivable because we saw it on television.

Perhaps there is a creeping futility about war reporting in an age of media torrent. No matter how hard you swim, how many risks you take, you can never influence the course of the events you are witnessing. You have your face pressed up against the window, but you are still an observer, still watching, still seeing images, not necessarily the reality as it is lived by the people who surround you. The French philosopher Jean Baudrillard caused controversy after the first Gulf War when he said that the conflict never actually happened. I was starting to understand how he felt.

The evening we were shown the mines in the mosque at Kadir Karam, the Peshmerga invited Tom and me up on the roof where they were making a dinner of meat stew. We stood around the pots on the fire, drinking tea and talking about war. I asked the commander when his men believed they would get to Kirkuk. 'When George Bush tells us,' he replied, with a faint, lopsided smirk.

As the Peshmerga spoke, one of his comrades began to gesture into the waning glare of the setting sun. A vapour trail was creeping steadily across the deepening blue of the evening sky. All eyes turned to look at the outline of the B-52 as it headed towards Kirkuk. Eventually, it began to bank in a gentle arc, and about halfway through its turn, we heard the drumbeat of detonation as its bombs hit their targets. From that roof-top, it all seemed to make sense.

The Iraqi mines piled high in the crypt, the lies of the Kurdish commander and the echo of American bombs. All of it fitted some perverted, imposed logic.

It was time to go home.

12

THE MEDIUM IS NOT THE MESSAGE

'War in Iraq.'
CNN

'War on Iraq.'
Al-Jazeera

We left without a full stop, with no cathartic moment of brutal finality. For the best part of two months in the Kurdish enclave, we had expected our war would end with a decisive US invasion of Saddam's northern strongholds, but that never happened. There were still important stories to be told in Northern Iraq, including the final march on Kirkuk, but the course of the war had changed. The value of our work had rapidly diminished even as the physical and mental strain increased.

Still, the logic behind the decision to leave had been of little consolation when we pulled up beside the PUK offices near the Iranian border. There was a short-lived compulsion to turn the jeep around, drive back to Sulaimani and wring the last drop of pathos from the story. But as the Kurdish official brought a final glass of tea, it became clear the main event was taking place somewhere else. Before the official returned to his office to process our paperwork, he turned on the television in the corner of the room. The Arab station Al-Manar was reporting that Baghdad was still firmly under the control of the Iraqi leadership, but with a quick flick of the remote the story changed dramatically. BBC World was running live pictures of American tanks rolling through the streets of Baghdad and Iraqi irregulars running along the banks of the Tigris, apparently in retreat. We could see the hole in the side of the Palestine Hotel, where a US tank shell had just killed two journalists.

As the curtain rose on the fall of Baghdad, there was a commotion in the hallway of the PUK offices. Two burly men with automatic weapons stepped through the door of the waiting-room and glowered at us. They were followed by a bearded cleric in brown robes and a black turban who sat down in the corner of the room without acknowledging our presence. Blnd said he was a top man with SCIRI, the Iraqi Shi'ite opposition group led by Mohammad Baqer al-Hakim, whom we had come across at Friday prayers in Tehran. The cleric sat quietly in the corner, but one of his minders got up and switched the television channel from BBC to Fox News. It seemed a bizarre choice for an Islamic activist, but we were in no position to pass comment, so we all sat in silence and watched Fox presenters cheer on the American invaders.

Greg Kelly was the Fox News reporter travelling with an advance party of US Marines. He had his videophone set up outside Saddam's Republican palace in central Baghdad (or 'downtown' Baghdad, as it was now) and was hosting a live celebration of the troops' rapid advance on the Iraqi capital. 'Saddam Hussein says he owns Baghdad,'

Lieutenant Colonel Philip de Camp declared live on air;
'Wrong. We own Baghdad. We own his palaces. We own
his hotels.' As the anchorman and studio guest back in
Washington showered tributes on 'these American
heroes', two Marines unfurled a flag carrying the emblem
of the Georgia Bulldogs, an American college-football
team. 'Go Dogs,' they chanted across the crackly video-
link. The SCIRI bodyguards looked on without any visible
emotion, as their boss sat reading in a corner of the room,
oblivious to the fact that the Georgia Bulldogs had just
conquered his nation's capital.

We set off for the border checkpoint a few minutes
later, where we said our goodbyes to Blnd and Mustafa.
On the Iranian side of the gate was the welcome sight of
my RTÉ colleague Philip Boucher-Hayes, who was in
transit to Sulaimani. We exchanged information and
equipment over lunch, and then Tom and I got into an old
Hiace van for the twelve-hour drive to Tehran. I slept for
most of the trip and went straight to bed when we reached
our hotel. During the night, I was woken by a nightmare.
Staring at the ceiling, in the pre-dawn gloom, the war
came to an end, at least for me.

The next day was April 9. Sometime in the early
afternoon, I fell asleep in front of the television. When I
woke, BBC World was broadcasting live pictures of an
American tank crew wrapping ropes around a statue of
Saddam Hussein in the centre of Baghdad. A few minutes
later, a happy crowd of Iraqis was dancing on Saddam's
head. Rageh Omar was broadcasting live from the scene
for the BBC on a dodgy satellite phone line. For once, he
was surplus to requirements. There was no need for
commentary at that moment. There was little or nothing a

reporter could tell you that you could not see with your own eyes, whether you watched from your front room in Ireland or a hotel room in Tehran.

It was possible to see these pictures and draw the wrong conclusion: that war was over. At the very moment the crowds were dancing on the head of the statue, CNN reported that a major military engagement was taking place just a few streets away from the scenes of jubilation. But the destruction of the statue was significant because there was no need for the media to interpret reality for their audience, perhaps for the first time in this conflict. Of all the coverage, on all the major networks, this was the first time I had complete confidence in what I was seeing and hearing.

During my final days in Northern Iraq, it was impossible not to feel depressed about how the war was being represented to the wider world. Listening to the voices of commentators on BBC World, CNN and Fox News and watching the pictures on a variety of Arab networks, including Al-Jazeera, was a lot like tuning into a movie programme where a sequence of film clips and banal sound-bites from the stars is followed by the loud din of opposing voices pandering to every prejudice in the audience.

The dark truth about rolling news operations is that the technology that delivers war with unprecedented intimacy is helping to kill off considered analysis and the concept of objective truth. CNN's star reporter Christiane Amanpour said it best when she described the message from headquarters: 'Keep it moving, keep it moving is what they tell us.' Live television delivers the story of war like a narcotic stimulant, but it leaves us confused about the exact location of the beginning, middle and end. Reporters on the ground are best qualified to sketch the bigger picture, but they are often prisoners of the technology they use, chained to their cameras on hotel roof-tops, serving constant rolling news bulletins with 'two-ways' when they would rather be out chasing the story. In our collective obsession with 'the latest', we frequently miss 'the context'.

In Iraq, it also meant missing certain facts or getting way ahead of them. Over a period of five days, British media outlets had the southern Iraqi city of Umm Qasr 'secured' nine times before it was actually captured. You cannot blame this entirely on military spin or the wishful thinking of pro-war media bosses. Reporters are faced with an insatiable demand for a fresh lead on the next dispatch or 'two-way'. They may be conscious of manipulation by their sources, but they know the bosses back home will balance any possible mistake against the fact that they were first. Anyway, the boss may have the attention span of a goldfish trying to stay afloat in the raging torrent of information from the war zone. Today's two-way is tomorrow's history.

The elastic truth of 'real-time' reporting makes it tempting for the military to try to sell big lies that would previously stand out. In Iraq, the easiest lies to sell were those that felt good in the telling. Private Jessica Lynch fought the Iraqis to the last bullet of her M-16 before being shot and captured. Her captors beat her up before she was brought to safety in a daring rescue operation. Probably the only part of that story (as reported by leading US newspapers) that was true was that Jessica Lynch was brought to safety. The Private Lynch episode showed how easy it is for spin to become fact in the age of instant news, but it also showed the extent to which the media is drawn to headlines that pander to audience sentiment. Private Lynch was of no consequence to the conduct or outcome of the war in Iraq, yet according to a study by the *Columbia Journalism Review* she had more mentions in major US papers in the two weeks after her rescue than Tommy Franks, the American general running the war.

Another peculiarity of instant news is how depersonalised it has made war reporting. You see the faces of those reporters in the battlefield so many times that they eventually become as recognisable as a close friend. You get to know a lot about their appearance, diction and endurance, but you learn very little about their personality, their influences or even the true measure of their ability as a journalist. Perhaps the only way to appreciate what we are losing in the rapid advance of technology is to read about war through the eyes of previous generations of war correspondents. Take this description of the aftermath of the D-Day landings from legendary US combat reporter Ernie Pyle.

'I took a walk along the historic coast of Normandy in the country of France. It was a lovely day for strolling along the seashore. Men were sleeping on the sand, some of them sleeping forever. Men were floating in the water, but they didn't know they were in the water, for they were dead. The water was full of squishy little jellyfish about the size of your hand. Millions of them. In the centre each of them had a green design exactly like a four-leaf clover. The good luck emblem. Sure. Hell yes.'

If twenty-four-hour news were around in 1944, a row of reporters would be hemmed in behind a military checkpoint a safe distance from the shoreline, shouting to be heard above each other. Half of them would focus on stiff German resistance; the other half would be telling us about the rapid Allied advance. None of them would have had time for a walk on the beach. They could give viewers their best 'guesstimates' on casualty figures but no sense of who those casualties were or how they had died. It would not matter anyway, because the channels would spend no more than a few minutes on the beach before switching live to Berlin for the latest defiant video from Hitler's bunker.

In my experience, most editors in these twenty-four-hour news outfits do want something more than the whiz-bang glimpse of live conflict, but the pressure to fill airtime means they are increasingly dependent on studio-based talking heads to provide the kind of context Ernie Pyle delivered half a century ago. While some of these guests widen our perspective, others never get beyond the glib response. A couple of days before I left Iraq, CNN plucked an ex-GI in a polo-neck from their vast collection of military analysts to discuss the latest events on the battlefield. He responded to a question with the immortal line: 'I will answer that conceptually.'

The same conceptual blather was pouring out of experts who talked about 'shaping the battlefield' as if they were redesigning their bathrooms, tank enthusiasts who extolled the virtues of the Abrams over the Bradley and armchair generals who were fighting a war without names, faces or victims. As American tanks rolled ever closer to Baghdad, the television viewer was treated to the grotesque spectacle of well-dressed studio guests slowly disappearing up their own conceptual arses.

The reliance on a dehumanised language of conflict, or 'warspeak', was not invented during the last war in Iraq. The term 'collateral damage' was used as far back as the Vietnam era (where US military spokesmen also talked of 'circular error probability' to explain unintended civilian casualties). However, by the end of the second Gulf War, the warspeak dictionary had expanded to several volumes. You could now discuss any act of modern warfare without ever having to confront the morality of that act. 'I think they got thwacked,' said one RAF officer when describing the outcome of attacks by Harrier jets on Iraqi targets outside Basra. In fact, US and British aircraft were not dropping bombs, they were 'kinetic targeting'; they were not killing Iraqis, but trying to 'attrit' them.

In the ground war, the terminology was even more obtuse. After a US marine was killed in a shoot-out with Iraqi irregulars in the town of Diwaniya, a military spokesman described the encounter as 'blue collar warfare'. This was clearly not the 'catastrophic success' that some of the American top brass had predicted but a long drawn-out series of 'hot contact points', in which Iraqi forces followed a policy of 'shoot and scoot'. It had become so hairy in urban situations that some US patrols decided to go 'mouseholing': instead of raiding houses through the front door, they blew holes in the sides of the building.

Back in Washington, the experts kept up the flow of conceptual nonsense. As the Marines closed in on the Iraqi capital, one retired general compared US forces to the big hungry dot of an old video game. 'I think you should Pac-Man the ring around Baghdad,' said General Barry McCaffrey in an interview with the *Washington Post*. There were also a few moments of quasi-Freudian insight from US policy-makers. In one celebrated instance at a Pentagon media briefing, Donald Rumsfeld turned to one of his generals and said: 'Calibrate me, Dick.' It was meant as a 'correct me if I am wrong' type of statement, but it came out as unnerving haiku: 'The Republican Guard has – calibrate me, Dick – they pulled south in the north and they went north in the southern portion of the country.'

The responsibility for exposing the bloody reality of 'thwacking' and 'mouseholing' fell to the seven-hundred-odd embedded reporters who were assigned to various British and American military outfits. In many ways, they were in a no-win situation. To opponents of the war, they were automatically compromised because of their dependence on the soldiers surrounding them (a perception reinforced by the occasional reporter in military fatigues). At the same time, military commanders were deeply suspicious of their presence on the battlefield. The impression of strained dependency was reinforced by accounts written by the reporters after the war. A columnist from California's *Orange County Register* said one of the Marines in the unit he was travelling with gave him a grenade to throw in case the Iraqis overwhelmed their position. 'I found myself falling in love with my subject,' said the same reporter. 'I fell in love with "my Marines".'

In spite of this, many embeds overcame the uneasy relationship with their hosts to deliver journalism that will stand the test of time. In one incident, US soldiers mistakenly killed women and children in a van approaching a checkpoint. US Central Command in Qatar said the soldiers had followed all the established rules of engagement. The next day, William Branigin of the *Washington Post* delivered a very different account in which he quoted a commander shouting at a sentry: 'You just [expletive] killed a family because you didn't fire a warning shot soon enough!' A *New York Times* reporter, Dexter Filkins, delivered a profoundly honest account of a tragedy involving the unit to which he was assigned. A soldier with the unit had shot and killed a woman who was standing near some Iraqi soldiers. 'I'm sorry, but the chick was in the way,' the soldier was quoted as saying.

Various embeds from the BBC, CBS and CNN exposed failures to supply troops as they advanced on Baghdad, broadcasting reports of one meal a day for hungry soldiers or raising awkward questions about whether or not there were enough troops to do the job properly. This was all in stark contrast to the first Gulf War in 1991, when not a single pool reporter produced a first-person account of the battle between US-led forces and Iraqi troops.

From the outset, too, too much was expected of embedded reporters, especially those working for television. Embeds were never meant to be the primary source of information from the battlefield because their battlefield would, by definition, be too narrow. 'The war is whatever piece of dirt you are sitting on,' said one American reporter. However, the insatiable appetite of live TV placed an unrealistic burden on them, and the pressure was heightened by the woeful inadequacies of official military sources in Qatar and Kuwait. Ultimately, the embedded reporters worked best where they were a part of the overall picture, but too often they seemed to be the entire picture. As one Fleet Street editor observed about reports from embeds, 'Drink one and you think it's wonderful. Drink six and you get sick and woozy.'

It is too easy to write off embeds, experts and warspeak as elements of a pro-war agenda on the part of the big Western television networks. These phenomena are better understood as a reflection of the competitive pressure on television to deliver a diet of instant gratification and wall-to-wall blather. The key word here is competitive. For the big players in television news, war is a commercial opportunity, a chance to build brand loyalty. Having the best equipment, the best reporters and the snappiest theme music is only part of the equation. On the most competitive fringe of television news, bias is no longer something to be kept hidden but something to be sold as a wartime commodity.

America's Fox News channel was most successful in exploiting audience sentiment during the second Gulf War. In the first week of the conflict, Fox was watched by an average of 3.3 million viewers every day. During the same period, CNN averaged 2.7 million viewers. At one point during the conflict, Fox's audience rose to 4.4 million viewers; a 242 per cent increase in audience in the space of a year.

Fox operated under the slogan 'fair and balanced', but it echoed President Bush's dictum that the world was either with the United States in the war on terror or against it. The network presented its explicit support for US military action as patriotic duty, but it was also commercial imperative. 'We have to feed the core,' was how one Fox producer put it during the US military campaign in Afghanistan; 'the core' being the millions of Americans who believed there was a liberal bias in the established media.

When anti-war protestors gathered in the Swiss city of Davos, a few months before the invasion of Iraq, a Fox anchor referred to them as 'hundreds of knuckleheads'. It was Fox that popularised the use of the phrase 'axis of weasel' to describe Germany and France – it even appeared at the bottom of the screen during coverage of pre-war diplomatic wrangling. When conflict got underway, one of the hosts of its discussion show, *Fox and Friends*, told the *Washington Post*: 'Right now, there is a wave of patriotism in the country. Our show is about patriotism.' If there was one line that summed up the Fox approach to this war, it came on the day that statue fell in Baghdad. One of Fox's star anchors, Neil Cavuto, had a message for those 'who opposed the liberation of Iraq'. He said: 'You were sickening then, you are sickening now.'

In spite of all the bluster, there are a couple of reasons we should be cautious about the perceived dangers of the Fox News phenomenon. First, it is part of the reality of US media coverage of the war in Iraq, not the entire reality: the majority of Americans still get their news from the big guns such as *ABC World News Tonight*, which averaged an audience of over ten million viewers during the war. Second, Fox News is not a threat because it is loudly conservative, but because it treats audience bias as a commercial tool. Ultimately, the biggest danger for American television is not some right-wing cabal, loyal to corporate America and George Bush, but the fact that making people feel good about their prejudice has become good business. On this side of the Atlantic, we could smugly write off Fox News as just another reason to hate the United States, but the truth is that this is no longer an exclusively American phenomenon.

Just as its American equivalents were battling for new viewers during the war in Iraq, the Arab satellite stations were fighting for a bigger slice of the pie, and they too laid it on thick with a blatant appeal to the biases of their audience. For stations such as Al-Manar, based in Beirut, Al-Arabiya in Dubai and Abu Dhabi TV, the last conflict was also a battle for the hearts and minds of the hundred million people in the Middle East with access to satellite television. The market leader was, and still is, Al-Jazeera. As the conflict began, it had an audience of thirty-five million people, and after the first week of the war, it

claimed to have signed up another four million sub-
scribers in Europe.

Al-Jazeera has been a positive influence on the Arab
world in so many ways. It widened the space for dialogue
in the Middle East by becoming the first Arab station to
interview Israeli politicians. It has considerable autonomy
from its sponsor, the Emir of Qatar, and so presents a
historic challenge to servile state broadcasters in the
Middle East. During the war in Iraq, it helped to correct
the mistakes of Western networks by reporting from places
CNN and the BBC could never get to. Al-Jazeera was the
first to expose premature claims of success in places like
Umm Qasr and Basra, first to reflect Shi'ite frustration
with the US invasion, first to report the mistaken killing by
US forces of moderate Islamists in Northern Iraq.

However, from the very moment George Bush
declared his war on terror, Al-Jazeera took a side, just as
Fox News was taking the opposite side. From the moment
the war in Iraq was a *fait accompli*, so was Al-Jazeera's
primary sympathy. One of its editors wrote in *The
Guardian* that 'Al-Jazeera has been alone in proceeding
from the premise that this war should be viewed as an
illegal enterprise.' Comments from US officials were
'claims'; it was always the 'so-called' war on terror; the
Americans were the 'invaders' or 'occupiers' while the
Iraqi military was 'the resistance'; estimates of casualty
figures were often based on mysterious 'medical sources'
or no source at all. In Baghdad, Al-Jazeera's correspondent
talked of the city as the pulsing heart of the Muslim
caliphate, as viewers watched pictures of American
bombings. 'Here in Baghdad,' said the reporter, 'a city
accused of hiding weapons of mass destruction is being
hit by weapons of mass destruction.' To reinforce the sense
of Arab resistance, Al-Jazeera broadcast lingering close-

ups of two dead British soldiers and was first with pictures of American POWs.

Just as Fox News was 'feeding the core', Al-Jazeera was playing to viewers' prejudice with images of plucky Arabs fighting the powerful infidel invader. By using historical and even religious imagery, the broadcasters were guaranteed the intended reaction from viewers. 'They know they're on the so-called right side,' said Abdullah Schleifer, of the Adham Centre for Television Journalism in Cairo, 'and if this means tilting slightly to that side, they'll do it.' In that sense, Al-Jazeera had a lot in common with its American counterparts: 'If you're getting your news and views from either Arab or American television,' said the editor of the Lebanese *Daily Star*, Rami Khouri, 'you're only getting half the story.'

Al-Jazeera probably reflected international opinion of the war far more than Fox News. It also supplied enough raw information and alternative opinion to allow viewers to make up their own minds on issues related to the war. However, this is still what is known in some circles as 'contextual objectivity': an attempt to reflect all sides of a story while never straying too far from the dominant sentiment of your target audience. No matter what label you put on it, you are presenting the world as your audience wants it to be and not how it is. That may translate into good ratings, but it is bad news, in every conceivable sense of the word.

The global revolution in technology was supposed to make the world a more connected and tolerant place, showing us how very similar we all were. But you could argue that the rise of satellite television and twenty-four-hour news has done the opposite, dividing us into markets in which truth is manipulated to suit brand loyalties and consumer sentiment. In Europe, we have the rolling reinforcement of our useful parody of the United States. In the United States, the militant tendency has helped President Bush to exploit legitimate fears about terrorism. In the Middle East, a dysfunctional media transforms legitimate fears into raw material for the fanatics and despots.

The Arab parody of Americans is similar to our own in that it has a factual element. When Arab satellite stations have shown US-made helicopters being used by the Israelis to kill Palestinians, or US soldiers firing on Iraqi civilians, they have supplied an important piece of the overall picture. But genuine grievance tends to get mixed with self-indulgence and exaggeration as it passes through the filters of the Arab media.

The problem goes far beyond the satellite news stations. In newspapers across the Middle East, coverage of the war in Iraq was a variation on the same theme: Arabs resisted and were murdered for it. 'The resistance of Iraqi cities demolishes the image of an invincible Rambo,' declared Moroccan daily newspaper *Al Ittihad al Ishtiraki* at an early stage of the war. Meanwhile, some Egyptian newspapers depicted President Bush in a Nazi uniform or referred to the war in Iraq as the 'American holocaust'.

There were voices of moderation, such as *Al-Ahram* in Cairo, which tried hard to retain some neutrality during the war, as did a few of the London-based Arabic newspapers. But by the time the statue had fallen in Baghdad, prominent Arab intellectuals were voicing deep concern about the media-sponsored rage, sensing that it would help radical Islamists and hinder the forces of democratic reform in the region. One of Egypt's most respected political scientists, Dr Abdel Moneim Said, said the brutal imagery would not breed people who 'are looking to develop our societies, but those who think how to sacrifice themselves'.

As with our useful parody, Arab rage at the United States has cultural factors built in. Part of America's image problem in the Middle East stems from the increasing penetration of US television imports, lifestyle brands and Hollywood blockbuster movies into the Middle East. When viewed from the Arab street, America looks simultaneously seductive and grotesque. The United States is Coke, car chases and cluster bombs to a generation reared on a diet of anti-American commentary and imported pop culture. It is often presented as an evil force that seduces Arab youth with the promise of material wealth and sensual pleasure. The fact that this promise will never be honoured strengthens the case against the United States.

The idea of America as a purveyor of immorality has influenced Arab political thought for more than half a century. One of the chief ideologues of radical Islam, Sayyid Qutb, spent two years studying in the United States in the late 1940s and returned to his native Egypt to preach against the degeneracy he had witnessed. Among his influential writings was a description of a dance in an American church hall: 'The dance is inflamed by the notes of the gramophone, the dance-hall becomes a whirl of heels and thighs, arms enfold hips, lips and breasts meet, and the air is full of lust.' Since Qutb's era, the CD player may have replaced the gramophone, but the mixture of fascination and repulsion remains the same.

If you buy into the concept of a sustained American assault on Islamic values and combine it with the prevailing Arab view of US foreign policy, it is not hard to see American actions as elements of a sinister imperial plot. The perception is strengthened by the vast array of rumour and conspiracy theories that are peddled by sections of the Arab media. A month after the attacks of September 11, I was in Egypt and heard a story that was doing the rounds across the Middle East: Jewish workers in the World Trade Centre had been asked to stay away from the office on September 11, and this was proof that the attacks were the result of a Zionist plot. Four months later, a CNN opinion poll carried out in nine Muslim countries found that three out of five people did not believe Arabs were responsible for September 11. In Cairo, a senior government official tried to persuade me there was no way Arab hijackers could have piloted those planes into the Twin Towers. The clear implication was that a Western intelligence service had some hand in the attacks.

It speaks volumes about the Arab parody of America that senior political figures bought into these conspiracy theories. In countries such as Egypt and Saudi Arabia, it suits authoritarian leaders to promote stories that reflect badly on the United States, Israel and the West. Anything that convinces their citizens that the Americans and the Zionists are responsible for their problems is helpful. That is why the plight of Palestine and the occupation of Iraq became the officially sanctioned causes. They are a safety valve that releases anger and resentment that might otherwise be channelled into domestic political dissent.

Of the twenty-two members of the Arab League, not one is a fully functioning electoral democracy. They suffer from a 'freedom deficit' that undermines human development, according to the United Nations Development Programme (UNDP). In a report written by a panel of Arab academics in 2002, the UNDP found one in five Arabs still lives on the equivalent of €2 a day. The report said the Israeli occupation of Arab lands is part of the problem, and logic suggests that US support for Arab autocrats doesn't help, but the freedom deficit is in large measure a self-inflicted wound. Consider this statistic from the 2003 Arab Human Development Report: five times more books are translated into Greek every year than into Arabic even though there are eleven million Greeks and more than a quarter of a billion Arabs. The UNDP believes solutions lie in women's rights and freedom of expression, or in other words, the liberation of Arab intellectual potential. That goal is the lifework of unsung heroes inside the Arab world, journalists and writers who struggle against the dead hand of political censorship and anti-intellectualism. Yet they must contend with an institutional framework which transmits the self-indulgent prejudices that sustain the autocrats and feed the radicals.

This is not simply an Arab 'thing', just as paranoid jingoism is not an American 'thing'; the media outlets that trade in bias have an impact well beyond the United States or the Middle East. It is a cruel irony that among the few winners in the second Gulf War were television networks that reinforced the prejudices that lead to war, whether that prejudice was the blind rage of radical Islam or the vengeful patriotism of the American fringe. Of course, there is a powerful countervailing force in the global media. Among the voices that acquitted themselves well during the war in Iraq were established broadcasters with a proven record in foreign coverage; non-partisan newspapers that encouraged old-style reporting; and the multitude of new media commentators and bloggers who kept the rest of us honest and pandered to no one.

Speaking a few weeks after the fall of the statue in Baghdad, then BBC Director-General Greg Dyke said the war in Iraq proved that people in the United States and Europe did want more than 'the Fox formula of gung-ho patriotism'. There was a market, he said, for broadcasters willing to 'temper the competition of live news with the considered journalism and analysis people need to make sense of events'. If you set aside the implied transatlantic snobbery, there was something profoundly honourable about what Dyke had to say. It was the belief that balance and context can survive immersion in the caustic truths of contemporary newsgathering (incidentally, a belief not restricted to the BBC). This optimistic assessment assumes there is a market for the uncomfortable truths that people need to make considered judgements about the world around them. But the problem is that what people want and what they need are often two very different things: increasingly so in Zulu Time.

PART THREE

AFTER

13

THE HOME FRONT

'I would be remiss if I did not point out that
America does not have a monopoly on all the
stupid white men. There are plenty of these
creatures who lurk throughout the Common-
wealth and on the old sod of Cork and Tipperary
that my great-grandparents called home.'

Michael Moore, *Stupid White Men*, 2001

It took three days and fifteen officials to get us out of Iran.
Our original visa expired, so we needed an extension of
our permission to stay in the country before we could
leave it. There was no logic to the process, but there was
also no point in arguing. At the Office for Alien Affairs in
Tehran, the most innocuous questions were met with
withering stares of indifference. We were told we would
have to plead our case with a magistrate before we could
get the necessary stamps on our passports. The prospect
of pleading with an Iranian judge for permission to go
home would have filled me with sickening dread just a few
weeks before, but the mind has a habit of adjusting to

suffocating bureaucracy, just as your eyes adjust to the dark.

At the court-house, there were no free seats in the waiting room, although there was a person-sized space on a bench at the back, right beside four young men joined together by manacles. After about an hour, we were sent to a courtroom presided over by a sombre young judge. He was taking copious notes as two men took turns to tell their stories. One of the men was accused of manslaughter by reckless driving; the other witness was a relative of the victim. The case involved the loss of a life, but you would never have guessed it from the subdued tones in that courtroom. I wanted to find out the penalty facing the accused, but our translator had taken advantage of a lull in the proceedings to approach the clerk of the court.

There was no interrogation, just a couple of curt questions from the judge to the translator. The judge signed a piece of paper and then returned to his manslaughter case. We still had to get through another five officials before the exit-visa stamp would appear in our passports, but the sound of the judge's pen skimming across that document was like the noise of a big jet plane heading towards home.

That night, as the lights of Tehran disappeared beneath the wing of the aircraft, my safe Western European life resumed, as if the previous two months had never happened. During the next twelve hours of travelling, there were intermittent reminders of global crisis. In Frankfurt airport, the shaven heads of American servicemen bobbed along the crowded concourse, either coming home or going to war. Beyond the window of the departure lounge, a German police tank was parked below the nose of an aircraft with the emblem of an American airline. The morning newspaper reported that Disneyland Paris was now under heightened police surveillance. While I had been away, Mickey Mouse had become a legitimate target.

On every front page, in every language, there was news about the fall of Baghdad and the peculiar mix of hope, suspicion and anger that came in its wake. The black-and-white certainties of war were being replaced by formless grey speculation about a fragile future, and the media focus was slipping back towards the usual parade of celebrities and sex criminals, despite the cloud of toxic fall-out polluting the affairs of the world. Trapped within the glass and steel brightness of Frankfurt airport, it was harder than ever to believe there had been a war at all.

In the office at my home, there was a large cardboard box waiting for me. It was overflowing with the British and Irish newspapers my wife had collected when I was away. It took me a few days to work up the energy, but eventually I pulled up a chair and began to rifle through the papers, searching for some sense of how this war had played out on the home front. The first important piece of news was that the Irish people shared my doubts that the war had actually taken place, or at least in the way the media had reported it. In an *Irish Times* on-line poll, taken a few days before the fall of Baghdad, 86 per cent of those who expressed an opinion said they did not trust the media's coverage of the war.

The second thing that stood out was the extent to which the Irish analysis of the war was shaped by the mutually exclusive fringes of the global media. To join the ongoing debate, it seemed you had to choose between two opposing visions of the war: the war according to Al-Jazeera or the war according to Fox News. In the starkest presentation of that choice, Eddie

Holt wrote a mid-war column in *The Irish Times* in which he contrasted the US networks with their 'American flags, patriotic sentiment and emotional support on the parts of the toothy "anchors" and breathless reporters' and the prevailing Arab perspective: 'Arabs watching Al-Jazeera ... see horrific images of burned corpses, the injured in hospital and general devastation. Same war, different story.'

Most Irish commentators seemed to have decided that the Al-Jazeera vision of this war was the objective truth, or at least the closest thing you could get to objective truth in the corporate-media age. The commonly expressed perception was that the American networks, and their fellow travellers in Britain, had served up a sanitised and imaginary version of conflict designed to justify the flawed assumptions behind Bush's war. If there was something distinctly Irish in this view, it was faith in the underdog. Even before the war, our prevailing world-view had factored in George Bush as the bully and the Arab world – specifically Iraq – as the struggling victim. As the war progressed, there was the added assumption that Arab views were more credible than American responses. Pro-war sentiment in the US was properly scrutinised for self-interest and short-sightedness, but the same filter was rarely applied to the anger of the Arab street. There was little or no attempt to separate the legitimate core of Arab rage from the traces of exaggeration and self-indulgence that were also present.

In the acres of Irish newsprint devoted to the war, all but a handful of commentators presented mutually exclusive choices to readers. You were either with Gerhard Schroeder or George Bush; you had to be with Berlin on this one or stand with Boston; there was no third option. In a country that jealously guards the concept of neutrality, there was a shortage of sceptical detachment from the conventional wisdoms peddled by the hawks in Washington or their opponents.

As I delved deeper into that box of newspapers, it became clear that a few enlightened souls had tried to create a space for an indigenous dialogue purged of imported influences. They had sought out contrasting opinions that were definably Irish, particularly when it came to this country's responsibilities in time of war. The eternal search for a good old row played a part in the search for home-grown viewpoints, but there was also an honest attempt to achieve balance and fairness, even if it was not always successful. The strengths and short-comings of this approach came through during the debate about the government's position on the conflict and the incendiary topic of Shannon airport.

For its part, the government argued that the withdrawal of landing rights and refuelling facilities from US military aircraft would 'create a precedent which would run counter to our long-term interests'. The day after the war began, Bertie Ahern told the Dáil that to deny American planes the use of Shannon could be seen by the US 'as the adoption of a hostile position', while also noting that the Americans were 'our biggest trading partners' and 'our biggest foreign investors'. There was no evidence American companies would have pulled out of Ireland if the US military was banned from Shannon, but in the pre-war debate, facts were never as important as appeals to gut instinct.

Even when members of the government tried to bring the debate beyond self-interest, they turned to information that was already shrouded in doubt. At the end of January 2003, the minister for foreign affairs, Brian Cowen, spoke in blunt terms about the threat posed by Saddam and his alleged arsenal of weapons of mass destruction. 'The possession of these dreadful weapons is the immediate threat which must be dealt with,' he told the Dáil. 'There is nothing abstract about this.' A few days later, the Taoiseach told deputies that he was 'far more worried about Iraq's weapons of mass destruction than about anyone else's at the moment'. Another week passed, and the minister for defence, Michael Smith, told the Dáil that the world 'will no longer tolerate a dictator threatening the world with these terrible weapons'. It was certainly the stuff of nightmares, but was the bogeyman real? Was there evidence to justify the manufactured fear?

On the other side of the debate, the anti-war movement was trying to convince the Irish public that a US-led war would create deadly anarchy in Iraq. Some of its predictions turned out to be correct; others that have since been discredited were based on international reports from respected sources, including one from UNICEF that warned that eighteen million Iraqis could go hungry. That said, there was a trace of scare-mongering in what some peace campaigners told the Irish people before the war. When it came to possible civilian casualties, estimates ranged from unreliable to grotesquely inflated, serving the needs of the anti-war movement far more than reasoned debate.

One international group of anti-war doctors claimed that as many as 86,000 Iraqi civilians would be killed when the British and Americans invaded. That meant 'Iraqi deaths may amount to more than 50 times' the number killed on September 11, said one Irish commentator, in a succinct demonstration of the competitive morality of 'body-count journalism'. During the various Dáil exchanges about the approaching war, one Fine Gael TD told his fellow deputies that a man on the radio had said up to 30,000 people would be killed in Iraq, 'similar to wiping out the population of Drogheda.' In another debate, a Labour deputy claimed 'there may be 100,000 direct casualties and 400,000 secondary ones'. Not to be outdone, a Sinn Féin TD predicted 'the deaths of Iraqi children, women and hundreds of thousands of other uninvolved civilians'. On the day before the war began, a left-wing activist was quoted in *The Irish Times* as saying millions of people would be killed 'on behalf of oil interests'.

In the end, the numbers of civilians killed during the American-led invasion ranged from 3,240, according to the Associated Press, to 9,152, according to a group of academics with the unfortunate name Iraqi Body Count. (In February 2004, this group claimed the ongoing guerilla war in Iraq had pushed the death toll above 10,000.) Of course, the conflict did not become any more moral because hundreds of thousands did not die. And perhaps, in ethical terms, it is wrong to compare exaggeration in pursuit of peace with government-sponsored spin. But think about the impact of all that short-term outrage on our society's long-term perspective. Whether the threat was civilian genocide or WMD, the public were confronted with scary stories that became increasingly shrill with each successive telling. By playing up their rival nightmares, the competeing camps progressively lost their power to shock. By scaring us once, they made it harder to scare us again. Looking back, we may have believed one more than the other, but we were left with the lasting impression that no one tells the whole truth in times of war.

The vast array of competing claims about WMD and imminent civilian massacre challenged the Irish media almost as much as events on the battlefield. The problem with providing a forum for all opinions about this war was that only a fraction could ever be tested for objective truth. The audience was left to judge conflicting opinions on the basis of its instincts, on the basis of what sounded true. We often assume that our exposure to outside influences has granted us an uncommon worldliness, but like everyone else on the planet, our instincts are also shaped by our inclinations. We may feel right, but that is because we choose to ignore the facts that feel wrong.

Different people made different judgements about Shannon and Saddam, but there was one beacon of absolute truth in the fog of commentary and debate, and that was the badness of Bush's America. As we saw in earlier chapters, instinctive hostility to the American president had been building for more than two years, to the point where it was effectively a universal truth of Irish life. After September 11, a *Sunday Independent* poll found that 56 per cent of the Irish people believed that George Bush was doing a good job in the fight against terrorism. In spring 2003, as US forces closed in on Baghdad, a poll in the same newspaper found 75 per cent disapproved of his handling of the war in Iraq.

Bush had become the bogeyman. In the grey gloom of an unstable world, he was a character drawn in black and white. He had shown himself to be an international outlaw, opposing the Kyoto Protocol, the International Criminal Court and fair trade for the developing world. Not only had he caused war in Afghanistan and Iraq, he had helped to create the conditions for war. According to an increasingly influential school of thought, Bush was not only making global problems worse; *he* was the problem.

Still, the judgements about Bush were nothing without

a convincing indictment of American society, and that
leads us right back to our useful parody. In an earlier
chapter, I skimmed over the 'useful' part of the equation,
but it is worth focusing on the benefits that flow from our
malign impression of Bush's America. To begin with, if we
can prove to ourselves that the United States – and not
just its president – is responsible for the most pressing
global problems, they become less complicated and less
intimidating. So, for example, global warming is easier to
understand when we discover that America causes 24 per
cent of the world's greenhouse gases but has only 5 per
cent of the world's population. Ultimately, the more blame
we can heap on the Americans, the lighter the burden on
the rest of us. They caused the problem, so it is up to them
to solve it. This is the really useful thing about the useful
parody.

Think about the single most persistent accusation that
was levelled at the United States during the war in Iraq:
the conflict was all about oil. There was circumstantial
evidence to back up this assumption, including the very
close links between the Bush administration and the US
oil companies that stood to benefit from the occupation of
Iraq. There was also the argument that the Bush
administration was forced to invade the country with the
second largest oil reserves because American society is
guzzling fuel at an unsustainable rate.

In Ireland and other European countries, these elements
of wartime debate pushed the audience towards a broader
conclusion. Bush, oil, Iraq and the reckless consumption of
energy fused with our fears about global warming to form
a gigantic indictment against the United States: the US is
now so dependent on oil that it has become the biggest
threat to world peace and the global environment.

It was not just civilised Europeans who were

approaching this conclusion. The Irish media reported that some Americans were agitated by their nation's polluting ways. In *The Irish Times*, Kathy Sheridan wrote a column about the most visible symbol of reckless energy use, the sports utility vehicle (SUV). She had just returned from a visit to southern California where she was shocked by their surging popularity on the highways.

The backlash had begun in the US, the article noted, with a grass roots anti-SUV campaign that was drawing support from many disparate groups. There was even a concerned group of Christians who ran an ad asking: 'What would Jesus drive?' Despite such enlightened appeals, the resistance movement had a mountain to climb. Kathy Sheridan noted that SUVs account for a quarter of all new car sales in the United States, and she bemoaned the fact that most Americans just did not seem to get the connection between this modern addiction and the problems of the world: 'This is Bush's America, after all, the one that walked away from Kyoto.'

This was a persuasive article written by a respected journalist, but there was something profoundly irritating about it. The biggest problem was the headline: 'US must end its affair with gas-guzzlers.' The sentiment was fine, but the words dripped dodgy self-righteousness, and they avoided the most important reality of all: Ireland is increasingly America, especially when it comes to our reckless use of energy, our polluting ways and our mutual love affair with the gas-guzzlers.

Back in 1992, there were 900,000 private cars in Ireland. Ten years later, there were around 1.4 million, with all the implications that has for pollution and energy use. Perhaps the most distressing trend is the rapidly increasing number of SUVs pumping greenhouse gases into the skies above us. To be fair to Kathy Sheridan, she did mention the appearance of these 'gas-guzzling, road-hogging' vehicles in Ireland, but her column did not reveal the true extent of our burgeoning romance with them. In the first five months of 2003, more than 3,600 SUVs were sold in Ireland (almost a thousand more than were sold during the entire twelve months of 2001), and a European marketing survey predicted that the sales of SUVs would double again on this side of the Atlantic by 2007.

Even if we factor in the increasing popularity of SUVs, there is no way Ireland is anywhere as bad as America when it comes to wasting scarce resources. Is there? Actually, in one vital respect we are worse. Ireland is the seventh most oil-dependent economy in the world. According to Amárach consulting, oil provides 60 per cent of our total energy requirements while it makes up 40 per cent of America's energy consumption. Not only are we more dependent on oil than the Americans, we are heading in the wrong direction at an increasingly rapid pace. Our oil consumption doubled in the last decade of the twentieth century while consumption by the EU and the world remained unchanged. Obviously, we will not be invading Iraq any time soon because of our dependence on oil, but these figures show that the average Irish person is contributing to the depletion of the earth's scarce resources at a faster rate than the average American. So much for our smug lectures to those American gas-guzzlers.

Yes, you might say, but what about the Kyoto Protocol? At least our country has backed this multilateral approach to global warming, unlike the United States. This much is true. However, despite our lip service to Kyoto, we are among the worst violators of the protocol in the European Union. In fact, every Irish person is doing almost as much damage to the world's climate as every American.

Ireland's per capita emissions of carbon dioxide are the highest in Europe and the fifth highest in the world. We are producing more than eighteen tonnes of carbon dioxide per person every year, which is almost twice the EU average and not far off the US rate of twenty-five tonnes. What's more, we are heading in the wrong direction at a much faster pace than any of our European neighbours. So while we spend a lot of time complaining about George Bush's rejection of Kyoto, our actions have made a mockery of the protocol and revealed a breathtaking contradiction between our aspirations on the world stage and our actual behaviour. It's too easy to blame it all on government, industry and agriculture (the methane coming out of cows' backsides is a big contributor to global warming, apparently). Ultimately, there is no solution without a change in our personal behaviour.

Kathy Sheridan observed in her column on SUVs that the view among 'thinking Americans is that it's well past time to start making the connection between consumption and social impact'. Maybe some day those 'thinking Americans' will pass on some tips to the 'thinking Irish', as our collective contribution to global warming depends on our everyday choices as consumers. Even if you don't own an SUV, you are almost certainly still part of the pollution problem. For example, when you step on to an airplane you make a contribution to climate change. If you want to know more about how much environmental damage we do on each of these flights, take a look at the web site set up by the British group Climate Care. Using their on-line calculator, you find that the average passenger on a return flight from Dublin to Tenerife is responsible for the same amount of carbon dioxide emissions as a motorist who drives from Dublin to Wexford and back ten times.

We have a right to feel aggrieved by American excess,

but we would also benefit from a long, hard look in the mirror. Our obsession with those 'gas-guzzling' Yanks has obscured the jagged edges in Irish life. Our complaints are in danger of becoming an alternative to action and weakening the cause we claim to believe in. As I see it, there is a more productive approach. Every time we get angry at the United States, we could make it our business to investigate Ireland's position on the same issue, and not just the government's stated position, but the reality as it relates to each individual citizen. The Americans may lead all those negative league tables, but all too often, the Irish are not that far behind. On so many of the big questions that face our world, their problem is our problem. In so many little ways, we are becoming just like them. And to prove the point, let's pay a visit to our favourite American town, Springfield.

14

HOMER SIMPSON IS IRISH

'Drunkenness, fighting and damage to property –
are these qualities we associate with the Irish?'
Newsreader Kent Brockman on St Patrick's Day
riots in Springfield, *The Simpsons*

It took me a couple of weeks to settle back in after my
return from Northern Iraq, and trawling through that box
of newspapers was a useful exercise in decompression.
But eventually, I could not read another word about the
war in Iraq. I decided to detoxify my system for a few days
and replace the guff and blather with some mindless
entertainment. Instead of long conversations about the
anatomy of war, it was dinner in front of the telly. In that
brief window of insignificance, the closest I came to an
intellectual challenge was a daily dose of *The Simpsons*.

In my childhood, Maureen Potter and her Christmas
pantomimes pioneered a brand of comedy that could be
appreciated by children and adults at the same time. The
occasional *double entendre* and the political jokes went
right over the kids' heads, but everyone laughed together

since the panto was greater than the sum of the individual parts. A couple of decades later, *The Simpsons* captured the Potter formula, and my teenage daughter and I had a television programme that was equally ours.

I am not sure exactly what she gets out of it, but to me, *The Simpsons* is one of those increasingly rare television shows that, in the words of its creator, Matt Groening, 'rewards you for paying attention'. In fact, so profound is the programme's intellectual reach that twenty great American thinkers teamed up to write a collection of essays entitled *The Simpsons and Philosophy: The D'oh! of Homer* (sample line: 'this essay will illustrate Aristotelian virtue ethics through a discussion of Marge's life in Springfield').

In my own rather limited attempt to extract meaning from *The Simpsons*, I have collected some of the most illuminating references to Ireland by characters in the show. One of my favourites involves Christian do-gooder Ned Flanders, who accidentally marries a hard-drinking, loose-living woman he meets in Las Vegas. On their first morning together, the Vegas wife tells Ned to 'Irish up her coffee' and he tells here there will be no use of the 'I' word in his house. Perhaps the most revealing example of Simpsonian Irishness is an episode featuring the Springfield St Patrick's Day parade. A float carrying 'The Drunken Irish Novelists of Springfield' stops, and a novelist bearing an uncanny resemblance to James Joyce jumps off to start a brawl.

There is a bitter lesson here, even if it is delivered with satirical sweetness. *The Simpsons* reminds us that Ireland circles the outer fringes of the American consciousness in an endless loop of jollity, drunkenness and dark genius. The more things change in our Ireland, the more they stay the same in their Emerald Isle. The unbreakable cycle that brought us *The Quiet Man* and *Darby O'Gill and the Little People* ('A touch O'Blarney ... a heap O'Magic and A LOAD O'LAUGHTER!') is brought bang up to date when Homer Simpson sneaks into a U2 concert wearing a green vest, speaking with an Irish accent and carrying a bag of potatoes.

The enduring American image of Ireland is broadly affectionate, and even if it comes across as insulting, it is certainly not meant that way. In my experience, the enduring Paddywhackery is part of that great American tradition of fun without significance. The real problem is that the Irish clichés are not restricted to the vast lumpen masses but spring forth from the minds of the most intelligent Americans (even the Harvard-educated writers of *The Simpsons*). In reviews of modern Irish literature in the *New York Times* or the *Washington Post*, every living Irish writer seems to be struggling with depression, drink or a 'bog-gothic' childhood. Take this inanity from the April 2000 edition of the *Atlantic Monthly*: 'It has been said that growing up in Ireland one learns sin from the priests, Latin from the nuns and passion from Edna O'Brien.'

Just as Americans help to feed the useful parody, we bear a share of the blame for the lasting clichés about Ireland. Like every Irish person who ever travelled to the United States, I have played along with the jokes about booze and brawling, just to prove that I had sense of humour (God knows, you are not really Irish unless you have one of those). We also have a habit of producing the dark geniuses that America so desperately needs to fortify its clichés. Colin Farrell is a case in point. It is hard to see how the mundane reality of Irish life can compete with the media focus on his prodigious appetites and talents, or his occasional typecasting. Take his role in the movie

Daredevil, a timeless piece of Irish caricature if ever there was one. We are introduced to Farrell's character, a brooding assassin with a Dublin accent, drinking and playing darts in a dive bar. A fellow drinker challenges him and ends up dead on the floor, impaled on a flying paper-clip. All this takes place as Irish American rappers, House of Pain, pump out their 1990s classic, 'Top o'the Morning to Ya': 'Ya see, I'm Irish, but I'm not a leprechaun/You wanna fight, then step up and we'll get it on.'

Is that it? Is that all we are to Americans? Maybe not. But let's not fool ourselves. Smart, sophisticated Ireland has not penetrated the broad American consciousness, except in the most superficial way. And before you cite the gains made during the glory years of the Clinton administration, you should understand Ireland's renewed irrelevance in Washington. An official in the Clinton White House once told me that he was advised to learn about Ireland and Cuba if he wanted to understand the complexities of American foreign policy. Under the Bush administration, it seems you do not need even the most basic knowledge of Ireland. Take the following exchange at a press briefing shortly before a war summit between Tony Blair and George Bush in April 2003.

'Where in Northern Ireland will the two leaders meet?' asked a reporter.

'Dublin,' replied White House press secretary Ari Fleischer.

'No, no ...' replied the reporter.

'I'm sorry. I'm sorry,' Fleischer said. 'I said "Dublin." I had written down Belfast and I said "Dublin".'

'A historic development, Ari,' joked one reporter.

For all our common history, Ireland and America have reached a point of profound misunderstanding where we seem to have nothing left to fall back on but our clichés about each other. There is no warm and fuzzy Bill Clinton to reach beyond the caricatures, no profound American engagement in Northern Ireland, and even our dependable supply of American tourists is drying up. Instead, Bush's America has become increasingly distant to us, and modern Ireland is ever more irrelevant to them. Yet, in reality, we are more alike than at any time in our history.

One night, while watching an episode of *The Simpsons* called 'Secrets of a Successful Marriage', it occurred to me that Homer's marriage was a lot like our relationship with America. In this episode, Homer is banished to the tree house in the back garden, and his wife Marge tells him he cannot return to the marital bed until he has convinced her that he brings some unique value to their marriage. After much anguish, Homer realises that what he alone can give his wife is 'complete and utter dependency'. Is there an echo of Ireland's submission to the US in Homer's words?

That seems to be the view of the former UN arms inspector Scott Ritter, a staunch opponent of the American decision to invade Iraq. During a visit to Galway a few months after the fall of Baghdad, he said Ireland had become a US colony. 'The US is out to seek global domination,' he said, 'and if it is not invading Ireland with its troops, it is definitely invading Ireland with its economy.'

On a superficial level, Ritter's conclusions dovetail neatly with four decades of US investment in Ireland. Before we got those EU billions, it was American companies that dragged our economy out of its agrarian funk. They helped to sustain the Celtic Tiger, and as Irish policy-makers prayed for an economic soft landing, they lit candles for the big American investors. If the Yanks had decided to take their $34 billion of investment and go somewhere else, 90,000 jobs would have been lost, and Ireland's economy would have been sent into a tailspin.

All this informed the government's attitude to the war on Saddam Hussein and provided *prima facie* evidence that Ireland is still a prisoner of US policy, perhaps even an American 'colony'. But, as ever, the easy assumption was also the wrong assumption. To begin with, there is no credible evidence that the withdrawal of facilities at Shannon airport would have affected US investment in Ireland. If the government had wanted to take an avowedly pro-war position, it could have done so with minimal short-term risks to our economy.

An even more compelling argument against the 'colony' theory is the shifting balance of Ireland's economic relationship with the United States. When our country was an underdeveloped backwater, investment flowed down a one-way street. Today, the money they pump into our economy is increasingly balanced by the money we pump into theirs. A study by Joseph Quinlan of Johns Hopkins University found that by 2001 Ireland had become the ninth largest source of foreign direct investment in the United States, with Irish firms sinking €16 billion into American ventures, four times the level it was in 1996. As Tánaiste Mary Harney pointed out in a speech at Harvard in April 2003, Irish investment in the US is responsible for almost as many jobs as US investment in Ireland.

America still has the upper hand in this relationship and will do so as long as it is our number one source of foreign investment. But the terms of our business dealings with the United States have changed dramatically, a process hastened by the emergence of new markets and business partners in Europe and Asia. In short, the colony has become one of the colonisers.

There is something else quite startling about the nature of US investment in Ireland. For years, the Americans made the most of our weakness: they gave us desperately needed jobs and in return received generous grants and big profits. But now, the Irish economy is profiting from American weakness. The weakness is not political or economic, but spiritual and physical. Put simply, we would not be where we are today were it not for the collective vanity of the American people.

Americans now spend more on beauty than they do on education, and in 2002, cosmetic surgery alone was worth $20 billion. So what has this got to do with Ireland? Well, the answer is that we lead the world in the manufacture of the gunk and gizmos those Americans use to reshape their bodies and cure their ills.

In 2003, foreign-owned pharmaceutical companies employed 20,000 Irish workers and accounted for almost a third of Irish exports, a large measure of which went to supply the endless American search for health and beauty. Take Botox: first developed by germ-warfare scientists, it is now the wonder drug of the cosmetic industry, banishing wrinkles across the world, but particularly in the US. The world's supply of Botox is made by Allergan at two factories in Westport, which between them employ more than 1,000 workers.

For years, Ireland has been producing collagen, which is implanted in skin to smooth out wrinkles and add a fuller pout to lips. It is made by Allergan and another company called Inamed. Inamed is also a world leader in breast implants, producing 40 per cent of the world's fake boobs at its plant in Arklow. Ireland also provides a manufacturing base for Pfizer, which makes the active ingredient for the anti-impotence drug Viagra in Ringaskiddy, and Zoloft, an anti-depression medicine that is popular in the US.

You would have to be a person of uncommon virtue not to treat yourself to a brief sardonic snigger at this point. For generations, we were appalled yet fascinated by the Americans' apparently unattainable wealth and easy living. Now all that easy living has caught up with them, and the deeper they sink into self-indulgence and insecurity, the more money we make. Of course, the good life eventually catches up with all of us. The richer we become, the more American we tend to become, in the broadest possible sense.

Just as the war in Iraq was coming to an end, a group of health professionals published a truly depressing report about the impact of Ireland's insatiable appetites. A working group established by the Department of Health found that the rate of obesity in Ireland almost doubled in the space of a single decade, from 11 per cent in 1990 to 18 per cent in 2000. Obesity, the group warned, 'is set to become the major health problem affecting our population this century', and the rising generation is already falling victim. One doctor from the National Children's Hospital in Dublin told *Prime Time* that he had treated a two-year-old who weighed four stone, a seven-year-old who weighed eleven stone and a fifteen-year-old who weighed more than eighteen stone.

Of course, we can console ourselves with the assumption that we are not as bad as the United States. That assumption is right, but only just. In a study conducted in 2001, the US Centre for Disease Control and Prevention found that 20.9 per cent of Americans were obese.

Remember: that official working group found that 18 per cent of Irish people were obese, just 3 per cent off the American figure.

Once more, we have a problem that is widely perceived as American but is, in fact, increasingly Irish. And once more, there is an element of self-delusion involved. Surveys show that Irish people have a more positive view of their personal health than all other Europeans, with four out of five people rating themselves as pretty healthy. That is a stunning conclusion, not just in light of our obesity levels, but because our premature mortality rate is the highest in Europe, and our rate of heart disease is double the European average.

As we obtained more disposable income, we consumed more, and the more we consumed, the more we began to resemble the fat, unhealthy Americans we love to parody. Logic would suggest that our addiction to stories of overweight Americans would diminish once we started to look like the people in the stories, but that does not seem to have happened. We have simply widened the search, literally. Not only do we want proof that there are more overweight Americans than ever before, we need them to be bigger than ever before. Once again, the parody allows us to feel superior, even though the distance between our society and the society it describes is closing all the time.

While self-delusion and the useful parody make it difficult to appreciate how profoundly American our society is becoming, occasionally the trend cannot be ignored. A case in point was the debate surrounding the ban on smoking in bars and restaurants, during which the public was reminded of how the government was aping California and New York. Opponents of the ban said it was a mistake to mimic this new puritanism, and there were even reservations within the cabinet. Environment minister Martin Cullen told the *Irish Independent* that he hated the importation of 'this American political correctness' into Ireland: 'I dislike it with a passion. I'm Irish and I'm European. I am very worried about this Americanisation.'

That fear of being overwhelmed by the unstoppable wave that is America is a common refrain in post-Tiger Ireland. But while the resentment is often well founded, it can also be very selective, missing out on the really destructive trends such as obesity and pollution. It also has a touch of knee-jerk paranoia to it. We often hear American influence being represented as a form of 'cultural imperialism', a process by which destructive habits are forced on the world by unseen and sinister forces. It applies to political correctness and all those other nasty American imports, such as the upward inflection at the end of every sentence or drinks made out of iced coffee.

This theory has renewed credibility in the era of globalisation. Using all the tools of the information age, US corporate pioneers have spread that uniquely American mixture of indulgence and novelty, finding a particularly receptive audience in a newly affluent English-speaking society such as ours. With the help of local apostles of the Gospel of Stuff, they have created needs we never knew we had, given us lifestyles instead of lives and turned us from citizens into consumers. The result is that unmistakable feeling of perpetual consumption that once seemed to define the United States alone.

As we begin to consume on an American scale, we become trapped in a repetitive cycle. The fancy advert on the telly persuades us to buy a new car, so we buy the new car. Along with thousands of other car buyers, we get stuck in a traffic jam. As we sit there polluting the atmosphere, we notice the new billboards along the side of the road. They are telling us to buy more stuff, maybe even a bigger and better car. And so the cycle continues. If all this sounds far-fetched, consider the fact that by autumn 2003 rush-hour traffic in Dublin was approaching levels the planners said we would not reach until 2016. Meanwhile, in the first six months of 2003, the money spent on outdoor advertising increased by 17 per cent on the same period in 2002. And if you are still sceptical about the link between the two, listen to an executive from one of Ireland's leading outdoor-advertising companies, quoted by *The Irish Times* in October 2003: 'The huge increases in cars on the road and numbers at work has resulted in traffic gridlock. This enables advertisers to reach their target audience in a meaningful way ...'

According to the conspiracy theory, the United States has created a world full of advertisers and consumers to make the world safe for its brand of capitalism. To paraphrase Scott Ritter, if they cannot dominate us with troops, they will enslave us with their economy and the values of rampant consumerism. If you accept this view, then you can console yourself with the knowledge that you are a victim of powerful forces, the same forces that fund George Bush and shape his vision of the world. Ultimately, Ireland is only getting fatter, buying more cars and wasting the world's scarce resources because the Americans made us do it. Perhaps it is the jaded consumer in me, but I just don't buy it.

We are like America not because the United States has cast some evil spell on us, but because we have chosen to deal with radical changes in our lives in ways that are commonly assumed to be American. Look at the manner in which we chose to run the nation's finances during the boom times. On that infamous spectrum between Boston and Berlin, Ireland drifted closer to the American economic model of low taxes and limited government. Our economic rebirth brought record levels of employment and disposable income, but the good times were better for some than for others, and Ireland's levels of relative poverty and income inequality were worse than almost every other country in the western world. In fact, according to a report from the UN Development Programme in 2003, the only other country that was worse was the United States.

You could say it was the government that chose to put us so close to Boston, but on key issues the popular will seemed very American. When the economy finally slowed down and the public finances were in a spot of bother, an *Irish Times*/MRBI poll asked people for solutions: 29 per cent said the government should borrow more, and 9 per cent said raise taxes (both good Berlin ways of sorting out the problem), but 48 per cent said cut spending, echoing Boston's preference for low taxes and smaller government.

In other important ways our boom-time choices followed the US model more than the continental European example, although some choices were forced on us, such as the mass exodus to those sprawling, low-cost suburbs. Anne Marie Hourihane came up with a telling description of the capital's increasingly elastic borders in her book *She Moves Through the Boom*: 'Flat, sprawling, confused and centreless, west Dublin is now New Jersey. Somewhere out there it's Frank Sinatra, it's Bruce Springsteen.'

I do not want to dwell on the dodgy options we chose during our Tiger years; others are better qualified (anyway, the great thing about choices is that you can always make different ones in the future). More important to me are the changing instincts and priorities of post-

Tiger Ireland, particularly the subconscious process that led us to a political culture that is increasingly American.

In the autumn of 2003, the foreign-news sections of the newspapers were full of car bombs and chaos in Baghdad, but there was a brief respite for a couple of days in October when Arnold Schwarzenegger was elected governor of California. He replaced Democratic incumbent Gray Davis after a bizarre recall process that had many Americans hiding behind their hands in embarrassment. On this side of the Atlantic, the idea that the citizens of California, the world's sixth largest economy, would elect 'The Terminator' was naturally hilarious and confirmed our already rock-bottom impression of American politics. The campaign, according to one Irish journalist, was 'as superficial as an ad for McDonalds', while the result was the 'decomposition of America's completely worm-eaten political system', according to a leading French newspaper.

The most commonly expressed conclusion was that Americans are so utterly obsessed by fame and celebrity they had abandoned democracy. A more thoughtful judgement was that Arnie's victory reflected the people's rejection of the American political establishment: the people of California were so frustrated by pandering politicians that they chose a screen hero with a history of groping and admiring references to Hitler. Of course, things like this only happen in America ... don't they?

In a fascinating article on fame in the *New Statesmen*, the author John Gray wrote: 'Where affluence is the normal condition of the majority of people, continued economic growth depends on manufacturing insatiable needs.' Gray says fame has been transformed into a luxury good that satisfies some of those needs. In the past, it was hoarded by an untouchable élite and held from the rest of us. These days, celebrity is like delivery pizza: it can be enjoyed in the comfort of almost any home. Reality television helps to narrow the gap between famous people and ordinary people, and according to John Gray, a programme like *Big Brother* instils 'the illusion that celebrity is a universal entitlement that everyone can enjoy if they are lucky enough to be selected by everyone else'. (Although, no one has explained what happens when everybody has had their fifteen minutes; do people then become famous for not being famous?)

Just before Arnold Schwarzenegger was elected, Ireland was treated to the Pat Kenny/Eamon Dunphy face-off on Friday-night television and the spin-off spectacle of *Celebrity Farm*. At the time, it seemed the only really passionate conversation I ever took part in concerned the outcome of these manufactured dramas. In retrospect, it seems to me there was an 'Americanism' at work here: as we leave behind the conflict and privations of the past, the world of celebrity seems so much closer than anything the political arena can offer. The process that led Ireland to this point seemed to take just a blink of an eye. One moment, we were all religious or secular, Nationalist or Unionist, right or left, and the next we are either Pat or Eamon.

There is nothing inherently bad about the democrat-isation of fame; in the best American tradition, it delivers fun without significance. However, the alarm bells ring when the populist ethos of celebrity culture imposes itself on other spheres of public life. As they compete for attention with wayward actors and busty models, commentators, politicians and advocates know that being controversial is so much more effective than being respected. One sure-fire way to register in the public consciousness is to associate with the 'anti-establishment' cause. In contrast to the old order of Dublin 4, the bishops, the gombeen men and the corrupt politicians, the anti-establishment is non-ideological, straight talking, punter-friendly and filled with outrage against 'the shower that runs this country' (of course, the synthesis of the populist dialectic is that the anti-establishment eventually becomes the new establishment, or in laymen's terms, 'that shower that runs this country').

The same populist dynamic has defined American politics for some time, arguably since Watergate. You have no chance of election to any significant office unless you define yourself as an outsider and your opponent as a political insider, one of that shower from Washington. This intense populism requires attack advertising and perpetual polling, but the central rule of the game is always, *always* give the people what they want.

But here is the paradox: if the politicians have become so attuned to the popular mood, then why have the American people turned away from politics in such consistently large numbers? The turnout in the 2000 US presidential election barely crept past 50 per cent, and in the mid-term congressional elections of 1998, just one in three voters turned up at the polls.

Fareed Zakaria provides the most compelling explanation of this phenomenon in his book *The Future of Freedom*. He points to surveys in the United States that show that the institutions which have pandered most to public opinion in recent years are the very institutions that have lost public trust, including the US Congress. In contrast, agencies that are insulated from the pressures of public opinion, such as the Supreme Court, the armed forces and the Federal Reserve (the US Central Bank), are most respected by the people. Zakaria concludes that 'the

American people have watched their leaders bow and scrape before them for the last three decades – and they are repulsed by it'.

This apparently American process is now an Irish process. As political culture is drawn into a populist cul-de-sac, important institutions are losing the respect of the people they are forced to pander to. During the second Nice referendum campaign in October 2002, an *Irish Times*/MRBI poll found that public trust in television had dropped by 32 per cent in the space of a year, trust in the press was down 20 per cent and there was a marked loss of faith in political institutions, with a 14 per cent drop in the case of the government and 16-point drop in trust of Dáil Eireann. The poll found that the most trusted institution in the state was the civil service. The trend was confirmed by a *Prime Time*/MRBI survey in September 2003, which asked the public to rate the importance of certain professions to the community. Journalists and politicians were at the bottom of the list (about one in five said they were very important) while doctors and Guards, the least likely to pander to the popular will, were at the top.

Winston Churchill was once told he should 'keep his ear to the ground'. He responded by saying that the 'British nation will find it very hard to look up to leaders who are detected in this position'. So it is with the Irish nation. Populist values now dominate our public discourse, forcing politicians to cater to our worst instincts and making us resent them all the more. The next logical step is to take the politics out of politics and elect leaders on the basis of their fame and independence; after all, that is how California got Arnie. The other possible alternative is the emergence of the 'anti-populist' populist: a candidate who wins our respect by relentlessly prescribing medicine that tastes awful and does us the world of good.

Imagine if the first words out of a politician's mouth were always: 'You are not going to like this.' Now just think what might happen if we actually voted for this person.

As we deal with being rich, Ireland does not necessarily have to make the same mistakes as the United States. We have already shown we can handle change in uniquely Irish ways, and we can draw on inspiration from our European neighbours with whom we are progressively more integrated, at least in terms of public policy. In fact, there are aspects of Irish life that are currently very American but becoming very European, for better or for worse. For example, Ireland and the United States have among the highest levels of religious practice in the western world, but the figures for weekly attendance at mass in Ireland have fallen dramatically in recent years while American rates of churchgoing remain the same.

That said, the exceptional pace of Ireland's development has generally made us more prone to American-style responses than other European nations, to an extent that does not yet seem to be fully appreciated. There are a few ways of getting our heads around the similarities between Yanks and us. The first is to appreciate how our trans-atlantic bond with the United States has become more like our relationship with Britain. They will always have more economic clout than we do, but the one-way dependence is long gone and so is the old inferiority complex towards the Brits.

Another way of coping with American trends is to stop thinking of them as uniquely American. The obesity epidemic in the United States was not caused by some genetic mutation in Americans. It was a nasty consequence of rising disposable income, an overabundance of food and a sedentary lifestyle, and there is nothing exclusively American about this any more. You can blame American corporations for conspiring to make us eat more, but you can't blame Ronald McDonald if you buy his burgers. Too many social vices are defined as American when they are simply flawed responses to a level of individual affluence that Americans happened to experience first.

So far, I have focused almost exclusively on the dark side of Americanisation. But to better understand the similarities between us, we should also look at some of the virtues that Ireland and the United States have in common. One of the most striking things about the Irish right now is our decidedly non-European level of optimism and self-belief. In the middle of the boom-years, one opinion poll showed that a majority in Ireland believed the world would be a better place if every country were like theirs, which was clearly the kind of messianic declaration you would expect of the Yanks. In the World Values Survey of 2001, almost exactly the same high percentage of Irish and Americans said they were very proud of their nationality (74 per cent in Ireland and 72 per cent in the US). To put that in context, only 20 per cent of the Dutch gave the same response.

The sense of optimistic patriotism that we often mock in Americans seems to have infused our traditional nationalism, and that self-belief and pride have filtered downwards. Rates of depression and anxiety fell during the boom-times, and while we may whinge about the loose ends of post-Tiger Ireland, we know things are better. In the most recent health and lifestyle surveys, almost nine out of ten people said their quality of life was either good or very good. Unlike those delusions of good health, there is empirical evidence to back up our contentedness, including the 2003 Human Development Index, which rated Ireland's quality of life 12 out of 175 countries.

There are many other positive aspects of Irish life that scream 'America'. The sense of living in an immigrant nation is one. The 250,000 new arrivals that landed in Ireland between 1996 and 2003 have provoked a measure of resentment, but also considerable hope. The American experience proves that, if we can overcome the obvious difficulties, immigration will guarantee Ireland a form of renewal and innovation that we have not had since the Vikings sailed their long-boats up the Liffey.

One of the best ways of understanding Ireland's uneven progress is by understanding America. Beyond our useful parody and their Paddywhackery, we are facing common realities and dealing with them in remarkably similar ways. In truth, it really does not matter if the Americans cannot see beyond Colin Farrell and The Drunken Irish Novelists of Springfield; they will hardly sink into the sea if they don't have a proper understanding of Ireland. But we do not have the luxury of misunderstanding America. If we cannot see beyond George Bush and *The Terminator*, then we are blind to our own future.

15

Us against the World

A chill wind ran through the crowded square, carrying the
discordant dirges of many brass bands. It was Good
Friday 2003, and the festival of Semana Santa filled the
Spanish town of Huéscar with a brash display of
ostentatious devotion. At that moment, towns and cities
across Spain were hosting processions of confraternities,
or religious associations, honouring Jesus Christ and the
Virgin Mary. Each confraternity spends months before
Holy Week preparing the float that carries Our Lady in an
almost competitive drive to perfect the most ornate
display of flowers and fabric. The floats moved as if by
divine guidance, with the bearers hidden from the eyes of
the crowd, and they rose, fell and paused in time with the
martial rhythm of trumpet and drum. Surrounding the
float were the hooded figures of men, women and

children carrying candles and the relics of their confraternity.

The festival of Semana Santa is a declaration of identity as much as an exercise in piety, and from my vantage point on that Good Friday, it inspired a sense of privileged wonderment. It was the same emotion I had felt a few weeks before while watching a group of returned refugees praying quietly in their bomb-damaged mosque on the mountain frontier between Iran and Iraq. I could hear the echo of those Islamic prayers in the cacophony of this Christian festival. As I stood with my wife and two good friends, a thought entered my head: the world is shrinking into vacuum-packed uniformity, but there are still places – be it a Kurdish mosque or a Spanish street – where history shapes the future, identity thrives and there is virtue in difference.

In the immediate aftermath of the war in Iraq, I went looking for proof that Ireland was still one of those places. Was there a uniquely Irish event that matched the significance of Semana Santa? Was there some popular nationwide celebration that you could point to and say this represents the traditions that make us unique? Don't worry. This is not a prelude to some ponderous lecture about the meaning of being Irish. There is just so much 're-imagining Ireland' you can do before you deserve to be locked up in the loony bin. Neither is this a Luddite rant; there are already far too many curmudgeons mouthing off about 'mod-ren' Ireland (they strike me as the intellectual equivalent of the bad-tempered neighbour who would never give you your ball back).

No, what interests me is how Ireland could become detached from the rest of the world while technically being among the most globalised nations. In the case of the Spaniards and the Kurds, you know where they stand and what they stand for; you know what values they will fight for and what traditions they would defend. We are still capable of good intentions (as the anti-war march in Dublin demonstrated), but is there something distinctly Irish that we actually contribute to the global commons? To put it bluntly, if Ireland disappeared tomorrow, would the world really lose out in any practical way?

During my search for something that summed up Ireland's distinct niche in the world, I kept seeing a television ad for MasterCard that intrigued me. It followed a scruffily chic young man who encountered all the usual tourist clichés as he walked through the streets of Dublin. He passed two American tourists in matching outfits, and the voiceover said, 'Two pairs of Emerald green trousers … €100.' Next up was an older woman in a souvenir shop holding a model of a thatched cottage in her hand. The voiceover line was: 'One authentic Irish cottage, made in China … €10.' As he neared his destination, the young man passed a group of rollicking hen-party-goers wearing floppy green headgear: 'Leprechaun hats,' said the voice, '€15.' The ad reached its climax in what looked like one of those designer Paddy pubs in Dublin's Temple Bar, where our hero met his equally scruffy-chic mates. As he sat down to a pint of plain, the voiceover delivered the pay-off line: 'Knowing what it really is to be Irish … priceless.' The camera zoomed in on the shamrock drawn in the head of the pint of Guinness, which quickly morphed into the MasterCard corporate logo.

I watched that advert ten, maybe fifteen times, and I was still left with unanswered questions. What did it really say about Irishness? Was my identity infused in that alcoholic beverage or summed up by the promise of easy credit in that corporate logo? Eventually, I decided the message was not in the words but the tone. What was uniquely Irish was the hero's knowing detachment from the foreigners and their clearly absurd notions of Irishness. Without stretching the words or images too far, you could come away with the following advice. Take their money. Laugh at their bad taste. Savour the irony. Have a pint. Get a credit card. Be Irish. Be proud.

The advert was a bite-sized summary of the principles that seem to underpin our attitude to the world. First, there is something special about Ireland. Second, foreigners think we are great. Third, we know them better than they know us. I think it quite possible that behind the fog of knowing detachment so effortlessly expressed in that MasterCard advert, there is a widening gap between the objective reality and the subjective perception.

Ireland has always had critics who tread the fine line between anti-national vitriol and bigotry, and to paraphrase Gerry Adams, they haven't gone away you know. The anti-Irish rhetoric occasionally rises above prejudice, but it can still be needlessly vicious on occasion. The real change has been in our response, in particular our developing nonchalance about the opinions of others, even the most incendiary kind.

We half expect it of Unionist leaders because we know they need to chuck a regular offering of red meat to their hard core. In a speech in November 2002, David Trimble described the Republic as a 'pathetic, mono-ethnic and mono-cultural state' that would have no reason to exist 'if you took away the Catholicism and anti-Britishness'. To be the fair to Trimble, he later said he did not actually utter the word 'pathetic'. Either way, the attack provoked a few tired sighs from Nationalists, but no real damage was done to the peace process.

There was the same storm-in-a-rather-small-tea-cup quality to the controversy surrounding British controversialist Julie Burchill. The London Irish Centre tried to have her prosecuted during the summer of 2002 after she described Ireland's national flag as 'the Hitler-licking, altar-boy molesting, abortion-banning Irish tricolour'. A year later, the same group was outraged when Burchill criticised the level of funding for the St Patrick's Day parade in the British capital. The thing is that neither of these comments appeared to excite any significant reaction back home in Ireland, except perhaps to drum up publicity for Burchill's usually excellent brand of tub-thumpery.

I don't know if Trimble and Burchill were guilty of bigotry, although they clearly harbour an instinctive mistrust of the Irish. To me, their crime was to undermine legitimate external criticism of Ireland at a time when we are growing complacent about the opinions of others. They helped to strengthen the myth that foreigners who criticise Ireland are motivated by an Anglo-centric tradition of anti-Irish prejudice. In truth, a growing number of foreigners have perfectly legitimate reasons for not liking the Irish very much.

Leaving aside the merits of Ireland's decision to reject the Nice Referendum in June 2001, it certainly did nothing for our image. By the time the government put the treaty to the Irish electorate for a second time, in October 2002, foreign commentators were queuing up to take a pop at this country. Peter Wilson of *The Australian* wrote that when outsiders thought of Ireland, they imagined a 'loveable, lyrical and generous people – everybody's favourite foreigners'. 'Think again,' wrote Wilson. 'How about "the most selfish people in Europe"? The meanest, most hypocritical nation in the European Union? That is a more accurate and honest picture of how Ireland stands today.' Just days before the second Nice vote, Polly Toynbee of *The Guardian* warned that if Irish voters rejected the treaty again, they would be cast in a harsh new light. 'As the Celtic mists clear, instead of green romance, Europe might see another side of the coin – a narrow-minded, nationalist and selfish country.'

In the end, Irish voters voted yes, but the genie was out of the bottle. Once they were forced to question Ireland's pristine image, those opinion-makers could never have quite the same view of the country again. You could make a strong argument that the likes of Polly Toynbee and Peter Wilson did not understand the motivations of the people who voted no to Nice. But even if you could give a persuasive explanation of the Nice experience, you would still struggle to explain other negative conclusions about the Irish national psyche.

If you know foreigners who live in Ireland, you will have heard about their process of awakening. It starts when an Irish person asks the recently arrived visitor what they think of Ireland and then radiates boredom or impatience when they hear criticism. After a while, the newcomer heeds the signals and drops some anodyne comment about the weather into the flow of saccharine-sweet compliments about Ireland. Meanwhile, they privately express frustration at the contradiction between the overwhelming friendliness of Irish people and their profound detachment. Eventually, they will become more Irish than the Irish, or else they will leave.

A Malaysian corporate lawyer, Ho Wei Sim, described the process in the *Irish Independent* in November 2002: 'You can have a long conversation with someone and presume that you have made a friend but for the Irish person it doesn't necessarily mean anything.' She went on to explain the art of conversation as a foreigner in Ireland. 'Stick to small talk, don't tell anyone anything you wouldn't mind the whole world knowing about, talk about the weather a lot. Be humorous. Talk a lot but say nothing.' In the end, she said, 'you simply learn to withdraw, to keep a distance, just like an Irish person would'.

The most compelling explanation of this process is that most foreigners take things literally, and that upsets the ambiguities that surround our self-image. We think of ourselves as the friendliest and most outgoing people in the world, but the directness of outsiders exposes our deficiencies. One Japanese woman, writing in *The Irish Times*, offered a rather charitable explanation of Irish hostility and indifference, saying we 'are scared of revealing our own lack of understanding'.

When I lived in the United States, the most common question from home was what did I miss most. My rather glib response was Tayto crisps and irony. Today, when I ask my friends from the US what they dislike about Ireland, they often say it is the Irish obsession with irony. At its best, irony is a way of keeping our feet on the ground, but it is also used to separate the insiders from the outsiders. There is nothing more isolating than a stranger who begins a sentence with a knowing smile and the phrase, 'Yeah, right ...'

The Irish use of irony is 'nothing more than insulting people by tone', or at least that's what an Irish film director once told an American friend of mine. For outsiders, the effect of prolonged exposure to double meaning is often paranoia and exhaustion. 'Here you have to be clever,' another resident foreigner told me. 'If you're happy you're not clever. You're a dickhead if you get sheer unadulterated happiness from things.' Note that use of the local idiom. If you can't beat them, join them.

In some ways, the reliance on irony has brought us closer to our nearest neighbours, the British. In his book *The Nineties*, Michael Bracewell suggests the Cool Britannia concept of the 1990s was a reaction to the widespread abuse of irony in public life: 'We were gorged on irony, sickened and bloated and cramped with snooty cleverness. Irony was our trapped wind.' There is that slightly uncomfortable feeling in the belly of Irish life right now, a symptom of the blocked-up mess of indigestible sarcasm and knowing mockery you face each time you open the Sunday newspapers or listen to an argument on radio.

The more irony defines our public discourse, the more our political culture is robbed of meaning and sincerity. The reliance on double meanings, the aversion to directness and the smug aloofness also makes it so much harder to engage with the literal realities that shape other countries. How can we have a sincere debate about our international responsibilities when the concepts of sincerity and responsibility are suspect? How can we directly engage with the rest of the world when we avoid directness? And how can they take us seriously if we are constantly mocking their seriousness?

At this point, you probably still have your doubts. You might find it hard to believe that the smart-alec tone of public conversations has any impact on our foreign policy, besides sharpening our irreverence towards the world's lone superpower. But something must explain our growing detachment from international affairs, and if 'snooty cleverness' is not the cause, then it is one of the most obvious symptoms.

You may also still need convincing about the scale of Ireland's detachment. On the surface, given the explosion in foreign travel by Irish people in recent years, you could conclude that we are more deeply engaged with the world than ever before. Just look to the experience of our backpacker generation; all those extra long-haul trips we are taking; all that skiing and scuba diving; those safaris and desert treks; and the dream honeymoons in Koh Samui and Mauritius. And thanks to those low-fares, nobody is excluded from the annual foreign getaway. Ireland truly has taken its place among the nations of the earth.

The problem with our obvious passion for travel is that we do not always travel well. In July 2001, the Internet travel agency Expedia produced a survey of seventeen popular holiday destinations to find out which nationalities were the best and worst behaved on holidays. The poll put the British at the bottom but then listed the Irish in joint second-last place with the Israelis. 'Irish and British travellers are some of the most widely travelled in the world,' Expedia's Dermot Halpin told the *Sunday Tribune*, 'but that doesn't mean they are good at it.'

In line with the bad behaviour, there is an emerging pattern of delusion that matches some of the trends we have already examined. In his 'European Diary' for *The Irish Times* in June 2001, Dennis Staunton described an encounter with the archetypal 'Ugly Irishman' in a bar in Budapest. He was complaining loudly about immigrants in Ireland and the other side-effects of prosperity. Staunton noted the similarities with the 'Ugly American' and the 'Ugly German' but said 'there is a fundamental difference between the Ugly Irishman and his counterparts elsewhere – he is convinced everybody loves him.'

That deluded sense of being special is sometimes mixed with mean-spirited mockery. In *The Irish Times* in July 2002, a letter writer described his encounter with other Irish tourists in Egypt. He noted their complete disregard for Islamic custom, their anti-Muslim jokes and their ostentatious drinking. He also described the 'slagging', which involved 'asking the lowly paid Egyptian waiters how much they earned and then laughing heartily at the reply. The fact that they were humiliating these men would never have occurred to them; it was just a bit of harmless craic.'

Some social critics have suggested this type of behaviour would not have happened if we were still the poor relation in the European family. They believe we have either forgotten what it was like to be the butt of the jokes, or we are drunk on the novelty of being 'superior'. Either way, the intensity of this behaviour seems to be linked to the speed with which the Irish mind-set has changed. We have been transformed from a nation of employees to a nation of consumers. In pre-Tiger Ireland, our future was determined in corporate boardrooms in other countries, but now our spending patterns shape the future of millions of people across the world. We used to be worried about impressing others; now we know it is up to them to impress us. It took other Western countries generations to reach this point, but the Irish seemed to make the transition overnight.

You could argue that it is only human to feel superior towards people who aspire to our standard of living, and once we get used to being a member of the exclusive club of rich nations the obnoxious streak will disappear. However, our growing retreat from world affairs will not be halted so easily. On the contrary, the wealthier we become the more detached we seem to be.

Earlier chapters dealt with the cultural roots of our growing alienation from Bush's America, but how do we explain the apparent drift away from Europe? Remember, our rich European benefactors pumped us full of Structural Funds and CAP money and in the space of thirty years helped drag our national income from about 60 per cent of the European average to 128 per cent. Why is it, after everything the European dream has given us, that we seem to be increasingly out of step with the drive for a closer union?

Recent opinion polls show the Irish are still relatively positive towards the European Union, but the trend is ever downward. In a Eurobarometer survey taken in autumn 2001, 83 per cent of Irish people said membership of the European Union (EU) was a good thing; by spring 2003, the figure had slipped to 67 per cent. What is remarkable is the speed with which Ireland's enthusiasm for Europe is waning. In autumn 2002, more than two out of three Irish people said they had a positive image of the EU; by the following spring, only half said the same thing.

Despite the benefits the Irish have derived from the European project, we don't seem terribly concerned about its long-term survival. When asked in 2002 how we would feel if the EU was scrapped, only 48 per cent said they would feel very sorry. The polls also found we don't have much confidence in our understanding of European issues; Ireland is now among the four member states with the most widespread lack of knowledge of the EU and its policies.

We are not so much euro-sceptic as euro-indifferent, and the most dramatic evidence of that was the rejection of the Nice treaty in June 2001. Far more telling than the margin of defeat was that 65 per cent of voters could not even be bothered to cast a ballot on the future of Europe (when the treaty eventually passed in 2002, the turnout was still under 50 per cent). In fact, at the time of that first

Nice campaign, Irish people seemed more interested in helping an Irish flight attendant, Brian Dowling, win *Big Brother*. As Fintan O'Toole observed at the time, it was a safe bet that more Irish people voted for Dowling than voted against the Nice treaty, and what's more, they paid for the privilege in telephone charges.

We seem increasingly indifferent to Europe because the tangible benefits of our involvement are in the past tense. We still believe the EU *was* a good thing for Ireland, but when we look into the future, we get nervous. The surveys show that among the things we fear about the expansion of Europe is the loss of national control over issues such as immigration. Put simply, self-interest trumps gratitude. But, once again, what fascinates me is not the incipient scepticism but the indifference, not simply to Europe, but to wide range of issues that are, literally, foreign to us.

In May 2003, the SARS crisis was sweeping across Asia, and there were concerns that visiting Special Olympics athletes might bring the virus on to Irish soil (although, as a guest on a radio programme noted at the time, there was as much chance of an Irish person dying from SARS as being killed by a falling coconut). Such was the level of paranoia that an *Irish Times*/MRBI poll found SARS was one of fifteen issues that would swing votes in the next general election. In fact, more people cited SARS than neutrality, the only foreign-policy issue to make it on the list. Think about that: more voters were worried about a disease that had never been recorded in Ireland than about our role in future wars.

They say the attacks of September 11 changed the world, but they could not shift Irish viewing habits. Just before 10 p.m. on September 11, 2001, *Prime Time* broadcast a special programme on RTÉ One about the momentous events unfolding in the United States; 372,000 adult viewers tuned in to watch. When they totted up the ratings, it was only the thirteenth most-watched prog-ramme that month, falling behind shows such as *Fame and Fortune*, *Treasure Island* and *Up for the Match*. In fact, earlier on the evening of September 11, an audience of 310,000 had tuned into Network Two to watch *Fair City*. A literal reading of those numbers tells us that the fall-out from the destruction of the Twin Towers on RTÉ One was a mere 20 per cent more interesting than the day's events in the fictional Dublin suburb of Carrigstown. This is the rule, not the exception. In April 2003, one episode of *Fair City* had 100,000 more viewers than the average nine o'clock news programme. It was aired the night before the Americans captured Baghdad International Airport.

There is perhaps no industry in the world today that is more attuned to the tastes of the market than television, and the tastes of the Irish market have shifted dramatically away from the coverage of foreign events. The only exceptions are events that appeal to the lowest common denominator of human compulsions (compare levels of interest in Jordan, the well-endowed British model, to Jordan, the strategically important Middle Eastern kingdom). The new dispensation is summed up by the advice of a television executive who once told me there are three subjects that make people change channels as soon as they are mentioned: Northern Ireland, Europe and foreign politics.

This loss of interest is closely aligned to the marked fall in demand for news and current affairs in general. And what's more, the growing public disinterest in news from around the world is magnified by the cut-throat atmosphere that prevails in the mainstream Irish and international media. In fact, in recent years, public indifference and a commercial dynamic have come together to create what you could call the 'vicious cycle of detachment'.

To get a place in the television schedules, a broadcaster must be able to prove that the subject of their broadcast will bring in viewers – or 'audience share', to use corporate jargon. Given the trends in recent years, there is a growing awareness of foreign affairs as a minority taste. This puts pressure on existing programmes such as RTÉ's *Prime Time*, which currently occupies a very valuable slot in the television schedule. If it spent too much time on subjects with which viewers do not connect, such as foreign affairs, then its ratings would fall, and some commercially minded executive might ask: why not move *Prime Time* to a slot later in the evening to make way for a programme that will definitely pull in the punters?

There is obvious pressure on news and current-affairs programmes to spend more time on bankable subjects such as crime, health and sport and less time on worthy but boring subjects such as the EU or the reconstruction of Iraq. It does not mean they are ignored, just that the story of a gangland murder generally gets precedence over the report on the European constitution (I can actually sense eyes glazing over as I write those words). It makes perfect sense on one level, but it is disturbing on another. The expansion of Europe will affect every Irish life in a variety of ways while it is unlikely that gangland assassins will murder a significant proportion of the population. Of course, that is just a hunch.

The decision to relegate foreign news stories because they generate lower ratings is a self-fulfilling prophecy with serious long-term consequences for the future. Less interest in foreign affairs leads to fewer programmes about foreign affairs, and that leads to less debate about foreign affairs, which leads to less interest in foreign affairs. And that is what I mean by the vicious cycle of detachment.

The broadcasters always get the blame for this. If they were more courageous, goes the argument, they would broadcast more news from around the world and break the cycle. There are people in the business who go along with that argument, at least to some extent. At RTÉ, *Prime Time* has hung on to its valuable slot (even though other European broadcasters are shunting their current-affairs programmes into the darkest recesses of late-night television), and it still devotes significant time to international events. Meanwhile, the RTÉ Newsroom is spending more time and money covering complex international issues in a way that is interesting and accessible. The efforts seem to have paid off. *Prime Time* has increased the size of its audience in recent years, and news programmes still have incredibly high ratings by international standards (I focus on RTÉ because it is the place I know best; there are plenty of others in the Irish media fighting the good fight.)

When it comes down to it, the vicious cycle of detachment is the result of conscious choices by the audience and a certain element of self-deception. Watching foreign news has become a little like physical exercise. We all agree it is very important, but we do a lot less of it than we actually think. And just as our health suffers because we cannot find the time to exercise, our standing in the world suffers because we devote less attention to international affairs. So does us our ability to deliver on our good intentions.

As Edmund Burke might have said, all that is necessary for war, famine and terrorism to thrive is for rich and influential countries like Ireland to shut themselves off from the world. It need not be this way: if we screamed and shouted in every available forum about developing threats such as AIDS in Africa or repression in the Middle East, then we could help to solve problems before they became international crises. But that does not happen. We seem to notice the problems only when a suicide bomber carries out a massacre or when American missiles fall on a distant city. Of course, by then it is too late. By the time the ninety seconds of death and destruction reaches our TV screens, we are powerless to act. So, instead, we curse George Bush or Osama bin Laden and switch over to *Teenage Celebrity Idol Fear Farm*, which in a strange way feels more relevant to our lives. It would be an exaggeration to say the vicious cycle of detachment will be the death of us, but it certainly will be the death of others. Thankfully, they live in places we no longer have to care about, or even understand.

Think back to those three assumptions that underpinned the MasterCard view of Irishness: we are special, everyone likes us and we understand foreigners better than they understand us. All the evidence suggests these three assumptions are no longer valid, yet, perhaps out of a sense of deluded nostalgia, they remain fixed in our national consciousness like an old song we just can't stop humming.

So, is it fair to say that the opposite is now the case: that we are no longer special, that we are generally disliked and that we have no clue what makes foreigners tick? I don't think so; that would ignore the nuances behind the depressing generalities. Our distinctiveness has been pushed back into the middle distance, but some traditions have renewed relevance (my daughter tells me her favourite school subject is Irish, and she is no longer the exception). All around the world, Irish men and women still live out their commitment to development, peace-keeping and justice and in doing so reflect goodwill back on their homeland. In this country, many people still consume news from around the world as if it were oxygen, plenty of Irish people have a profound welcome for the foreigners in their midst and there is an intoxicating feel about Ireland's newly acquired sophistication and openness.

Yet, while this is all true, we cannot ignore the broader truth. Despite the surface calm of our expressed internationalism, Ireland is caught up in a powerful current. A deceptive sense of well-being has left us blissfully unaware of the quickening pace of our detach-ment, but eventually we will have to look around and ask ourselves, how did we get here?

In the meantime, there is always the consolation that we will never be as bland, disliked and insular as the United States. But such comforting assumptions only make the problem worse. As I have outlined in previous chapters, the only thing more dramatic than the Americanisation of post-Tiger Ireland is the extent to which we are still unaware of it. For example, in light of all those horror stories about the American grasp of world geography, take note of the results of an *Ireland on Sunday* poll published the day after the big anti-war march in February 2003. Only one in five people questioned on the streets of Dublin could locate Iraq on a map, and one person mixed it up with the American state of Utah. One man was told he had picked Saudi Arabia. 'Well, it's close enough, isn't it?' he replied. 'I bet if you asked Bush he'd have less clue than me where Iraq is.' Good old Dubya. As long as he exists, we get to be model citizens of the world, no matter what.

This brings me back to the question I posed at the beginning of this chapter: how could we become so detached from the world when we are clearly among the most globalised countries in it? Well, for the same reason the United States is one of the most diverse nations on the planet while also being so insular. The US has reached a point in its history where it can afford to pick and choose from what the world has to offer without being compelled to adapt its way of life to external norms. This is the 'limited liability' connection to global cultures that now defines Ireland.

Around the time that MasterCard ad was being broadcast, there was another television commercial featuring two Irish holidaymakers taking a boat ride past a riverside market in South-East Asia. To their amazement, the traders called out to them in Moore Street Dublinese. The ad was selling a new cracker called 'Thai Bites', which the voiceover told us was 'Thai with an Irish accent'. These days, it seems everything we take from other cultures gets an Irish accent. And when we travel, we no longer need to be strangers in strange lands, not as long as we remember to pack the county football jersey, the suitcase full of Denny sausages and the address of a good Irish bar. To be Irish in the era of globalisation is to conquer the world without ever having to leave home.

This brings us to the ultimate irony of being Irish at this point in history. We have never been so wealthy, so confident or so independent, yet we have never been so confused about our global responsibilities. For once, we have the economic muscle and political capital to make our ideals count, but we seem to have lost the collective will. We loudly reject the values of Bush's America while instinctively following its lead. As it stands, there is no great incentive for us to confront these contradictions, not as long as the blame for the problems of the world can be laid at the feet of one country. And yet what is wrong with Zulu Time only appears to be exclusively American. In truth, it is increasingly Irish.

Of course, it does not have to be this way, not for us and not for them. There are ways that the United States, Ireland and Europe in general can work together to confront the delusional and dangerous realities of Zulu Time. There are ways we can both move the clocks forward if we are willing. The question is: are we willing? And are the Americans able?

16

THE AMERICAN EVOLUTION

'A state without the means of some change is
without the means of its conservation.'

Edmund Burke, *Reflections on the
Revolution in France*, 1790

Airports do not exist. They are black holes created when
the glamorous novelty of air travel collapsed in on itself,
leaving a vortex of constant motion and generic bland-
ness. The airport is not a place; it is a non-place, a
bubbling stream of opposites that suggest everywhere but
nowhere. There is no beginning or end, just an infinite
amount of journeys. People surround you at all times, yet
you are often profoundly alone. The clock on the wall
keeps the time of day, but every day is the same day – one
vast, unending Tuesday.

Once in a while, the airport vortex spits out a reminder
of external forces. For a brief moment, you catch a
glimpse of a world where people have names and life
stories instead of flight numbers and seat assignments. I
had one of those moments at Gate 20 in Heathrow's

Terminal Three on June 3, 2003, as I stood in line for a flight to Washington DC.

The two American servicemen ahead of me were conspicuously inconspicuous. Their build, posture and haircuts suggested they were members of an élite military outfit, but they were dressed in 'sports casual' outfits of short-sleeved shirts and light-coloured chinos. If it were not for the heavy desert boots, they could have been office buddies returning from a golf holiday. They blended in perfectly with the anonymity of the non-place until a third soldier came out of the vast expanse of nowhere and shattered the illusion.

He was not loud in a vocal sense, but he dominated the space around the final security check like an actor who owned the stage, and instead of perspiration, his pores oozed confidence. As the line moved slowly towards the walkway to the plane, he chatted with airline staff and security guards like a visiting celebrity. In contrast to the golfing attire of his friends, he wore shorts and a T-shirt. On the back of the T-shirt was a map of Iraq and the words 'Operation Iraqi Freedom'. On his face was a look that seemed to say: 'job well done'.

The contrast between the three soldiers would stay in my head during the next ten days as I travelled around the east coast of the United States. It was supposed to be a holiday, but it was also a chance to plug into the mains of American life for a little while. The war had been over for almost two months, but its effects were still working their way to the surface in confusing patterns. The confidence that I had witnessed in the face of that imposing Marine at Heathrow came across strongly in media commentary. But there was also something else, and it was similar to the reserve of the other soldiers at the departure gate in London. On that June visit, America seemed cautious; the war was officially over, but the uncertainty remained, and it did not take long to see it.

On the morning after my arrival, the *Washington Post* carried an unsettling story on its inside pages: 'Many Washington area residents may find their sleep interrupted by the roar of Air Force F-16 fighters tonight as the Pentagon conducts a 90-minute air patrol exercise ...' The drill, called Falcon Virgo, was just the latest test of a general overhaul of air defences in the wake of September 11. 'The US military now maintains irregular patrols over Washington, New York and other cities and deploys Avenger artillery batteries equipped with Stinger missiles at various locations ...'

For a visiting foreigner, the extent of this institution-alised paranoia was hard to fathom. But then again, which was more valid: my scepticism about the level of threat levelled against my American friends or their insecurity about the immediate future? If you lived in Ireland, it seemed the Americans had lost the run of themselves in the wake of September 11, and all that talk of air defence drills was part of an attempt to terrorise the public into supporting extreme responses, at home and abroad. As usual, the truth was a little more complicated.

A lot had changed since I lived in Washington, and it was not until my visit in June 2003 that I properly understood the extent of the transformation. At the end of my posting in January 2001, the United States was still enjoying the longest economic boom in its history and maintained unrivalled dominance on the world stage. America's ruling class, the middle-class 'baby boomers', were reaping the rewards of a decade of peace and prosperity and preparing for extravagant retirements funded by the paper riches of their Internet stocks.

Within months, their easy-living dream suffered the first in a series of mortal wounds. In May 2001, the stock market began a dramatic tumble as the Internet bubble burst with unanticipated violence. September 11 rattled the American psyche like an earthquake and was followed by a sequence of tremors: Anthrax, Enron, Afghanistan, Osama's survival, the Washington sniper, Code Orange alerts, SARS, the Space Shuttle disaster, anti-American rage and then the war in Iraq. The cumulative impact of these seismic shocks was best expressed by a fifty-eight-year-old technician called Alan Jacobs, quoted in the *Washington Post*: 'Years ago you felt safe and well off as an American. All this stuff happened in Israel, Africa or Ireland. Now we're part of the real world.'

Even that expression of changed realities does not do justice to the radical transformation of the American psyche in the first years of the twenty-first century. In fact, it is almost impossible to find language that does. It does not help that Americans themselves seem confused by their own predicament and increasingly alienated from the bitter political confrontation that characterised the Bush years.

This disenchantment should come as no surprise given the polarising bitterness that has infected public discourse in the United States. Democrats (and Europeans) are described as weasels and worms on Fox News while liberal pundits accuse Republicans of being liars and thieves. In response, ordinary citizens are tempted to switch off. With each partisan dogfight, the alienation and indifference that already characterise American political culture grow stronger and more debilitating. The impact is greatest on the substantial moderate core that backs the aims of the war on terror but has big doubts about the Bush administration. You could think of this conflicted middle-ground as the silent Americans.

During my June visit, I went back to my favourite bar in Washington, the Capitol Lounge. What was always so intriguing about the Lounge was the presence of the slickest young politicos in Washington, who were attracted by the promise of beer, music, the opposite sex and an occasionally partisan row. On my return, nothing seemed to have changed. There was still the same peculiar mix of sexual tension and shabby cool. From the jukebox came the sound of 'Alternative Ulster' by Stiff Little Fingers, and the portrait of the late John Belushi still sat behind the bar. Then I noticed a blackboard on the wall that I not seen before. I leaned over to get a closer look and saw that it had 'Bar Rules' written on it in chalk. Rule number one: 'No Miller Lite.' Rule number two: 'Be polite or you will be asked to leave.' And rule number three: 'No politics.'

What if the silent Americans gave up on politics altogether? It would be left up to the opposing fringes to battle it out for the political soul of the United States. This would descend into a bare-knuckle brawl played out for the benefit of the partisan fringes of the American electorate. It would be cynical, vicious and manipulative, and the odds would favour the American right, if only because of the gale-force wind of patriotism that has blown through American life since September 11.

On the train between Washington and New York, the slick young man with the mobile phone talked his way across three state lines without drawing breath. He had taken his fellow passengers hostage, making us prisoners to his loud one-sided conversation. Worse still, he was oblivious to his transgressions. At the end of one particularly animated monologue, two of his fellow passengers looked around pointedly, but he was too busy dialling his next victim to notice. He was brash, rude and completely lacking in manners. And he was Dutch. Don't you just hate those loud Europeans?

I was feeling a lot closer to Boston than Berlin by the time the Metroliner pulled into Manhattan's Penn Station, but up on the station concourse those European gut feelings about post-September-11 America returned once more. Yellow ribbons had been attached to the main departure screen, and the slogan 'God Bless America' kept appearing underneath details of trains to Philadelphia, Miami and Baltimore. In front of me, soldiers in camouflage fatigues and black berets strode across the concourse as if their very presence was some form of guarantee. It was the same all over Manhattan; an off-putting blend of patriotism and paranoia in the world's most blasé city.

When American patriotism turns this 'garrulous', Alexis de Tocqueville once observed, it 'wearies even those who are disposed to respect it'. But that is the perspective of the outsider. To most Americans, there is nothing sinister about their patriotism even if it occasionally drifts into the realm of kitsch. When we see the American flag, it is very often sitting on top of a tank. To Americans, however, the flag is primarily a 'badge of belonging', according to media analyst Todd Gitlin, 'not a call to shed innocent blood'.

Patriotic fervour can, of course, be exploited as a means of suppressing protest, and during the war in Iraq it seemed that dissent had become officially un-American. A frequently cited example of the creeping repression was the treatment of country rockers the Dixie Chicks. Just before the war in Iraq, singer Natalie Maines told concert-goers in London that the members of the band were ashamed that George Bush came from their home state of Texas. When the comment was reported back home, the Dixie Chicks faced death threats, their CDs were burned and there were calls for a boycott of their tour. Writing about the controversy in the *Sunday Tribune*, an Irish journalist observed: 'This mob rule is the most effective form of censorship, and is profoundly dangerous in a society so introspective and yet so powerful ...'

Yet the critics in Ireland seemed to have missed something. After an initial dip in sales, the Dixie Chicks album *Home* returned to the number-one spot on the country chart and stayed there for weeks. During the summer, the band travelled across the US on the highest-earning tour in the history of country music. As the *New York Times* noted in July 2003, 'The Dixie Chicks may be bigger than ever.'

Natalie Maines was not the only American dissident to emerge from the patriotic wringer with enhanced popularity. One of loudest anti-war voices in Hollywood belonged to comedian Janeane Garofolo. Among other things, she went on live TV and described the Bush administration (led by America's forty-third president) as the 'Forty-third Reich'. Rather than destroying her professional reputation, dissent was a pretty good career move. 'Before this I was a moderately well-known character actress,' she said. 'Now I'm almost famous.'

Reports of flag-waving, troop-supporting, music-suppressing patriots were certainly overplayed, but the portrayal of wartime America as naïve and misinformed was not altogether false. Thanks to substandard media scrutiny of White House spin, many Americans ended up believing that Saddam Hussein was involved with the attacks of September 11. Still, the caricature of the ignorant and misinformed American was increasingly crude in the aftermath of war, when critical analysis began to flourish again.

If you turned on CBS News or its competitors on any night during the summer of 2003, you were given graphic descriptions of life for American soldiers in the firing line. In small-town newspapers, the families of servicemen and women began to articulate the uncertainty facing their loved ones in Iraq. The big-city broadsheets were asking tough questions about the intelligence used to justify war, and *New York Times* columnists such as Maureen Dowd, Tom Friedman and Paul Krugman kept up a drumbeat of criticism of the Bush administration. Even the Pentagon-financed newspaper, *Stars and Stripes*, was reporting that half the troops they had polled in Iraq complained of low morale.

The critical awakening seemed to have a limited impact on the behaviour of the Bush administration. To critics around the world, Bush's America was still guilty of arrogance on an imperial scale. In the words of one Irish academic, the 'US is unquestionably an empire in the making, exploiting its fabulous wealth and power to fashion a world in its own image and interests'. However, the notion of empire failed to take account of the fact that the United States was increasingly two distinct entities: the US inhabited by the Washington policy-makers and the US in which hundreds of millions of ordinary Americans lived. When it came to this issue of imperial ambition, the differences between these two entities could not have been greater.

In June 2003, the German Marshall Fund began work

on a survey of transatlantic trends. The results showed that 'Americans, on the whole, are neither isolationist nor unilateralist.' Less than half the Americans surveyed believed their country should be the only superpower, and more than one-third wanted to see the emergence of a European superpower, even if it sometimes opposed US policies. The survey also found that the American public was more willing to be involved in world affairs than at any time in half a century.

Clearly, most Americans were not in an imperial mood, no matter how their leaders might act, but an overwhelming majority still felt bound to support the use of their nation's unrivalled military might. What lay behind that apparent contradiction was the constant flow of incompatible messages coming from competing extremes. The silent Americans were being pushed and pulled from every direction. Faced with a torrent of angry rhetoric, terror alerts and patriotic appeals, some were being seduced by the simple answers to the complex questions.

In December 2003, I returned to the US to find out whether George Bush could be beaten in the approaching presidential election campaign. Within minutes of landing at Chicago, it became clear the ground had shifted since my last visit. On the television screens in the airport restaurants, CNN was playing the same pictures, over and over again. A down-and-out Saddam Hussein was standing in front of a US Army medic with his mouth wide open, apparently unconcerned by his sudden change of circumstances. Unconfirmed reports of Saddam's capture had come through as I left Dublin that morning; here was the proof, on an endless loop of videotape.

On the way to my connecting flight, I set off a metal

detector, and a security guard ordered me to take off my shoes and walk through again. Struggling with my laces, I became aware of disapproving stares behind me. A line of business travellers stood with their slip-on shoes in their hands, silently cursing my clumsy attempts to cope with the new reality of air travel in America.

In the days that followed, the celebration of Saddam's capture was replaced by tales of impending doom. The US Department of Homeland Security had imposed a national Code Orange alert in response to intelligence reports of an imminent terrorist attack on American cities. The result was the same institutionalised vulnerability I had seen back in June, but now it was more virulent and had seeped into unexpected corners of public life.

Two days before Christmas, the New York *Daily News* carried a front-page story that summed up the developing madness. It featured a suspected mobster called Louis Barone, known to his friends as Louie Lump Lump. On the night of December 22, Lump Lump was sitting at the bar in Rao's, a legendary Italian restaurant in Harlem, listening to Broadway actress Rena Strober singing 'Don't Rain on My Parade'. He got involved in a verbal confrontation with a fellow wiseguy called Albert Circelli, who had loudly mocked the singer's performance. At the end of the night, Louie Lump Lump allegedly followed Circelli to the door, pulled out a .38-calibre handgun and shot him dead. After Lump Lump was arrested, the police asked him why he had been carrying a gun in a restaurant. 'Didn't you guys hear?' he is reported to have said: 'We're at Code Orange.'

The fog of threat that had settled over America in the dying days of 2003 made the most ridiculous situations seem almost normal. To a visiting foreigner, it was impossible to imagine a real-life threat that justified the extremes, but in a city like New York it was enough to think about how you felt before September 11 and how you felt after. If the price of vigilance was occasional farce and slip-on shoes, then so be it.

During the weeks before Christmas, it began to feel as if there were no moderates left in America, which I suppose is hardly surprising since I spent a lot of time in West Texas. The first omen came outside the oil city of Midland, where a highway sign announced the app-roaching town of Stanton: 'Home to 3,000 good people and a couple of old soreheads.' Here was the characteristic dry wit of a practical people, telling the visitor, 'As long as you accept us for who we are, you are very welcome.'

On a hillside outside the town of Big Spring, there is a memorial to the local boys who have been killed in almost one hundred years of foreign wars. Their faces line the walls of a small chapel on the grounds of the memorial. The most recent picture is that of a nineteen-year-old Marine called Chad Bales-Medcalf, who died when the truck he was driving crashed in central Iraq on April 3, 2003.

Chad was raised in the nearby town of Coahoma by his mother, Ginger, and stepfather, John. A few minutes in their presence was enough to renew my faith in the essential goodness of humankind. They have a quality that first strikes you as innocence, but could also be a complete absence of cynicism. There is no calculation or judgement in their welcome. You have come to their house with a clean slate, and they have no reason not to like you.

'I would never have kept him from it,' Ginger said when we sat down together at the kitchen table. 'That's what we're for, that's how we're here, it's for freedom.' As she talked about her dead son, there was a visible contradiction between her words and the crushing loss in her eyes. Chad was just out of high school. He died in a senseless accident in a place Ginger had never heard of. But at least she had an answer to the question, 'For what?' In her mind, there was such a thing as destiny.

Like millions of Christian Americans, John and Ginger believed that President Bush and his war on terror were God's response to the terrorist assault on America. 'It needed to be stopped,' John said. 'I really think that's why God has allowed him to be president, and I am so thankful that he is the president.' Where world events brought doubt and pain, John and Ginger responded with faith. They also had their patriotism, although the America they celebrated was not a jumble of identities but the essential decency of a tiny place called Coahoma.

Before I left Ginger and John, they showed me a map of Iraq with the site of Chad's death marked with a red dot. I asked would the family consider travelling to Iraq to see the place where Chad had died. They seemed taken aback and both shook their heads. Something told me this was the first time they had ever considered the possibility of leaving the United States.

If you just had a single word to describe Ginger and John, it would be 'decent'. If you had a few more, you might consider 'honourable' and 'idealistic'. But 'sceptical' and 'worldly' would not be among them. Where you might expect a fierce curiosity about the war that claimed their son, there was only a deep sense of loss and God's plan for humanity.

John and Ginger are a living illustration of the forces that suppress the moderating instincts in the American psyche. As well as that belief in America's destiny and fear of unseen threats, there is the absence of uncomfortable questions about America's vulnerability and a reluctance to see the world as it actually is. If the United States ever really becomes the prisoner of political extremes, you might blame it on a basic lack of curiosity.

For an outsider, it is easy to conclude that curiosity and moderation have been driven from American life, and all that is left are those with unshakeable faith in George Bush and those who hate everything he represents. One popular theory is that years of polarising debate in America have created a 'fifty-fifty country', evenly divided between those who vote Republican and those who back the Democrats. But take a moment to consider this possibility: the US is a 'thirty-thirty country', where 30 per cent of the population is staunchly Democratic and an equal proportion is rock-solid Republican. The rest of the population tends to lean one way or the other but is generally turned off by partisan rhetoric and ideological certainty. And, depending on the issue, they are willing to break ranks. For example, they may generally vote Republican but support the Democrats on health care; they may be traditional Democrats who like Republican policies on crime. Find these silent Americans and you have the key to America's ongoing evolution.

Take the lunch-time crowd in Ginny's diner, just outside Louisville, Kentucky. It was December 15, the day after Saddam Hussein was captured, and the clientele was predominantly white, middle-aged and male. You would not expect to hear any serious criticism of George Bush or the war on terror, but middle America is often full of surprises.

Stuart was a retired accountant who had voted for George Bush in 2000. Yet, as 2003 came to a close, he was angry with the president because of the war in Iraq. 'I was led to believe that the Iraqis had huge stores of poison chemicals,' he said. 'Once they got in there they couldn't find them so then I felt betrayed.' Despite that sense of betrayal, Stuart felt Saddam's capture was a turning point, a partial answer to the many questions raised by the war. Like most of the diners we talked to, he was now more likely to vote for Bush in the presidential election.

Over lunch in Ginny's, a pattern began to emerge. Most of the customers were backing Bush, some for no other reason than a basic affinity. As one diner put it: 'He's not polished, he screws up talking, he's a regular guy.' Yet in almost every conversation, there was ambivalence about Bush and his main rivals. 'I'm not a huge President Bush fan,' said Mike, an engineer who had just flown in from Michigan, 'but he's the best choice right now given what I have been presented with.'

In the weeks that followed lunch at Ginny's, I passed through eight US states and heard a variation on the same theme from almost every middle-ground American I met. Whether or not they leaned towards Bush, they always expressed frustration with the agenda of the political and media establishment. Even where the memory of September 11 was strongest, there were complaints that America's priorities had been knocked out of kilter by the relentless focus on war and national security.

The first weeks of the New Year brought me to rural Pennsylvania, a place so full of iconic American images that it feels like a Hollywood creation. As we arrived, a bitter wind sent snow squalls crashing against the wooden farmhouses and grain silos ranged across the pale-yellow cornfields. Driving through that bleak landscape, the rest of the world seemed very distant, but in the placid little town of Shanksville, there were vivid memories of the day that changed America.

Ernest Stull was the elderly mayor of Shanksville, and

in a methodical, almost theatrical way, he described the morning of September 11, 2001: 'I went to the post office and Judy stuck her head out and said aren't you glad you live in Shanksville where nothing ever happens? I said "Yup". Then I came home, started to open the mail and it *did* happen here.'

Moments after Ernest returned from the post office, United Airlines flight 93 crashed into a field outside town and disintegrated. Hijackers were flying the plane towards Washington when some of the forty passengers on board tried to retake control of the airliner. Their final moments and the town of Shanksville were linked forever in one of the most enduring legends of September 11. 'This is where the war on terrorism began,' was how Ernest put it.

Ernest Stull knew something about war. He still suffered the effects of leg injuries he received in the Second World War, although it was the memories that troubled him most. In a dead monotone, he told me about the friends he lost when his Airborne unit stumbled across a Panzer division during the Battle of the Bulge. 'Seven of us from this area went to war together,' he said. 'On that one day, five were injured and one was killed.'

Ernest was wearing a sweatshirt with the logo, 'Proud to be American,' and at the outset of our conversation, he said he was a life-long Republican. Yet this patriotic and conservative war veteran was not sure if he would back Bush in the upcoming election. No matter how strong his support for the war on terror, other issues would decide his vote. In this corner of Pennsylvania, what mattered most was the terminal decline of the coal and steel industries and the resulting slide in local fortunes.

'My family were Dodge dealers for sixty-seven years,' he said. 'Today you go to buy a Dodge truck and nine out of ten are made in Mexico. Somebody has got to stop this exodus of jobs.' I began to say that it seemed people in these parts were quite happy with the war on terror but not quite happy with the economy. Before I could get the last words out, Ernest finished my sentence. Then he went on to explain why he was considering a break with tradition. 'I told you I am a life-long Republican,' he said, 'but when I vote, I always vote for the best man.' I asked him if the best man in this coming election might be a Democrat. He nodded his head and said, 'It could well be.'

The process that might lead Ernest Stull to break ranks is being replicated all across America right now, in both directions; there may be Democrats considering a vote for George Bush. What is important is that there is a momentum inside American political culture that is not readily apparent from a European perspective. It is driven by the escalating impatience of the silent Americans, who continue their search for credible answers in an era dominated by faith and fear. Their choice in the coming election was best expressed by a Muslim American woman I met in Iowa in January 2004: 'While we may be presented with black and white options, we will have to choose something we can all live with.' These silent Americans may stick with their current president. Then again, they may not. The important thing is that they will continue to drive forward the society they live in, no matter who occupies the White House.

It goes without saying that the Americans could be far more curious about the world around them. A recent study by the Pew Institute found that roughly one in five Americans had travelled to another country in the previous five years. However, behind the headline figures there are important trends. According to the US Census

Bureau, the number of its citizens travelling outside North America increased by 67 per cent between 1990 and 2000. Meanwhile, the growing popularity of alternative news sources, such as the BBC and Univision, and the multitude of foreign programmes on cable TV are testament to the increased appetite for views and news from abroad.

There is also a heightened multicultural feel to American life, thanks to a recent historic change in its ethnic make-up. By 2003, thirty-three million US citizens had been born outside the United States, and there were five times as many Americans of non-European descent as there were in 1960. You could think of this wave of immigration as a renewal of American political culture. Because these new arrivals have no established group allegiances, Democrats or Republicans must work harder to reflect America's growing diversity or go out of business.

There are also developing changes in the complex American relationship between religion and politics. Polls show that the US is an overwhelming devout nation and will remain profoundly religious long into the future, but it would be a mistake to simply equate its prevailing faith with bible-thumping conservatism. Those trends in immigration have led to a surge in religious diversity. For example, there are now between six and eight million Muslims in the United States, and Islam is rapidly winning converts in the African American community.

There are also powerful moderating influences at work inside American Christianity, which, according to Fareed Zakaria, 'has become doctrinally pluralistic and highly attentive to the beliefs, desires and wishes of its people'. A growing number of Americans with a deep devotion to God are now endorsing social trends that run counter to established religious doctrines. So, for example, opposition to gay marriage has fallen by 12 per cent since 1996, and the Episcopalian church now has its first openly gay bishop.

In fact, on a range of social issues, increasing numbers of Americans are defying our stereotypes. Support for the death penalty has dropped by 14 per cent since 1996, with almost 40 per cent of Americans now opposed. And consider this assessment of Americans, taken from a recent survey by *The Economist* magazine: 'Support for the idea that "women should return to traditional roles in society" has fallen from just under a third in the late 1980s to about a fifth now. Both Americans and Europeans overwhelmingly disagree that when jobs are scarce men should be given priority.'

In fact, in one very important way, the United States is far more open to change than Europe. Polls show that Americans tend to be fairly positive about the contribution of immigrants to their society whereas, in most of the rest of the industrial world, similar surveys show that more than half the population think immigrants are bad for their country. And there is the germ of truth in 'American exceptionalism': the understanding that to live in the United States is to live with change.

The key players in this process are the silent Americans, searching for answers that match the realities of their lives rather than black-and-white doctrine. As the US population grows ever more diverse, their ranks look set to swell, and that means a growing proportion of the American population is likely to fall outside the narrow parameters of our caricatures.

Make no mistake. The United States will change on its own terms, not ours. Having lived through a different collective experience, Americans will not necessarily come to the same conclusions as us. God and country will still dominate the world-view of millions of ordinary, decent Americans. And where there is pressure for change, the US political system has a habit of warping the popular will (thanks in part to the corrupting influence of corporate media and big money).

Yet in this nation's profound diversity is the greatest guarantee of continuous change. As the US evolves, it is quite possible we will be confused, perplexed and perhaps irritated by the next stage of its development. The important thing is to stop thinking of the United States as a monolith and start thinking about it as an evolutionary process open to the right types of influences and, crucially, the right type of example.

Conclusion

Beyond Zulu Time

'We have it within our power to begin the world
over again.'

Thomas Paine, writer and political theorist, 1776

By the autumn of 2003, it was official: George Bush was
Ireland's most hated man. OK, so I exaggerate slightly.
The American president was the person whom Irish
young people least admired, according to an MRBI/*Irish
Times* survey published in September. He led the poll by a
significant margin, beating off competition from Saddam
Hussein and Osama bin Laden. Against a domestic
setting, he was nine times more unpopular than Charlie
Haughey or Liam Lawlor.

With each passing day, it seemed that Bush's America
was growing ever more loathsome to a growing number of
Irish people, and in almost every conversation there was
deepening anger at the US role in Iraq. Before long, the
opinion polls appeared to reflect this. In October 2003, a
Eurobarometer survey found that 60 per cent of Irish
people believed the US was a threat to world peace (right

behind Israel and North Korea), making us significantly more suspicious of the Americans than the average European. Meanwhile, just 13 per cent of Irish people trusted the United States with the task of rebuilding Iraq.

And yet, behind Ireland's apparently united front there were mixed messages. While we were more sceptical of America's post-war plans than other Europeans, we were far less sceptical about the initial US-led invasion of Iraq. Forty per cent of Irish people in that Eurobarometer survey thought military intervention in Iraq had been somewhat or absolutely justified, while the average across the European Union was just 29 per cent. The anti-war cause still had the support of the majority of Irish people in the months after invasion, but there was a substantial minority that was of a mind to give the US mission in Iraq a chance. My bet is that this division was partly generational. Despite the onset of Zulu Time, there are still many people who had grown up in an era in which America was nothing but hope, opportunity and shiny innovation.

Even among younger Irish people, who came of age some time between Reagan and Bush Junior, the loathing had reached saturation point. Any form of sustained indignation will eventually be tinged with weariness, and from late summer on, you got the feeling that Yank-bashing was becoming ever so slightly *passé*. The underlying foundations of our disdain were never really in danger, but there was a tangible sense of boredom with hectoring lectures about American excesses. Maybe it was just bloody-minded contrariness, but a small expression of anti-dissident dissent crept up on our feverish monologue about the US like a gentle gust of wind on a hot day.

The emergence of Irish ennui would eventually confront Michael Moore. In October 2003, the follow-up book to *Stupid White Men* was published and, as you might expect, *Dude, Where's My Country?* went straight to the top of the bestseller list in Ireland. Yet in some of the reviews there was impatience with Moore and a suspicion that, in his desire to extend his fifteen minutes, he had crossed the fine line between parody and travesty.

Michael Moore was still a hero to a legion of Irish people, and yet even among his admirers, there was a growing awareness of his limitations. 'Outrage only goes so far, Michael,' wrote *Irish Times* correspondent Derek Scally. 'It's time to change the record.' In the words of another *Irish Times* journalist, Moore had become 'the idol of the smug, hypocritical US middle classes who say they object to Bush's foreign policy but do little to stop it'. To his credit, Moore tried to dispel a few complacent clichés in *Dude, Where's My Country?* The book has some good things to say about ordinary Americans, who Moore believes are essentially closet progressives. As Diarmuid Doyle observed in the *Sunday Tribune*: 'It is fascinating to hear someone who has made a name as a severe critic of his nation, and who has contributed to an image of America as backward and stupid, argue that in fact it is a liberal country waiting for its moment to come.'

Things are a little more complicated than that, but it is refreshing to hear some recognition that Bush's America is just one chapter in an ongoing story. Perhaps it is wishful thinking, but it seems to me that more and more Irish people are looking beyond their preconceptions for lessons about the future, lessons they can learn from the silent Americans.

The ability to see beyond Bush's America will help liberate us from a limiting fantasy that is implicit in our prevailing world-view: if George Bush were removed from the equation tomorrow morning, the problems of the world would disappear with him. In its place, let me suggest another way of looking at the world around us.

Zulu Time is defined by simple-minded solutions to complex problems. The axis of evil, the useful parody and holy war are highly addictive concepts because they act as filters for inconvenient facts and relieve us of the burden to change. On one level, these seductive rallying calls are more powerful after a sustained period of war and global upheaval, but there are evolutionary movements chipping away at the clichés. Our individual actions, whether we live in Europe, America or the Islamic world, can nudge that process of evolution in the right direction. Real progress may depend on changes in our personal behaviour where it will make a difference, hard political choices where they are needed and allies where we never expected to find them.

I am well aware that my idealism may seem a tad naïve, so this book comes to an end with a few brief, practical suggestions that go beyond saccharine-sweet appeals for global understanding. In the great tradition of self-help treatment, let me set out a five-point plan designed to wean us off the depressing realities of Zulu Time.

Step one: dump the parody

If you are not convinced of the danger of our useful parody at this point, then allow me to appeal to your sense of self-interest. If we continue to believe US society is beyond reform, then we effectively surrender the world's most powerful nation to the very Americans we fear most. Equally, if we are waiting for all those good Americans to rally the masses in revolution, then we are in for an awfully long haul. Forget about those New York liberals. If salvation exists, it lies in the quiet expanse of middle

America where conservatism comes with a small 'c' and a side serving of decency.

Understand the value of the useful parody to our enemies inside the United States. Many Americans have developed a deaf ear to the substance of our criticism, but their hearing is finely tuned to the high moral tone that sometimes accompanies it. Consequently, the neo-conservatives can make a convincing argument that America must go it alone, since most of its supposed allies are blinded by smugness and resentment.

Finally, it is worth noting how the useful parody obscures our own process of evolution. By thinking about problems such as obesity or car pollution as innately American, we have desensitised ourselves to their impact on Ireland. By ignoring the good things about America, such as its experience of immigration, we have diminished our ability to learn valuable lessons about our own future.

Step two: send the media a message

These days, our preferences as consumers seem to have more impact on society than our values as citizens. What newspaper you buy in the morning, what form of transport you take to work, what school you send your child to and what television programme you watch in the evening, all these decisions shape the world around you. With that in mind, think carefully about the message you want to send to the people who run the media. To get more good journalism, you have to consume it when it is offered. If you want something more than a shallow and parochial view of the world, then reward the media outlets that offer you foreign coverage.

If and when you do consume coverage of world events, you will be faced with more choices. In an effort to make foreign stories interesting, there is a creeping tendency to make them shocking and simplistic or, worse, to make them conform to our preconceptions. Such pandering is sometimes hard to detect, but here are some tell-tale signs.

- The reporters with the strongest opinions are given the most space.
- The news reports sound like the editorials.
- One group of victims is favoured over another.
- There is no analysis, just pictures and human-interest stories.

The worst type of pandering is the 'bodycount journalism' I mentioned earlier, where stories of human suffering are used to prove the journalist's point of view or the audience's bias. To America's critics, the war in Iraq was defined by victims of US aggression. To America's defenders, it was simply about the victims of terrorism. Either way, with this type of competitive outrage victims are no longer human beings; they are just Arabs, Americans, Jews or Palestinians, digits in an endless sectarian body count. Whether it is suicide bombing or cluster bombing, there are no longer objective wrongs, just crimes your enemies committed first.

You have a choice when confronted with these tell-tale signs, just as you have a choice when overwhelmed by all that whiz-bang 'instant news' from the battlefield. You can turn off the channel or change the newspaper. You could also go on-line in search of extra sources from abroad (and there are plenty of foreign opinions beyond *The Guardian* and *The Daily Telegraph*). When you find a media outlet that does not insult your intelligence but does challenge your preconceptions, reward it with your business. The message will eventually get through, if not to the panderer, then to the panderer's competitor.

Step three: talk less, act more

There is a temptation to judge the quality of our foreign policy by how loud we shout rather than by how much we achieve. Maybe that explains why our behaviour often falls short of our aspirations. The first step in resolving that contradiction is to check Ireland's position on an issue before we criticise others. The next step is to find actions that match our fine words.

Take our role in Africa. We are justifiably proud of Irish aid workers, peace-keepers and missionaries, and we maintain our tradition of giving, but we also seem fatigued by the images of endless suffering beamed into our homes. The more we see, the more powerless we feel. This is a shame because there are many ways we can make a difference. In the first place, we could pay more attention to our overseas aid programme. The government has pledged to increase our aid contribution to 0.7 per cent of GDP, but in 2002 it cut the programme by €40 million. As well as keeping an eye on what we give, we might also ask questions about where the money goes. Should we give money to governments that are accused of human-rights abuses, corruption or promoting war? I don't know, but it is worth thinking about.

Too often we give with one hand and take back with the other. For example, while we talk about our commitment to help developing countries, conservationists warn that European trawlers are seriously depleting fish stocks off West Africa. The largest boat of all is the *Atlantic Dawn*, which can catch in one day what ten Mauritanian fishing boats catch in an entire year. Guess what? The boat is Irish.

There is another contradiction between our expressed desire for peace and Ireland's role in the business of war. According to the Irish section of Amnesty International, in the years between 1997 and 2003 this country exported

€240 million of military goods. Amnesty says that among the goods made in Ireland were triggers for Tomahawk missiles and vital components of the US-made Apache attack helicopter (an aircraft used by the Israeli Defence Forces in assaults on Palestinian targets).

Why do these contradictions remain unresolved? Well, in addition to that growing detachment from foreign affairs, we seem confused about our responsibilities even when we are roused by world events. For example, in the middle of October 2003, almost two out of three Irish people in a Eurobarometer survey said they were in favour of sending Irish troops to maintain peace in Iraq. Within a fortnight, two out of three Irish people were *against* sending troops to Iraq, according to a *Sunday Tribune*/IMS poll.

The issue here is not our attitude to post-war Iraq, but the inability to resolve our desire to make a difference in the world with our aversion to military conflict. We are proud of our peace-keepers, but we still cannot agree what objectives justify the sacrifice of Irish life (a 2003 survey showed that one in three Irish people opposed Irish involvement in any war, under any circumstances). The polls show we are prepared to join a future EU common defence, but we have also voted not to deploy our troops without UN approval (a decision that kept Irish troops out of the EU's first formal peace-keeping mission in Macedonia).

An honest debate about our role in the world might help to resolve those contradictions, but as long as foreign policy stays at the bottom of the list of voters' priorities, we remain full of pious intentions yet incapable of effective action.

Step four: make Europe count
Here is one of the big problems we face right now: the

United States tends to overreact to certain types of international crises while Europe appears unwilling to respond to them at all. Afghanistan is a good example. Before September 11, the country was rotting alive, yet no one seemed to care. After more than twenty years of war, and three successive years of drought, a million people were at risk of starvation and millions more had fled their homes. At the beginning of 2001, the UN made a desperate appeal to the international community for $250 million in emergency aid. By May, it had received pledges of just $40 million.

The US had walked away from Afghanistan when the Soviets left in 1989, and Europe had turned a blind eye to two decades of murderous chaos. We all know what the consequence was. When the Americans responded to September 11 by bombing the Taliban out of power, there was a chorus of indignation from Europe in response to the plight of ordinary Afghans. But where were the Europeans when they could have done something? Where was our concern for ordinary Afghans when it really mattered? The lesson from Afghanistan is that it is not enough to wait for the Americans to screw up; we have to respond to problems before they become crises.

Europe's powerlessness in the face of genocide and ethnic cleansing in the Balkans shows why the EU needs a military capability (it was European weakness that paved the way for the massacres at Srebrenica and American firepower that broke the log-jam in Bosnia and Kosovo). However, most international problems do not require a military response, and this is where Ireland can help to make European leadership count. There are developing crises in the world today that require diplomatic and humanitarian responses, or what diplomats refer to as 'soft power'.

Take the rise of a homicidal brand of Islamic militancy.

Al-Qaeda did not come into being because of a clash between Islam and the West. Instead, it is a symptom of a civil war between moderates and radicals in Islamic civilisation. Just as Europe and America helped to create the conditions for that battle, so we have a role in bringing it to an end and a stake in its outcome.

Of course, our response has to have an overtly political element to it. One way of helping those moderate forces is to continue pushing for a lasting settlement between Palestinians and Israelis and lobbying for a responsible American policy in the Middle East. But other elements of 'soft power' are perhaps even more important, particularly when it comes to the Arab world.

Progress requires an economic strategy aimed at fostering freedom and knowledge. Instead of dumping cheap beef in Arab markets, Ireland would be better served by a trade-and-investment policy that promotes research and development and high-tech skills in Arab nations (there are 280 million Arabs, which is also a pretty good market for Irish companies). Perhaps Ireland should consider the creation of a direct-aid programme that concentrates on specific targets, such as female literacy. Where we offer direct aid, we could make it clear that our donations would be withdrawn if there were an increase in military spending or abuse of civil liberties.

Last but not least, we could make an effort to understand Islam better than we do now, particularly the difference between the prehistoric ramblings of the radical fringe and the historic vitality and future potential of the vast, moderate middle. Ultimately, it is possible to promote freedom of expression and women's rights while respecting the right of Arabs to build democracies that are consistent with their own traditions. All this has a name: it is called 'draining the swamp'. Yes, the Americans should have tried this a long time ago, but then again, so should we.

Step five: help America to save the world

One of the most disturbing figures I have ever met was a mid-ranking Taliban official called Sher Mohammed Abbas Stenakzai. In Kabul, in April 2001, he told me why his government was still protecting Osama bin Laden. 'If Osama is a problem, he is a problem for Americans but not for others,' Stenakzai told me. 'Osama is the enemy of Americans, not of Britishers or French people, so why do they all blindly follow the Americans?'

On that late-spring morning, six months before September 11, this Taliban official was speaking directly to the growing number of Europeans who no longer shared a common bond with America. In his words was the calculation that drives the Islamic radicals: we will succeed because we are united by belief; the West will fail because it has nothing to keep it together.

The first step in mending the transatlantic relationship is to realise that we will not resolve our differences over the war on terror without understanding why they exist. Europeans do not feel the threat of terrorism like Americans do, just as Americans do not appreciate our feelings about the 'war' part of the equation. To borrow a phrase from our own dirty little conflict, if Europeans and Americans continue to focus on 'the politics of the last atrocity', then we are doomed to Zulu Time for eternity.

Even if you believe that Osama bin Laden is not a genuine threat to our way of life, you still stand to lose if Europe and the United States do not re-establish a genuine partnership. Take the long-term view for a moment. We live in a world where there are almost a billion motor vehicles, but almost five thousand species of life are threatened with extinction. It took all of recorded history for the world's population to reach six billion people; within fifty years it will reach ten billion. Half the world's forests have disappeared, and the Arctic ice sheet has thinned by more than 40 per cent in the past thirty-five years. Yes, I know the United States bears an inordinate amount of responsibility for global problems, but that is precisely why we cannot simply throw up our hands and curse those damn Yankees.

So if we cannot live without them, how do we live with them? I think the question implies a certain lack of ambition. If we are really serious about saving the world, let's consider a few tactics that might persuade the Americans to be a force for radical change. First, live up to the standards that we demand of the United States. Second, convince the Americans that change is in *their* interest as much as ours. Third, play to our respective strengths (they have the 'hard power' and we are good at the 'soft power'). Finally, find some level of communication with the Yanks that is not based on smug superiority.

That last principle is perhaps the hardest part of the equation to put in place. Everything we know about America tells us it is a big, lumbering simpleton that inherited all the physical power but none of family smarts. That parody tells us dialogue is pointless because they are not our intellectual equals.

If that is still your view, then there is little I can do except appeal to your self-interest one last time. If you just want a bogeyman to fear, America will provide you with endless nightmares. But if you genuinely want the United States to become more responsible, you might consider new ways of communicating with it. Are you horrified by the death penalty? Forget the letters page of Irish newspapers: write directly to the *Dallas Morning News*. Instead of sending money to a human-rights group here, find out if you can help a legal defence fund in the States. If you have relatives in the US, try to persuade them to write to their congressman. If you're a member of a trade union, find the affiliated union in America and make contact. There are two important principles here: match your aspirations with action; and bypass the politicians to appeal to the basic decency of ordinary Americans.

That is not to say we should give up high-level political dialogue between Europe and America. Our own foreign minister, Brian Cowen, has called for the appointment of a deputy EU foreign minister with specific responsibility for the US. Europe would then have a face and voice in Washington, not just to lobby the White House and Capitol Hill, but also to reach out to the pressure groups and opinion formers who set the political tone in the American capital.

By far the most effective proponent of enlightened dialogue between Europe and America is Bono. He pitched camp at the heart of American power during the Clinton years and maintained that influence over the current US administration. This remarkable act of endurance paid off when President Bush announced in January 2003 that the US would allocate $15 billion over five years to fight AIDS. When it appeared that the commitment was slipping, Bono went into the Oval Office and had what he later described as 'a good old row' with Bush.

Not even heads of state get this kind of leeway with an American president, so what is it about a Glasnevin boy called Bono? There is certainly the reflected glory of his rock stardom and his obvious charisma, but what seems to set him apart is his gut feeling for what makes America tick. Writing in the *Washington Post*, he said the fight against AIDS was 'a chance to show what America is for, not just what America is against'. Bono also cast his eye beyond the grey men of Washington while travelling around the American Midwest talking about AIDS: 'In the heart of America we felt the decency and generosity that springs from the soil. We saw the values that set the moral compass for the rest of this country. And we heard the rumblings of a movement.'

On this side of the Atlantic, the rumblings of a movement sounded very different. For an influential group of Europeans, the war in Iraq crystallised gut feelings about Bush's America. In their eyes, the US had become a bigger threat to global security than the unsavoury characters it had declared war on. This was no time for accommodation, they said; as long as the United States was bent on revenge, it must be resisted.

Sometimes it feels as if this has become the only authorised European critique of US foreign policy, as if intellectual discourse was mediated through one very angry voice. Perhaps I am wrong, but there were other voices from the remarkable movement that flooded the streets of Dublin in the weeks before war. I heard friends who had shed tears on September 11, who saw logic in America's long-term aims, who despised Saddam but could no longer suppress their anger. Bush was throwing it all away, they said, by fighting an unnecessary war. Where did it all go wrong?

If something did go wrong, perhaps it was that some very important people in the United States lost sight of what makes their country great. When George W. Bush was still a presidential candidate, in November 1999, he made a remarkable statement of intent at the Ronald Reagan Presidential Library in California: 'Let us reject the blinders of isolationism, just as we have refused the crown of an empire. Let us not dominate others with our power or betray them with our indifference. And let us have an American foreign policy that reflects American character. The modesty of true strength. The humility of real greatness.'

Think about this for a moment. George W. Bush was saying that if America wanted to stay great it could not be imperial or arrogant; it would have to be modest and humble, pay attention to the world around it and stay true to its friends. It is a speech you would like to see tattooed on the forehead of some high-ranking White House adviser, just so the president would see it on a regular basis.

It is the kind of speech that I wish someone had shown the president as he formulated his strategy towards Iraq. From my standpoint in Northern Iraq, concerns about betrayal or indifference were drained from American policy. The US strategy was remarkably introverted, with all that self-serving exaggeration about Ansar al-Islam, al-Qaeda and WMD. Perhaps they had been wearing the 'blinders of isolationism' for too long, but the Washington strategists were so obsessed with finding enemies that they forgot their friends. And when the troops finally stumbled into the moral quagmire, there was precious little sign of modesty or humility on the part of their political masters. So if you ask me where did it go wrong, I would have to say it was the moment someone mislaid that speech, when they forgot why America is great.

We would have less to worry about if we heard more rhetoric from Washington about the 'humility of greatness'. I know that US politicians sound crass when they talk with missionary zeal about the United States as a 'city upon a hill', but when set against the broad sweep of history, the world has done very well out of American self-belief. It is too easy to look down at the balance sheet and see that single word: 'Bush'. Look closer and there is a jumble of words hidden in the margin: Jefferson, Paine, Douglas, Lincoln, Twain, Wilson, Earhart, Roosevelt, Marshall, Presley, King, Kennedy, Armstrong and Ali. As I write those names I can hear the voices whispering, 'We will never see their like again,' but I just don't buy that. Beyond the self-perpetuating cycle of deception that is Zulu Time, the world will begin again.

While there is always a place for scepticism, I find it hard to be pessimistic for any length of time. In spite of all the bitterness and malevolence that fill the air at this moment in history, my travels through Zulu Time have shown me the common decency of people who face very different realities. I still believe in the Irish capacity for reinvention, America's propensity for evolution and the desire of the Arab world for a better tomorrow. If we have lost our way, it is simply because we have forgotten what it means to be us.

However, there is one thing that still eludes me at the end of this journey, and it is faith in my own business – not the profession of journalism, but the environment in which we work. I have been honoured to meet people who have the courage to tell inconvenient truths, reporters with the strength to pull back the rock to reveal the thousand shades of grey. I have been humbled by the quiet integrity of some unsung heroes, a quality that never announces its presence on screen but is there nonetheless. And I have been pleasantly surprised by how many of these people are Irish (perhaps the genes of William Howard Russell are piped through the air vents in our journalism schools).

Yet, at this crossroads in history, the storytellers seem to be losing their capacity to present the world in a way that makes objective sense. It is not for want of trying, but objectivity can be hard to maintain when everything is live and personal, intimate and shocking. As for the audience, the perpetual drip-feed of instant news has delivered so much pain and suffering that our senses have been dulled. The more detached we become, the more the storytellers are forced to act like a classroom of hyperactive children, competing for a moment of attention.

On a personal level, the war in Iraq made me claustrophobic, something I first noticed in the 'hostile environment' of Longmoor. War had been familiar on an intellectual level, but it was always somebody else's reality. But over a matter of months, it became the sound in my ear, the reality under my feet and the ambiguity in the faces around me. As war closed in, so too did the oppressive realities of wartime debate. History was last night's headlines, and balanced perspectives were lost in the torrent of competitive outrage. By war's end, we were all locked in a black-and-white box containing all the opinions we would ever need.

There were moments when the claustrophobia was tinged with fear. Personal fear is momentary, but what really stayed with me was the feeling that we were reliving the same mistakes, over and over again. I started to wonder whether we really do have that capacity to change, since we find it so hard to learn from the inconvenient details of the world. At certain dark moments, it seemed there was no way out.

That was the fear that clouded my brain the night I listened to Alistair Cooke in a hotel room in Sulaimani. On the anniversary of genocide in Halabja, I listened to the patrician tones of a wise old man laying bare the missed opportunities of that international conference at an old Georgetown mansion called Dumbarton Oaks. The world's great powers had emerged from the Second World War determined to install the United Nations as a bulwark against future conflict. On a desolate night half a century later, the greatest power was about to bypass the UN in a headlong rush to war. The same night, Bono's voice came through the speakers of that transistor radio singing about the moment that you can't get out of. It did not seem possible I would ever find words that so perfectly summed up Zulu Time.

A few months later, I was back in Washington, where I found myself walking beneath the lush canopy of green that framed a Georgetown street. The rain had been falling in the American capital for weeks, and there was a peppery smell of tropical leaves in the air. Just as I turned in the direction of the Potomac River, my mind made the mental leap to that night in Sulaimani. Two blocks away was Dumbarton Oaks. Even in the unseasonal gloom, I could see the walls of the mansion, which was now a centre for international studies. On one of those walls, there was an inscription I had never noticed before, a mission statement in the name of one of the original owners of the house: 'To clarify an everchanging present and inform the future with wisdom.'

The 'everchanging present' often seems like a variation of the same nightmare, but the words on that wall reminded me that, while we often repeat our mistakes, there is always some force pushing us forward, hinting at the right direction. Some call it divinity. I put it down to basic human curiosity. As long as there are ideas that make us shift in our seats and facts that challenge our assumptions, as long as there is a market for clarity about the present and wisdom about the future, there is a future beyond Zulu Time. I do not know what it is, but it is there.